INTIMACY IN AMERICA

INTIMACY IN AMERICA

Dreams of Affiliation in
Antebellum Literature

Peter Coviello

University of Minnesota Press
Minneapolis • London

A shorter version of chapter 2 was published as "Poe in Love: Pedophilia, Morbidity, and the Logic of Slavery," *ELH* 70, no. 3 (2003): 875–901. Reprinted with permission by The Johns Hopkins University Press.

An earlier version of chapter 4 was published as "Intimate Nationality: Anonymity and Attachment in Whitman," *American Literature* 73, no. 1 (March 2001): 85–119. Copyright 2001 by Duke University Press. All rights reserved. Used by permission of the publisher.

Passages from "Agonizing Affection: Affect and Nation in Early America," *Early American Literature* 37, no. 3 (Fall 2002): 439–68, appear in the Introduction and in the Epilogue. Copyright 2002 by the University of North Carolina Press. Used by permission of the publisher.

Published by the University of Minnesota Press
111 Third Avenue South, Suite 290
Minneapolis, MN 55401-2520
http://www.upress.umn.edu

Library of Congress Cataloging-in-Publication Data
Coviello, Peter.
Intimacy in America : dreams of affiliation in antebellum
literature / Peter Coviello.
p. cm.
Includes bibliographical references and index.
ISBN 0-8166-4380-6 (hc : alk. paper)
ISBN 0-8166-4381-4 (pbk. : alk. paper)
1. American literature—19th century—History and criticism.
2. Intimacy (Psychology) in literature. 3. National characteristics, American, in literature. 4. Difference (Psychology) in literature. 5. Interpersonal relations in literature. I. Title.
PS217.I52C68 2005
810.9'3553—dc22   2004022511

to Alison Ferris

Contents

Acknowledgments

Intimacy in America has led a peripatetic life. The book was conceived in Ithaca, kick-started in San Francisco, revised and revised again in Chicago, and finally brought to anchor here in coastal Maine. Through the whole course of these perambulations I have been favored by the kindness, patience, and generosity of an astounding collection of people, who together have taught me volumes about the sustaining power of far-flung intimacies. For a very long time now I've been anticipating the pleasure of thanking them for their wise counsel and heroic good humor. Of course, not all of those listed have read what's in here; several, I'm pretty sure, wouldn't care to. But they have all afforded me the most precious kind of inspiration: they've made me happy.

First thanks go to my teachers—Stuart Davis, Helen Deutsch, Debra Fried, Ellis Hanson, Mary Kinzie, Shirley Samuels, Robert Strunk, Julia Stern, Wendy Wall, and especially Mark Seltzer—to whom I am indebted not only for their encouragement and rigorous instruction. Their willingness to believe in me, however baffling it sometimes seemed to me, was also always heartening. I'm a teacher now myself; I hope someday to be as good at it as they are.

In among all their other gifts to me, my parents, Anthony and Josephine Coviello, have somehow managed to make me feel loved every day of my life, and for that there will never, ever be adequate thanks. I love them dearly, as I do my brother John and his son Gio, and hope this book makes them proud. And to my whole fantastic family, my cousins and uncles and much-beloved aunts—specifically the Carcusas, Carrieras, Ciprianis, Coviellos, Scognamiglios, Sterners, and more recently the Ferrises, Coops, and Hamlins—I offer the most expansive thanks for all these years of love and forbearance, and for a world in which such wide allowance has always been made for celebration and joy. If there is anything better a family can give you, I couldn't say what it is.

I know that writing a book is meant to be a forbiddingly solitary and lonesome experience, but I can assure you that writing this one wasn't. It has felt more often than not like the continuation of many years-long conversations—so much so that I sometimes fear that the very best parts of the book have been left untranscribed, and hover even now in the ether above blessed places like the Ritz, the Wild Side West, the Edgewater, the Hopleaf, and Joshua's. To the friends who shared countless joyful hours in these and other establishments, I offer abounding love and gratitude, and a promise to stand the next round: from the days in Ithaca, David Alvarez, Katherine Biers, C. A. Carlson, Paul Downes, Mark Essig, Jody Greene, Misha Kavka, Dana Luciano, Scott MacKenzie, Donal McQuillan, Anna Neil, Kevin Ohi, Catherine Rice, Heather Roberts, Adam Schnitzer, Heather White, and especially Bonnie Blackwell, who was very much a part of the project's nascence; in Cambridge, the incomparably hospitable Pamela Thurschwell and Jim Endersby; in Connecticut, Joe Jankovsky and Adam Shopis; in New York, Sandy Zipp and Ilona Miko (and Chris Spilker, when he's in town); in California, Mark Goble and Elisa Tamarkin; and in Chicago, my home away from home, Jim Arndorfer, Laura Kepley, Jobi Peterson, Lyle Rowen, Paula K. Wheeler, and the ever-miraculous John Dorr.

Alec Ramsdell lived in Chicago too, until his death in October 2002. His presence made this book, and me, substantially better than they could otherwise have been.

It's no exaggeration to say I've loved being at Bowdoin College—the punishing winters notwithstanding—where it seems to me I've found an environment that combines, in the happiest proportions, collegiality and conviviality. Former president of the college Robert Edwards, along with deans Chuck Beitz and Allen Wells, took a chance on me in 1998; I am lastingly grateful for that gesture of great good faith. It was my good fortune, too, to have arrived at the college with an excellent cohort of folks, whose company has been sustaining and, really, joyful. My thanks to Joe Bandy, Rachel Beane, Susan Bell, John Bisbee, Eric Chown, Carolyn Coleman, Pamela Fletcher, Paul Franco, Eddie Glaude, Suzanne Globetti, Marc Hetherington (a surprisingly literate political scientist and ideal partner in misdemeanor), Liz and Matt Jacobson-Carroll, Joe Lane, Matt Lassiter, Henry Laurence, Genny LeMoine, Dan Levine, Scott MacEachern, Madeleine Msall, Patrick Rael, Sarah Rivett, Jonathan Weiler, and Mark Wethli; to Scott Dimond, Alison Ferris, Amy Honchell, Katy Kline, Chad MacDermid, Emily Schubert, and everyone at the Bowdoin College Museum of Art; and to my wonderful students who, unknowingly or otherwise, helped me clarify many of the book's most crucial arguments. Five formidable graduates in particular—Willing Davidson, Abby Davis, Molly Hardy, Chad MacDermid, and Nate Vinton—have my eternal gratitude for helping to smooth my transition (such as it has been) from grad student to grown-up professor. And finally a great many more thanks go to my gracious and inspiring colleagues in the English department, who make Massachusetts Hall such a lively place to work: Burl Barr, Aviva Briefel, Franklin Burroughs, Tess Chakkalakal, David Collings, Mary Agnes Edsall, Celeste Goodridge, Ann Kibbie, Aaron Kitch, Liz Muther, Terri Nickel, Mark Phillipson, Marilyn Reizbaum (provider of sure-handed guidance through the straits of tenure), Anthony Walton, Bill Watterson, Kevin Wertheim, and our coordinator extraordinaire, Cynthia Johnson. Frank's kindnesses to me exceed any accounting; so does my gratitude to him, for each and every one of them. It's not really enough to say that I'm thankful to Ann for her friendship, and for all the care and protection and encouragement and loving guidance that have gone with it. She is an ideal colleague, a hostess beyond all compare, and a friend I cherish.

Glenn Hendler read the manuscript several times; his meticulous care and exacting intelligence improved it inestimably. I look forward to more accidental rendezvous with him on North Clark Street. I feel certain that without the heroic interventions of Michael Moon, this book would not exist. Michael guided me with great patience, and even greater generosity of spirit, through the terrors and mysteries of first-book publication and for this, as for his many other kindnesses, he has my deepest gratitude. Many thanks go as well to Richard Morrison of the University of Minnesota Press for the care he's taken with this book, and me.

Dana Luciano's unswerving friendship and fierce intelligence were indispensable to me at every stage. I'm proud to call myself her paisan. With respect to kindheartedness, brilliance, hilarity, and general human splendidness, I sometimes feel I've spent the better part of my life trying to come up to the standard set by John Dorr and Mark Goble. What I owe them is, alas, beyond words.

On the homefront, Sophie and Eliza provide useful and regular reminders of all that I don't know. I'm more thankful for that instruction than they yet suspect. And to Alison Ferris, whose passion and brilliance and radiant grace have been inspiring me for years now, and who daily affords me a more expansive joy than I ever knew possible—to Alison I offer a world of love and thanks. This book is for you.

Introduction
"What Is It Then between Us?"

Intimacy between people, like occult phenomena,
is fundamentally bewildering.
ADAM PHILLIPS, *TERRORS AND EXPERTS*

In the summer of 1856, one year after the first publication of *Leaves of Grass*, Walt Whitman wrote a political tract entitled "The Eighteenth Presidency!" Though the piece went unpublished in Whitman's lifetime, making it only as far as printer's proofs, it nevertheless finds him in characteristically high rhetorical form. But rather than praise the singular grandeur and native genius of the American nation, as he had done so unabashedly in his preface to *Leaves of Grass*, Whitman here gathers his verbal forces for very different purposes. What he offers is not the nationalist panegyric of the previous year but instead an attack—an uncommonly vitriolic attack—on the dreadful state of American governance. "Today, of all the persons in public office in These States," he writes, "not one in a thousand has been chosen by any spontaneous movement of the people, nor is attending to the interests of the people."[1] Nothing of the exuberance or splendid lexical inventiveness of the "Song of Myself" catalogs is lost as Whitman trains his sights on the "nominating dictators" of American political life, who are "poisoning the politics of these States." Under the heading "WHO ARE THEY PERSONALLY?" he writes:

Office-holders, office-seekers, robbers, pimps, exclusives, malignants, conspirators, murders, fancy-men, post-masters, custom-house clerks, contractors, kept-editors, spaniels well-trained to carry and

1

fetch, jobbers, infidels, disunionists, terrorists, mail-riflers, slave-catchers, pushers of slavery, creatures of the President, creatures of would-be Presidents, spies, blowers, electioneers, body-snatchers, bawlers, bribers, compromisers, runaways, lobbyers, sponges, ruined sports, expelled gamblers, policy backers, monte-dealers, duelists, carriers of concealed weapons, blind men, deaf men, pimpled men, scarred inside with vile disorder, gaudy outside with gold chains made from the people's money and harlot's money twisted together; crawling, serpentine men, the lousy combings and born freedom sellers of the earth. (1337–38)

The sheer range of villains listed here, from lowly "mail-riflers" to "creatures of the President," appears to leave little margin for the existence of any uncorrupted national citizenry, anywhere at all. But Whitman keeps faith and assures his readers of the imminent "COUNTERACTION OF A NEW RACE OF MEN," who are "soon to confront Presidents, Congresses, and Parties, to look them sternly in the face, to stand no nonsense" (1336). It's clear, however, that the successes of this "new race" will stand not as confirmation of the ultimate promise of American political forms but in dire opposition to a hardened system of official governance that seems to Whitman all but unredeemable. "Where is the real America?" he demands in the midst of his polemic. "Where is the spirit of the manliness and common-sense of these States? . . . It does not appear in the government" (1334).

It may strike us as peculiar that the poet who only one year earlier proclaimed the United States the world's "greatest poem" should have such unrelentingly venomous things to say about the American state itself, as it actually existed around him. From another point of view, though, the story Whitman tells in "The Eighteenth Presidency!" is an old and familiar one: it is the story of the anguished difference between the virtually limitless *promise* of American freedom and its failure ever to be realized in any but unjust and diminished forms. Whitman's nationalism, which retains all its stridency and conviction, simply opposes itself to the state, and in particular to the way that state has seen to the systematic betrayal of a better America, "the real America." His is the story, then, of an America made somehow less than the scope of its promise, and Whitman was by no means alone in telling it.

In fact, anti-state nationalism of the type Whitman here exemplifies flourished at midcentury and came from an amazingly diverse range of sources. A spirit of elevated dissent from the hopelessly small-minded machinations of the state was of course part of the patrimony of hallowed literary ground like Concord, and the writers who came near this circle—Bronson Alcott, Margaret Fuller, Hawthorne, Melville, Emerson, and, most defiantly, Thoreau—would all at one time or another ring changes on this story, pausing amid their other intellectual labors to decry the state and its invidious pretenses.[2] But so too would very differently motivated (and very differently appraised) authors of the antebellum nation: writers such as Frederick Douglass, early black nationalist Martin Delaney, and of course Harriet Beecher Stowe, whose anti-state fervor found at moments a pitch of biblical apocalypticism that fully matched Whitman's venom.[3] And though the local reasons for such political discontent were very clearly plural—imperial aggression, an increasingly divisive party system, and the continued presence of chattel slavery were three of the most prominent[4]—it is nevertheless true that in this shared sense of deep aggrievement with respect to the extant American state we discover a striking kind of unanimity among an otherwise terrifically heterogeneous collection of authors and texts. If there is any common denominator linking the many different canons, modes, styles, and genres of antebellum literary endeavor, it would appear to reside in the conviction that the American state, however promising it might once have seemed, no longer provides for, accommodates, or adequately expresses the substance of American nationality.

Consequently, these authors, along with Whitman, find themselves confronted with a basic problem: how to establish a conceptual ground, not territorialized by the state, on which the coherence of a national citizenry might be imagined. If together such writers form anything like a movement, it is because they share in the problem Benedict Anderson identifies as that of a distinctively modern nationality, one whose distinctiveness Anderson helps us to specify when he writes of "that remarkable confidence of community in anonymity which is the hallmark of the modern nation." In these terms, America was not only a distinctively modern nation, in several senses, but also, in Seymour Martin Lipset's resonant phrase, "the first new nation."[5] Unable to draw on those "massive and dense structures of inherited customary practices" that were to be the mainstay of European nationalisms, cut off as well from any storied, usable past, Americans found that, in the place of these traditional forms of nationality, they had only their sense of a kind of present-tense mutuality, of a far-reaching connectedness, to vouch for their coherence as a nation.[6] (As we will see in the epilogue, this is precisely the moral John Winthrop preached in 1630 to his Puritan flock aboard the *Arabella*, then approaching the shores of the New World.) What the anti-state authors of Whitman's day confronted, and what Anderson intimates when he writes of that *"confidence of community in anonymity,"* is the fact that modern nationality acquires meaning and gravity not least as a quality of *relation*: as an affect or attachment, a feeling of mutual belonging that somehow transpires between strangers. But this raises other dilemmas: for what kind of bond is it—or, as Whitman would have it, what kind of intimacy is it—that can subsist between people who have never met, between strangers? What exactly is the nature of such an unlikely, downright occult attachment? As Whitman himself framed the matter, in the simple, haunted words of "Crossing Brooklyn Ferry," also from 1856: "What is it then between us?" (310).

Though he would offer many answers over the course of his career, Whitman himself gives us one clear version of how this riddle might be solved when, in "The Eighteenth Presidency!," he speaks more particularly of that heroic "NEW RACE OF MEN," referring his reader to "the true people, the millions of white citizens" (1335). This picks up on James Kirke Paulding's belief (taken up more fully in chapter 1) that "the government of the United States, its institutions and its privileges, belong by right wholly and exclusively to white men." It is one of the principal ambitions of *Intimacy in America* to show how these assertions are not merely racist boilerplate, or revamped versions of an old American exceptionalism. Just as dramatically, they are *dreams of affiliation*. What race describes for these authors, and for a whole range of antebellum writers, is not only an identity or a moral distinction but a state of being-in-relation, a way of being attached: it names for them a quality of inborn connectedness to others, even those one has never met. As such, the language of race provides antebellum nationalists a way to corroborate the dream of an America made coherent not by the decrees of the state but by that peculiar bondedness that joins its dispersed and mutually anonymous citizens, fusing them into what we might call an *affect-nation*. Race comes into prominence at midcentury, in other words, as a language of affiliation. It gives even those who revile the state a way to believe in a unified, incarnate America, one whose substance is not the government and its institutions but the specifically affective ties that knit its citizens, its *white* citizens, into lived cohesion.

These, then, are the most basic premises of *Intimacy in America*: that for a range of antebellum authors dissatisfied with the claims of the state, American nation-ness existed, and had meaning, as a kind of relation—for some, an intimacy—that bound together a scattered, anonymous citizenry; and that the language of race, with its progressively escalating aggrandizement of whiteness, provided one powerful way to realize this unlikely dream, that of an intimate nationality. Among the startling things the literature of antebellum America might suggest to us, then, is that race comes into meaning in ways our present critical models tend to underemphasize, or simply misperceive. We are by now used to thinking of race, on the one hand, and affect or affiliation, on the other, in two very different critical registers. To set race in the register of attachment, intimacy, and affect more generally is to frame it with a critical language inflected more by psychoanalytic methodologies than by the protocols of history and historicism, a language attending above all else to the elastic, infinitely nuanced vagaries of relation and states of relatedness. (Adam Phillips imagines psychoanalysis as a discipline given structure by a single human puzzle, by "the question that exercised Freud": "in what sense do we have what we prefer to call relationships with each other?")[7] But in the antebellum writing this book considers, race very clearly traverses these different conceptual terrains, which is to say that any understanding of race that excludes its affective and relational dimensions will of necessity remain damagingly partial, whatever its claims to historical acuity and breadth. These theoretical collisions are taken up throughout the readings that follow as occasion requires, but my prevailing sense has been that an understanding of race as a language of affiliation, called on to serve the needs of a particular moment in American life, may help to ease the division between historicist and psychoanalytic approaches and may perhaps afford us a broader perspective on what we have come to know, somewhat complacently, as the "social construction" of race in America. And that may provide us, in turn, with a new and enlarged vision of what race has been, is, and does.

Part of the endeavor of the readings that follow is thus to

describe what happens to the social meaning of race as it comes to answer to certain of the specifically nationalist imperatives of antebellum America. But throughout the arguments of the book I suggest as well that this description can fully emerge only through an equally thorough understanding of the peculiar notion of intimacy—of national intimacy—for which race was increasingly made a vehicle. Of course, "intimacy" is itself a notoriously slippery conceptual category, as any number of writers and critics have noticed.[8] This is so in large part because of what we might call its referential capaciousness—the way it gestures, in one complex motion, toward modes of attachment that are diverse, mobile, difficult to isolate from one another, and often elementally resistant to taxonomy and neat systemization. On this point, we need only think of the lush abundance of terms that, in the antebellum nation, could have traveled under the sign of "intimacy," each with its own distinctive resonances and protocols. Were we to define intimacy as, at base, an affective exchange understood to be reciprocal and recursive, its most immediate cognates would make up a veritable "keywords" for antebellum culture: these would include sympathy (and *its* cognates: sensibility, sentiment, feeling, benevolence, compassion, friendship); belonging, allegiance, and fraternity; as well as the more familiar connotations of a mutual bondedness inclusive of nurturance, lifelong proximity, and sexual exchange, whose provinces would include matrimony, motherhood, and domesticity.[9] "Intimacy" may thus designate a kind of connectedness between persons whose proper vehicle is feeling but, in the antebellum republic at least, the exact nature of the feeling meant to carry that connection was, to a remarkable degree, unpredetermined. Indeed, the particular kinds of affective investments implied by "intimacy" could, and did, vary tremendously: they ranged from the suffering and tearfulness of sympathy to the passion of desire, from the affective intensities of sentiment to more affectively neutral states of relation, such as "belonging." To conceive of American nationality in the way many antebellum authors did, as a kind of binding intimacy extended across a far-flung citizenry, was thus not to determine absolutely the proper affective tenor of American national life, or to insist on a single kind of feeling around which some form of coherence might gather. It was, instead, to make available for the purposes of nationalist imagining the whole unruly range of affects from which some variety of affiliation might be thought to follow.[10]

One of the major stories *Intimacy in America* tells, then, is of the sudden rise of whiteness as a vehicle for exactly this sort of nationalist intimacy: race, I argue, becomes its own affective language, a way to describe one's intimate connectedness to the distant and anonymous citizens of the republic. This shift in racial meaning is surely dramatic, and chapter 1 is taken up almost entirely with the description of its long trajectory. But the readings assembled here endeavor to tell another story as well. For these extensive changes in the relational meanings of race are themselves nested within a profoundly unsettled, interstitial moment in the history of intimate relation itself—within a long and remarkable moment, that is, in the American history of sexuality. For instance: however the racialist utopia of national affiliation might project a vision of civic harmoniousness and unruffled white mutuality, the question of any person's intimate, affective relation to any other was, by midcentury, scarcely so free from complication, volatility, and a whole range of newly born social anxieties. "What is it then between us?" Whitman wonders, and if his question dilates over the oddity of that anonymous nationalist intimacy for which race became both emblem and vehicle, it ramifies as well along significantly different lines of stress. In its slightly teasing interrogation of the nature of a particular kind of relation, Whitman's question both anticipates, and adds still another degree of piquancy to, those charged but provokingly inexplicit scenes he would author in 1860, in the "Calamus" poems: scenes of passionately embraced "comrades," songs of "manly affection," and of strangers somehow drawn to one another by a mysterious love. As I argue extensively in chapter 4, what these half-concealed though undisguisedly impassioned scenes of male exchange bring most vividly into relief—what provides for much of their charge—is precisely the epistemological transformation unfolding alongside the evolutions in racial meaning: a transformation in the meanings, parameters, and social codes of intimacy itself.

We can see this perhaps most immediately in the range of antebellum cognates for intimacy we have already listed: sympathy, friendship, matrimony, allegiance, and so on. There is in these categories of relation an essential rift, certainly more visible from our contemporary perspective, but beginning to open up even in Whitman's time, to eventually dramatic effect. We notice, that is, how the relations gathered here fall indeterminately across the divide between those that might include physical sexual exchange and those that categorically do not: Does the intimacy of friendship preclude physical passion? Does sympathy, which forever tugs at the body, carry that agitated body over into states of desire? Whitman's query—"What is it then between us?"—leans suggestively on exactly this indeterminacy, but it does so here, as in the "Calamus" poems, with a certain wariness, audible even through the winking humor. The very need to pose the matter *as* a question begins to suggest that this is, in fact, an increasingly fragile indeterminacy, one that Whitman must develop strategies to hold open and insist on, in the face of imperatives that would foreclose it. Though he responds to them with unique acuity, Whitman was not alone in registering the first rumblings of a major conceptual shift in America. (Thoreau's *Walden*, as Michael Warner suggests, responds to them as well, with similar wariness.) At the heart of this shift was, above all, a gradually more intense scrutiny of the nature of any attachment, of its qualities, its extensions, and, eventually, its propriety. As the century went on, that is, one's attachment to any other person would increasingly take its identity, its taxonomic designation, according to one basic measure: the presence or absence of sexual intent, of *desire*. One result of this, of course, was a progressively more systematic reprobation— or, at the very least, chastening—of any and all same-sex intimacies, a gradual purging of those relations of any quality of attachment that veers too close to the sexual.

What we see when we read the literature of the antebellum nation is that this hardening of intimacies into identities, of kinds of relation into kinds of people —which is a movement Foucault would say reached its culmination in the later nineteenth century—is quietly underway in America, in the middle of the century, and that the nationalist authors of the period respond to its charged anatomies.[11] How could they not? The affective mutuality implied by the notion of an intimate nationality necessarily broaches, for all these authors, the suddenly anxious question of the propriety of any given attachment, particularly those between persons of the same sex. Their writings thus define not only a moment of confluence between nationalist and emerging racialist languages, but also a particular moment in the development of American sexual ideology: a moment *before* it was assumed that every individual (and every intimacy) could and must be assigned either a hetero- or homosexuality, but in which the stirrings of that taxonomical imperative could already be felt. At the crossroads of these two distinct upheavals in America, one in the meaning of race, the other in the meaning of intimacy, the great colloquy of antebellum nation-languages takes its form.

Intimacy in America addresses itself, then, to the contours and complexities of a particular model of the nation—what I have called the dream of an intimate nationality. It is concerned, in part, with the specific conceptual histories of race and sex, though its angle of approach to them is somewhat oblique: most immediately and persistently, the book is concerned with the way this peculiar mode of nationalist imagining *intervened* in these histories, the way an affective vision of national coherence drew into its orbit languages of race and sex and invested them with its own imperatives. More precisely still, it is concerned with the layered intricacies of ambivalence, antipathy, and enthusiasm with which a small handful of white and male antebellum authors inhabit that dream: how, quite variously, they inflect the ideal of an intimately experienced mode of national belonging, and with what competing or complementary sets of conceptual terms—race and sex are two of the most prominent—they endeavor to embody it. This is to say, then, that the book does not presume that this conjunction of conceptual vocabularies resulted in anything like a dominant or "hegemonic" nation-language for antebellum America. (With respect to an era so marked by fracture and disunity, such totalizing claims seem particularly tendentious.) Nor does it presume that the relation of any of these authors to an ideal of intimate nationality is identical to that of any other. On the contrary, in a way that I think is revelatory, the three authors given broadest consideration here—Poe, Melville, and Whitman—approached these configurations of nation-language in ways both utterly particular to themselves and subject to substantial alteration over the course of their respective careers. If the vision of an America made coherent by virtue of a special bondedness between its mutually anonymous citizens was a prominent ideal—and I think it was—the question of the proper form of its realization was, as these authors amply demonstrate, very much open to contestation.

The attempt to follow out this basic fact has structured the book's premises, arguments, and methods in several important ways. A brief look at another kind of approach to these matters may help to illuminate something of the idiosyncrasy of my own.

In *National Manhood: Capitalist Citizenship and the Imagined Fraternity of White Men*, Dana D. Nelson amasses a powerful and wide-ranging argument about the nationalist purposes to which whiteness was turned in antebellum America. She too is interested in the cultivation of whiteness as a vehicle for "fraternity," a term she uses to describe an essentially affective coherence among differently situated men. In her reading, this new language of race forges among men a sense of "sameness" that works to counteract their increasing separation from one another as atomized subjects of an expandingly capitalist market society. For Nelson, the rhetoric of white manhood ameliorates the growing anxiety among antebellum men that their fellow men were to be considered less comrades than competitors, rivals in the market-driven economic sphere; and it does so, she contends, in the same movement by which it answers to the "national need to cultivate sameness." Of course, the conceptual category "white manhood" that issues from these compounded imperatives is itself chronically fragile and ever in need of shoring up—Nelson herself allows, quite remarkably, that "it is a nearly impossible . . . subject position to achieve and to maintain"—and this is much of the reason why white manhood is so frequently tied, in her account, to the stabilizing discourses of professionalism and an emerging "professional authority." Whiteness in this way comes to promise "a reassuring unity in the brotherly exercise of rational, managerial authority."[12]

Nelson's thesis is a powerful one, in part because the "national manhood" it theorizes, whatever its lived fragility, is also unassailably solid: it is an entity assembled in a range of rationalist discourses, ratified by the decrees of the state, and thereby broadly translated, Nelson suggests, into an insisted-on national imperative. I think white manhood can indeed be described in these ways, but my approach to what Nelson calls "the nationalization of whiteness," while attending to many similar concerns, follows out different interests and critical affinities.[13] Most immediately, where Nelson underlines the managerial and rationalist aspects of an emergent state-sponsored whiteness, I find the development of whiteness as a specifically *affective* language—a language of intimate attachment and affiliation—to be among its most crucial (and as yet undertheorized) nationalist dimensions. In this, I follow the lead of Julia Stern, Bruce Burgett, and Glenn Hendler, all of whom have troubled the Habermasian emphasis on the civic sphere's disembodied rationality, in order to show, in Hendler's words, "the way publicity, despite Habermas's emphasis on 'rational-critical discourse,' has always had a crucially affective component."[14] Relatedly, my reading of the shape of the nation—of the relations that comprise nationality—develops along a different course. For Nelson, the nation is primarily the site of an "imagined affiliation" between "men who have power over groups of people—the power to objectify, to identify, to manage."[15] In her account, the social bond around which nationality gathers is fundamentally managerial and, in essence, authoritarian. Such a conception of the nation does without question give us real purchase on some central aspects of antebellum state ideology; but I think there is a good deal to be gained by approaching the affiliative bonds of nationality at a slightly different angle, and in particular by paying a more finely grained attention to what Christopher Nealon, in a splendid turn of phrase, calls "the interiors of the social bonds that make up 'American history.'"[16] I am interested, that is, in the play of relations that course through the social bond of nationality, for which whiteness was one kind of shorthand, and "authority" was one kind of code, among varied others.

These differences of emphasis are perhaps most concisely expressed in a basic terminological distinction. Nelson understands "white manhood" as, precisely, a "subject position": an identity conferred by an assemblage of coordinated state edicts, professional protocols, and assorted discursive practices. But what Nelson calls a "subject position" I find to be both more precisely and more suggestively understood as an *identification,* a term of psychoanalytic origin, which I find to be especially useful inasmuch as it holds together both the sense of seizure and administration (as when one is "identified") and of a complicated, never entirely voluntary kind of self-nomination (as in to identify *as* or *with*). This turn toward the more nuanced and variegated terms of identification means, in the first place, to keep open and alive the question of any person's *relation* to the range of available socially coded descriptions of him- or herself (a relation that the term "subject position" tends preemptively to assume). More than this, though, one of the new stories *Intimacy in America* wishes to tell about the antebellum nation is precisely the story of an identification: the story of how whiteness became what we might call an *enforced* identification, an identification from which one increasingly could not demur.[17] If, as I contend, national belonging becomes more and more a function of the whiteness tying together the dispersed citizenry into an intimately bound collectivity, then white antebellum citizens, of *every* class, could not as easily conceive of their whiteness as a matter of only passing or negligible importance, useful perhaps in a number of contexts but finally less self-revealing than, say, one's occupation, gender, property, or family history. We see, in other words, that as the dream of an intimate nationality attaches more fully to the language of race, whiteness becomes an aspect of the self one may no longer, or not as easily, decline to cathect.

In a real sense, that enforced cathexis, mediated by an ideal of intimate nationality, is at the center of the book's varied readings. I am interested in what happens when whiteness ceases to be a category whose privileges accrue largely through its putative invisibility and insubstantiality, and emerges as a positive and embodied attribute of the self, through which one is invited to understand oneself as intimately connected to the anonymous others who, in their mutual attachment, comprise the nation; and I am interested, at the same time, in how that imagined intimacy puts pressure, of various kinds, on the operative codes of masculine sexual propriety that were forming and reforming in the antebellum republic. More particularly still, in the chapters that take up the works of Poe, Melville, and Whitman, I am concerned with the detailed and idiosyncratic relations of each of these authors to an ideal of intimate nationality, because those relations tell us, in turn, a great deal about the varied dispositions toward "white manhood" that were yet available at midcentury. Thinking about the nation, I am suggesting, became very suddenly—and for some, very uncomfortably—a way of thinking about whiteness, and about the proper relations of masculinity. The uniform whiteness and maleness of the authors given broadest consideration here is thus neither an accident nor an unintended slight nor an oversight: it is above all else an archival strategy, one that means to foreground, and then bring into sharper focus, some of the consequences, the lived intricacy, of this compulsory identification.

To read the trials of antebellum nationalism in and through a story of identification is of course to approach historical questions and concerns from an angle that may seem, again, oblique—and it is here, I think, that we arrive at the book's most strident idiosyncrasies. For what most differentiates the work of *Intimacy in America* from scholarship attending to similar concerns is not, in the first place, its move away from questions of race and subjectivity or identity. (Russ Castronovo has recently argued that an attempted turning away from the "clichés" of race, of which "racial identity" is one of the most prominent, is in fact a hallmark of much current Americanist work.)[18] The book's largest departures from prevailing scholarly models are instead bound up with its attention to and investment in the primary texts themselves, and with the quality of historicism that differently calibrated attention means to sponsor. That is, the Americanist reader of these pages is apt to notice most immediately that the readings of Poe, Melville, and Whitman assembled here, whatever else they may do, dilate on the peculiarities of idiom, figure, syntax, and diction—essentially, over the mechanics of close reading—far more extensively, and more unhurriedly, than is now customary, at least in work purporting to offer substantial claims about history and its movements. These readings follow an opening chapter that is more familiarly historical (engaged as it is with a broad swath of nonliterary sources and contemporary historiographic literature) but do not seem to follow from it, methodologically. What is at stake for me in these modulations of method is not, however, a turn away from historicism, and much less a turn away from history. On the contrary, in a way that I think bears some preliminary explication, my aim has been to explore the possibilities of a different sort of historicism: one that looks to elaborate new forms of historical meaning, and make visible new and compelling stories of the era, by evading a few of the now-habituated movements of Americanist new historicism.

The emphasis on detailed textual reading is intended, most basically, as a corrective to the reductive tendencies that any stridently contextualizing textual interpretation risks. I am thinking of interpretations that reduce not only the internal complexity of a given work in the rush to collate its major moments or themes with one or another nonliterary text or imperative, but reduce as well the kinds of mobile responsiveness even the most apparently acquiescent or "hegemonic" texts and authors regularly display with respect to the conceptual contexts in which they are situated. On the first point, the readings offered here have meant to trouble the presumption of a kind of undistorted transparency between text and context, according to which works that are unresolving, internally unstable, studded with paradox and ambiguity and aporia, come to function essentially as "vivid illustration or prestigious confirmation" (in Adam Phillips's phrase) of claims about the contexts in which the critic situates them.[19] By this approach, the identifying singularities of a given text—the idiosyncrasies of its very construction—are of consequence only to the degree that they confirm or extend the impulses of contextual placement and exemplification. Attending closely to the ground-level idiosyncrasies of idiom, syntax, and structure by which each author's work is distinguished has seemed to me one strong way to resist the potentially flattening effects of contextualization and, in so doing, to nourish the contrary proposition: that the relations between text and context are considerably more fraught and "thick" than a mere placement or dating can suggest, not least because of the performances—what Eve Kosofsky Sedgwick calls the "stylistic agency"—of the texts themselves.[20]

Such readerly procedures are in no sense designed to dismiss history, or to derogate "culture" in favor of "literature." I think of these procedures, to the contrary, as historical methods in themselves, inasmuch as they mean to restore to the texts at hand precisely the kinds of "thick description" that many of the progenitors of what came to be known as "new historicism" insisted on as methodological imperatives.[21] I take this method to push against the implications of Walter Benn Michaels's infamous, influential quip that "the only relation literature as such has to culture as such is that it is part of it," insofar as the line has been taken to argue for a kind of inescapable determinism—"Always historicize!," as Jameson had it—and not to suggest that literature and culture are bound by an inextricable but fundamentally indeterminate relation. (Michaels's interpretive practice, it ought to be said, is often its own argument against this latter, more capacious reading of the line.) The aim throughout *Intimacy in America* has been to generate a more finely calibrated sort of literary historicism, one rooted in the premise that no text, properly conceived, is a "window" to any historical passage but is rather an unruly collection of dispositions *toward* it (a premise that, as Bakhtin reminds us, means neither to exonerate nor heroicize any author or text but to save them from such unenlivening simplification).[22] Along these lines a guiding presumption here has been that it is precisely at the level of words, in their smallest arrangements, that the deep particularity of any author's engagement with the salient languages of his or her day most meaningfully expresses itself. Writers, Vladimir Nabokov once suggested, have only their style to leave behind, and I have followed Nabokov in looking persistently to what Mary Kinzie calls the "small and local movements" of style as something like a fingerprint, as the surest map to the singularity of each author's complex relation with his world.[23]

These, then, are the motivating textual concerns. Embedded in them, though—particularly in the attention to the complexity of relation *between* text and context—is a claim about "the historical" and its conception in literary criticism. For the forms of emphasis outlined above begin to suggest as well that the story about antebellum history I wish to tell here is not, or is not solely, a story about "power," at least not in the ways that story has become familiar to us. It is instead a story about the intricate and particular forms of relation that were mobilized in and around a newly available set of conceptual descriptions of the nation. That is, the principal object of study in *Intimacy in America* is neither a hegemonic formulation nor an isolated arc of cultural time, but something less teleological and a good deal less presumptively determining. It is, precisely, an *ideal*: that dream of a nation given coherence by the intimacies somehow tying together its scattered citizenry. This is "history," then, though it is history of a sort that tends not to yield regimented subjectivities or implacable forms of order and authority. What it produces instead—and what I wish to study in their particularity—are exactly those splintered allegiances and speculative inhabitations we noted earlier in relation to Dana Nelson's work on "white manhood."

Here again, another brief counterexample may be useful. In what follows, I do not explain or approach "whiteness" and "heterosexuality" solely as reciprocal "structures of oppression." I share with Mason Stokes, whose terms these are, a strong interest in the interpenetrations of race and sex, many of which he describes acutely in his recent work, *The Color of Sex*, a book whose arguments follow inventively and productively from Nelson's. For me, however, such interest is not the equivalent of a desire to anatomize these categories through a mapping of their location "within a larger system of oppressive and normalizing structures." Very obviously, heterosexuality and whiteness are in large part "structures of oppression," but sex and race are also—less obviously, more ambivalently, and in a ways less easily "exposed"—dreams, ideals of affiliation, speculative vehicles that shuttle unresolvingly *between* structure and fantasy, institutions and sheer imagination. Race and sex are also, that is, identifications, which take place under the rubric of structure and discourse and ideology, but are not for that reducible to their terms.[24] Again, this is not to say that race and sex were not apt vehicles for power, or for the consolidation of state authority, or that they cannot and should not be read as such. But it is to say that the turning of "power" into history's master-trope has tended to obscure rather than illuminate these other stories of race and sex, as forms of power that work in and through the more delicate, unstable operations of affiliation, attachment, identification. (And it has tended to do so, I would argue, through a narrowed reading of history itself as, finally, a colloquy of legible codes: as ideology, structure, discourse.)[25] If I have attended more assiduously than is now usual to the textual peculiarities that distinguish each author's work, it is not because I have wished to insulate them from their history but because that methodology has seemed to me best suited to the telling of this other, differently historical kind of story.

In making the case for close reading as a way of doing history—a way of reconsidering not only what approaches count as historicist but, more generally, what forms of meaning and experience count as history—I have had in mind a specific allegiance with aspects of the work of Michel Foucault, and a specific demurral from the often misbegotten inheritance of that work in America. It may of course seem odd to demur from a strictly power-based reading of history *and* to claim Foucault, since Foucault is, as Christopher Nealon observes, "the scholar best known for having . . . subjegated 'history' as theory's master code to some other term, usually *power*."[26] This is certainly the Foucault we have come to know in America; but Foucault was also a theorist whose works, though we rarely remember this, take up not "history" or even "power" per se but the *dreams* of modern power and discipline, the abstracted ideals of their operation. A power that exerts itself at the level of "the heart, the thoughts, the will, the inclinations" is for Foucault modernity's fantasy of perfected self-elaboration, and it is from the vantage of that ideal of operational efficiency that Foucault endeavors to write his assertively counterprogressive history of the West.[27] But to mistake an account of modernity's dream for, say, the historical unfolding of the modern era is to simplify Foucault grievously, as a critic of the West and as a theorist of subjectivity, by turning him into a much more conventional historian than he was. For inasmuch as we ignore the fact that Foucault's focus is on power in its idealized form—on modernity's fantasy of perfected discipline and marginless control—we misunderstand the crucial ways that Foucault's work leaves open and unforeclosed the question of any individual's relation to the constitutive imperatives of his or her world. Throughout its course, and especially in the too frequently ignored second and third volumes of *The History of Sexuality*, Foucault's writing accepts as a premise that persons sustain a capacity for unpredetermined relation to the forces of their world, leaving it to us (as I have argued elsewhere) to notice that not everyone goes to prison, joins the army, or stays forever in school.[28] Foucault's work has thus seemed to me to make ample provision for the different kind of story about history I wish to tell, a story that, paradoxically, the too-strict reading of history as that which aggregates into one or another "discourse" can obscure. What I fear has dropped out of American historicist versions of Foucault, in other words, is the sense (which would be so crucial to contemporaries of Foucault like Deleuze and Guattari) that the matters that travel beneath the notice of what Lévi-Strauss famously called "the historian's code" are made no less consequential, *and no less historical*, by virtue of their obliquity to or within that retrospectively assembled structure of meaning.[29] Such matters—identifications and disidentifications with proffered languages and terms of self-apprehension, investments with no voice in the code we will later come to read as a discourse, relations *to* power—are nonhistorical only according to a necessarily limiting predetermination of what history actually is, what counts *as* history.

Primarily through the methods of close reading I have described, I have tried to attend as scrupulously as possible to the kinds of investments my three featured authors sustained in and toward the stuff of their history—toward idealizations of whiteness, evolving codes of sexual propriety, dreams of mutuality and national belonging; and I have done so out of the conviction that such investments themselves *are* history, are the often occluded interior forces that work to give shape and texture to the broader movements we later fit into governing abstractions and call by proper names. In this I take myself to be following in the path of other critics who have wished to worry over the narrowing effects of certain kinds of "historicism," without for that ceding the matter of history: Eve Kosofsky Sedgwick, Michael Moon, Mark Seltzer, and, most recently and incisively, Christopher Nealon, whose work on Hart Crane, for instance, draws us away from the proper names of history, and toward "the unnoticed sensory experiences out of which historical narration emerges"—toward a sense of "what complex code for the traffic between the large and the small, the inapprehensible and the concrete, the proper names compress." For Nealon, Crane teaches us how to begin to write a different kind of history, one that involves us crucially in "the study of details undignified by contact with History": intensities of sensory experience, unsanctioned affiliations, fantastic attachments.[30] From his supple formulations I take for my purposes the sense that the finely grained affective relations *to* the names of history, to its ideals and insisted-on imperatives, are not history's remainders but, more properly, the conditions of its possibility, the traffic from which it eventuates.

My insistence on close reading as a way of doing history devolves, then, on some very basic points, obvious enough in themselves but consequential when taken seriously. The most basic of them is that "history," properly conceived, is more and other than what condenses into "discourse." Our varied cathexes to such discourses and their objects—often passionate investments for which we have only the clumsiest terms, like "opposition" and "acquiescence"—tend to travel under the radar of current practices of contextualization but are for that no less a part of the substance and texture of "history." (Indeed, if Deleuze and Guattari are correct, such cathexes are rather history's engine, the agents of its propulsion and rhizomatic expansion.) Following this line of thought, I have tried to suggest, first, that the very grammar and syntax, the peculiarities of form that characterize a particular author tell us immensely consequential things about that individual's relation to the notions, objects, and ideals that we will later come to think of as history; and second, that the peculiar intensities and obliquities of that relation are, again, not exterior to history but the conditions of its emergence. So it has been to the contours of such obliquities, and to their diverse expressions, that I have tried to be most attentive.

The four succeeding chapters and the Epilogue address these complexities from a number of angles. To preview them briefly: Chapter 1 looks to establish the provenance of the idiosyncratic conceptual vocabulary of race—in which race figures less as an identity-marker than a form of affiliation—that is employed throughout the rest of book's readings. It gives a prehistory to the invention of race as a language of attachment and affiliation, returning to the revolutionary era to show how the notions of property and self-possession, which were of defining importance to the civic epistemology of the early republic, came to inflect the social meaning of race, investing it with significance, first, as a quality of self-relation, and then, by extension, as a capacity for relation to others, for affiliation. Chapter 2 turns to Edgar Allan Poe and reads his disdain for the idea of a national literature in concert with the uneasiness in his writings with the very notion of affiliation, of human intimacy and its dangerous encroachments. Here, I examine Poe's monstrous re-animate women as projections of an acute anxiety about the uncertain aliveness of the slave, and I show how Poe's drive to sequester a racialized corporeal turbulence in the bodies of women means, in turn, that only little girls (not yet burdened with the depredations of adult femininity) appear to him as suitably unthreatening objects for intimate, sexual investment. Chapter 3 follows the ardent, though strangely voided nationalism of *Moby-Dick*, a novel whose rhetoric seems intent on inventing an absolutely original America by consuming, and then systematically dissolving, every imaginable literary or discursive precedent; America is original, the novel implies, to the degree that it outstrips any of the terms in which it could possibly be described. For the novel's difficult task of translating this agnostic, epistemological nationalism into the knotted terms of social *relations*, I argue that Melville turns to the impious, matrimonial, suggestively inexplicit intimacy of Ishmael and Queequeg as a model for a kind of relation designed, like Melville's America, to defy any of the terms that would explain it. Chapter 4 returns to Whitman, for whom the idea of an intimate nationality was a career-long dream. Here I take up the movement from two different languages of affiliation—the language of race and the language of sex—as it unfolds in the different styles of assertion and encryption that define, respectively, the 1855 *Leaves of Grass*, and the "Calamus" poems of 1860. The Epilogue frames the readings of antebellum nation-language that precede it by looking at the centuries-long tradition of imagining American cohesion in terms of suffering, loss, and grief. Moving from the Puritans through Thomas Jefferson and up to our contemporary stories of relentless casualty and trauma, I place the work of antebellum nationalists in the context of an old and still remarkably vital, remarkably current vision of America as affectnation, a collectivity of the mutually wounded and bereaved.

Particular themes thus recur throughout the book (aspects of the gothic in chapter 2 and the Epiliogue, suggestive sexual inexplicitness in chapters 3 and 4) as the interdependent variables of race, nation, and intimacy collide and realign in each author's work. These trajectories are eclectic, but within them are two interlocked "plots" that the arguments of the book mean to trace. The first of these involves the three authors presented at greatest length here, in consecutive chapters. As noted already, *Intimacy in America* attends to the shifting entanglements of race, intimacy, and nationality primarily as they unfold within the works of Poe, Melville, and Whitman. Among the other telling interrelations the book observes, the work of these three authors maps out with almost diagrammatic precision an extended continuum of response to the ideal of an intimate nationality: we move from Poe's gothic antipathy to the very notion of anonymous intimacies, to Meville's boisterous but finally agnostic regard for any concrete model of American coherence, to Whitman's passionate, though mutable advocacy of, precisely, an intimate nationality. The tracing of this movement of identifications and investments—crudely, from antipathy to agnosticism to advocacy—means to afford us both a cumulatively encompassing perspective on the promises of an intimate nationality and an opportunity to see in close detail the range of particular entanglements (of race, sex, gender, geography, and much else) that variously contribute to each author's nationalist disposition.

The second plot of *Intimacy in America* is larger in scale. Although its primary focus is the mid-nineteenth century, the book means also to suggest the outlines of a broader pattern of transformation: the gradual movement into, and then out of, the use of race as a primary means to confirm and substantiate the dream of an intimate nationality. Thus we begin with an account of the movement in early American civic epistemology from the ideal of property to the ideal of whiteness, but end with a consideration of Paul Gilroy's polemical notion of the "fading sign of 'race,'" examining the way other modes of attachment—particularly those having to do with shared suffering and loss—have come to prominence in several crucial, though widely dispersed, moments of American history, including of our own. That race no longer definitively provides for the anonymous mutuality of American nation-ness does not mean, then, that we have exhausted or renounced the ideal of an intimate nationality. On the contrary, such visions of an affective national coherence continue to thrive, and are in fact frequently offered, today, in the very name of an anti-racist, more broadly humanist rendering of solidarity rooted in the shared human vulnerability to injury, loss, and extinction. The course of the book's arguments—its look into the nineteenth century's tattered utopias of intimacy and nationality—leads me to be less sanguine about such renderings than contemporary theorists like Gilroy and Richard Rorty (whose premises, I suggest in the epilogue, can at moments look remarkably like those of sentimental visionary Harriet Beecher Stowe). Nevertheless, their concerns do remind us that what has been at stake—across these centuries, and throughout the American literary archive—are what we might call *the ethics of national belonging*: those expansions and contractions in our imagining of the circumference of human obligation and mutuality, into whose movements the career of race in America has been thoroughly interwoven.

The theoretical and scholarly debts of such a project as this are of course considerable, and I address myself directly to many of them in the work that follows. Two rather new traditions of Americanist scholarship have been particularly important and are worth mentioning. First, a range of dynamic new work on whiteness, often classified as "white studies," has been especially useful to me, even when I have diverged from it. (These divergences are taken up explicitly in chapter 1.) Works by such scholars as David Roediger, Eric Lott, Theodore Allen, Noel Ignatiev, Ruth Frankenberg, Dana Nelson, and Matthew Frye Jacobson have been of interest to me not least for their sometimes vexed engagements with a tradition of African American scholarship ranging from Du Bois's *Black Reconstruction* to Toni Morrison's *Playing in the Dark*—the latter a book whose contentions about the signal importance of race in the literary fabrication of a new America, or a new American, opened up many of the interpretive possibilities I attempt to pursue here.[31] A second strand of scholarship, which is especially prominent in my concern with affective attachment and its nationalist applications, involves work in a subfield Julie Ellison has called "sensibility studies." This tradition, which begins in the seminal examinations of sentimentality by scholars such as Ann Douglas, Jane Tompkins, Cathy Davidson, and Carrol Smith-Rosenberg, has brought the rigor of feminist analysis increasingly to bear on the affective codes that inform the citizenship of men as well as women, in asymmetrical but also sometimes surprisingly contiguous ways. Informed as well by pioneering work in gay and lesbian studies, works by Ellison, Claudia Johnson, Lauren Berlant, Julia Stern, and Elizabeth Barnes (to name only a few) have done a great deal to place the protocols of sentiment—of affect and attachment—at the defining center of the emerging ideals of liberal citizenship and democratic nationality.[32] And I am, of course, deeply indebted as well to the literary-historical tradition of Americanist work that begins with F. O. Matthiessen, to whose initial identification of the midcentury as a period of conjoint cultural unrest and nationalist literary quickening this book owes many of its most ground-level formulations.[33]

The deepest intellectual debt in these pages, and so the one most difficult to specify, is to the vision of nineteenth-century America W. E. B. Du Bois offered just after that century's close, in *The Souls of Black Folk*. In its most basic terms, Du Bois's book is a history lesson, one that anatomizes the steady revocation, from African Americans, of virtually all the rights and privileges that Emancipation had seemed to offer. But this history lesson, unfolded across a massive and varied terrain of American experience, is invested throughout with a singular moral preoccupation: a concern not with the dates and names of times past but with the very fate of intimacy, of human relations, in a racially stratified America. "Between me and the other world," the book's first chapter begins, "there is ever an unasked question," and it is precisely the question of that *between-ness* that *Souls* again and again poses and dissects. (In this way, it reiterates Whitman's theme: "What is it then between us?") In a way that criticism seems to me only beginning to delineate, Du Bois's abiding preoccupation in the book—his prevailing point of moral absorption—is with the career of race not only as an actor in history or as a vector of self-relation but as an agent and element of other-relation. It is a preoccupation, that is, with the often tragic entanglements of race with virtually every aspect of intimate life, entanglements that have resulted in the frightening specter of a nation in which the races live "side by side, united in economic effort, obeying a common government, sensitive to mutual thought and feeling, *yet subtly and silently separate in matters of deeper human intimacy.*"[34]

Intimacy in America inherits Du Bois's contention that the intimacies both promised and disrupted by race have been essential to the stories America tells itself about its past, its present, and the nature of its improbable cohesion. I have followed Du Bois particularly in the hypothetical wager that there is a great deal to be gained interpretively by suspending for a moment the familiar questions of race and identity or identity-"construction," in favor of a counteremphasis on race and affiliation, on race as a language of anonymous attachment. But above all else the readings that follow attempt to make sense of a few of those abidingly strange American stories, in the hope of understanding more fully the project of national self-invention of which they were a part. As the epilogue to the book suggests, and as probably no one needs to be told, that project unfolds around us even now.

CHAPTER 1

Intimate Property: Race and the Civics of Self-Relation

Under these conditions, is it possible to conclude that the reputation of being white is not property? Indeed, is it not the most valuable sort of property, being the master-key that unlocks the golden door of opportunity?
ALBION TOURGÉE, "BRIEF FOR HOMER A. PLESSY" (1895)

By the standards of mid-nineteenth-century America, Thomas Jefferson failed in many respects to recognize or represent himself as a properly white man. Or, to put it a little less obliquely, Jefferson carried his whiteness in a manner that would seem to the generation following him not merely anachronistic but, in a fundamental way, insupportable. While defending the nobility of the American "Indian" from the attacks of an ill-intentioned French naturalist, Jefferson found himself indicting, with only slight qualification, the tendency to understand race as a necessarily determining moral category. "I do not mean to deny," he writes in his 1787 volume, *Notes on the State of Virginia*,

that there are varieties in the race of man, distinguished by their powers both of body and mind . . . I only mean to suggest a doubt, whether the bulk and faculties of animals depends on the side of the Atlantic on which their food happens to grow, or which furnishes the elements of which they are composed? Whether nature has enlisted herself as a Cis or Trans-Atlantic partisan? I am induced to suspect, there has been more eloquence than sound reasoning displayed in support of this theory.[1]

25

Though a great deal more complex, in its context, than the Enlightenment anti-racist rationalism for which it is often mistaken, Jefferson's pointed dismissal strikes one as no less remarkable when compared with, say, the phrenological exegeses of one George Combe, who, in 1839, would locate in the elevated and large central forehead of "the Caucasian race" the source for that "facility with which it attains the highest intellectual endowments."[2] And how could Jefferson have responded to Senator Benjamin Leigh, from his own Virginia, who proclaimed to Congress in 1836, "It is peculiar to the character of the Anglo-Saxon race of men to which we belong, that it has never been contented to live in the same country with any other distinct race, upon terms of equality"?[3] The matter is not simply that white men of the mid-nineteenth century were racist with respect to non-white peoples in a way Jefferson, the good republican, would have found distasteful. On the contrary, Jefferson the slaveholder was willing to venture in print that between blacks and whites "the difference is fixed in nature," the result of which "difference" was the irremediable inferiority of blacks to whites. What we witness instead in the breach between Jefferson and men like Combe and Leigh is a profound mutation in the nature, place, and social meaningfulness of whiteness: the racial trait that, for Jefferson, had clearly limited explanatory powers, was understood by the phrenologists, politicians, naturalists, and literary nationalists of the mid-nineteenth century as an innate, embodied, and powerfully determining moral attribute.

This was not all. By midcentury whiteness was coming also to define the very substance of American coherence—of American nation-ness—in a way it never had before. Jefferson himself had from the first been greatly concerned with the question of America's cohesion, of what manner of connectedness might transform the unjoined citizens of disparate colonies into one nation under God. "These facts have given the last stab to agonizing affection," he writes of the lacerations of the split with England in his initial draft of the Declaration of Independence. "*We must endeavor to forget our former love*," he declares, and thus imagines the citizens of America as a nation, capable of declaring itself—as a "we"—by virtue of a shared experience of loss, of severance and its attendant griefs.[4] But this kind of nation-making affective bondedness is significantly afield of the "spontaneous allegiance" (in Theodore Allen's phrase) sprung up between antebellum laborers on the basis of their shared whiteness; nor does it square at all with the notion that America's distinctiveness and autonomy as a republic were a function of its distinctiveness as a singular and separate race, grown on but broken away from the Anglo-Saxon tree: "a unique blend," as Reginald Horsman writes of midcentury racial nationalism, "of all the best in the white European races."[5] Jefferson may well have felt, or longed to feel, tied to those distant, unknown others in the early republic who, like him, were melancholically endeavoring to forget their former love; but as a country gentleman whose moral contempt for the nonagrarian laboring classes was undisguised, he would not have thought the mere fact of whiteness made sufficient provision for any substantive sense of affiliation or civic mutuality. That whiteness could indeed function as a premiere vehicle for the nation's unifying cohesion—that it could take shape as a kind of inborn connectedness between mutually unknown citizens—this was the invention of an America Jefferson would not live to see.

The story of these transformations is, unsurprisingly, a fantastically complicated one, complicated by the delicacies of postrevolutionary polity, as well as by subsequent convulsions of the nation by mass immigration, a market revolution, crises over slavery and Indian relocation, and the pressure to invent a distinctively American cultural identity—and this is not even to mention the concurrent transformations in the social meanings of gender, sex, and intimacy itself. Accordingly, there are a number of ways one might wish to tell the story of how and why a qualitatively different sort of whiteness began to emerge in the early nineteenth century, and to alter significantly the fabric of political life. One version has come into real prominence in the last decade and has in fact sponsored the emergence of an entire critical subgenre. Driven mainly by sociohistorical concerns and methodologies, work in what is often called "white studies" has been especially successful in showing whiteness to be a decisive element in the often agonistic relations between labor and abolitionist movements—movements whose collaboration, as Du Bois long ago noted, *could* have resulted in a workers' coalition of epoch-making breadth and power. In this version of the story, whiteness comes to heightened prominence in the antebellum era as a means to extend civic entitlement, of a sort, to the ever-expanding percentage of the public who were unpropertied, not of noble birth, and worked for wages.[6]

This version of the story, as offered and refined in a number of important and inventive studies, has made profound affordances for literary and historical reinvestigations of the antebellum era and its authors. But it is also a story with some significant limitations. First, as Matthew Frye Jacobson rightly observes, work in white studies has tended to lack a sufficiently "broad historical backdrop"—a sense, that is, of the very long history behind many of the startling transformations in nineteenth-century racial thought. Little has been done, for example, to link the stark racial discriminations of antebellum polity to the civic order that preceded it, whose organizing premise was not race but property. The genealogy of race in early America has yet to be written, in other words, in concert with a genealogy of early American political economy. Related to this elision has been a second, perhaps more inhibiting "theoretical" lapse, which manifests itself as an inattentiveness to what we might call the affective dimensions of race—to its status not only as a language of location and identity but as one of attachment and affiliation. Though many writers have taken pains to describe the class-consolidating power of whiteness (as in Allen's notion of "spontaneous allegiance" or Dana Nelson's of the "imagined fraternity" of white men), the notion that the very agency of race in the antebellum nation might be *relational*—the notion that whiteness might give name and embodied place to a shared affective bond between persons not proximate or even known to each other—has remained notably marginal to most contemporary accounts of racial meaning. This has made it difficult, in turn, to speak of these class-bound transformations of whiteness in concert with not only the amplified nationalism of the day but with other significant vectors of relation, especially those of gender and sex, which were themselves undergoing significant and interrelated transformations.[7]

In the pages that follow, I want to amend these shortcomings and to tell a different story about the complex process that culminates, I think, in the installation of "race" at the very center of the distribution of social meaning in American life. I am concerned in particular to tell how the antebellum transformation of race into a language of attachment, of inborn connectedness, also finds its roots in the republican political principles of the eighteenth century. To do this, I will ask, first, how a nation whose political economy was grounded in the idea of property could in such a short time be transformed into a republic suited exclusively for "the Anglo-Saxon race of men" invoked by Senator Leigh. Part of the answer, I suggest, lies in the gradual emergence of race as a specific kind of property, one whose political meaningfulness is largely derived from the conceptual economy of republicanism. For property, as I will argue, was the republican civic ideal not simply because of the wealth it represented but also because of the quality of self-relation it was understood to guarantee—a self-relation that was "virtuous" to the degree that it was *possessive*. Looking first at texts by Benjamin Franklin and Thomas Jefferson, and proceeding then to a handful of documents concerned with the white "labor republicanism" that emerged in the Jacksonian era, I mean to show that the transformation of race into a heuristic of unparalleled social efficacy and force turns on the bonding of race to manifestly possessive states of self-relation—and turns in particular on the invention of whiteness as a kind of ineradicable material property in the self.[8] By providing the initial terms in which race could be read as a kind of relation—a self-relation—Jefferson's republicanism, I contend, plants the seeds of the very different racialist order that followed it, in which race becomes increasingly meaningful as, precisely, a language of other-relation, of attachment and affiliation. I look in conclusion at how this unique racial property in the self comes quickly to represent the locus of a capacity for attachment, across landscapes and epochs, which alone enables citizens to partake in the embrace of American nationality.

RACE AND SELF-POSSESSION

Hortense Spillers has remarked that "the synonimity struck between Africanness and enslavement by the close of the seventeenth century" stands among the most powerful investments in race in modern history.[9] The answering investment, in American history, would have to be the synonimity struck in the first third of the nineteenth century between white masculinity and a capacity for virtuous citizenship. To say as much, though, is to make any number of tacit claims about the political life of revolutionary and postrevolutionary America. We might wonder, for instance, what sense it can make to speak of the era of the founders—the era just previous to the ascendancy of white masculinity—as anything other than the era of white men.

It would, after all, be absurd to deny that race was central to both the polity and self-perception of the fledgling nation. Winthrop

Jordan has argued eloquently that in their errand into the wilderness, early Americans made new use of Native and African Americans not only by material exploitation but as beings upon whom they might project an almost ungovernable fear about their own susceptibility to the impulsive, carnal, instinctual life they knew it was their duty, as God's representatives in the New World, to restrain. "We, therefore, we do not lust and destroy," Jordan writes in the voice of white colonial America, "it is someone else. We are not great black bucks of the field. But a buck *is* loose . . . either chain him or expel his black shape from our midst, before we realize that he is ourselves."[10] In addition, as Matthew Frye Jacobson reminds us, "the word 'white' did attain wide usage in New World political discourse, and it was written into an immense body of statutory law," including laws concerning marriage, voting, and, of course, indenture and enslavement.[11] Add to this the pointed excision of Jefferson's remarks on slavery from the Declaration of Independence, along with the heated factional debates over the Constitution and its "three-fifths" clause, and it becomes clear how central to the very founding of the nation the question of race actually was.[12]

What we sometimes forget, though, is that race was not—or was not yet—"the prevailing idiom for discussing citizenship."[13] It would become so after 1840, as Jacobson and others have observed. But before that a different civic order, involving race but not reducible to it, held sway. The free and enfranchised black citizen, for instance, was an entity vastly more conceivable in the 1780s than in the 1830s.[14] Similarly, white maleness, though it did indeed offer many privileges, such as naturalization and the freedom from enslavement, *did not itself guarantee an individual's civic status*. The social structure of the new nation made ample use of the discriminations of race, to be sure; but the essential principles around which the nation sought to organize its civic life were simply not identical to the discriminatory powers of race or gender. They had to do more directly, instead, with the qualifications of property.

It's striking to consider how troubling these plain, unremarkable facts can be to any systematic understanding of the period. On the one hand, we must keep before us at all points the fact that whiteness and maleness did indeed allow a unique access to the privileges of property and ownership and carried with it none of the stigma (of dependence or savagery) associated with Native and

African Americans. At the same time, however, we need to resist the urge simply to presume the unspoken whiteness of the originary American citizen—again, not because the determinations of race were inoperative in early American polity, but because such presumption renders invisible the specific conceptual involutions that allowed property and race to circulate in a mutually elaborating economy of social meaning. Call that economy what you will—for shorthand, I will be calling it "republicanism"—the fact still remains that any one of these categories is inadequately grasped in the absence of an understanding of its conceptual imbrication with the other. This is simply to say that any avowals of the prominence of "property" as a means of determining civic status need not be understood as somehow competing with an interest in the discriminatory utility of race, or for that matter of gender or of sex. I would argue, quite to the contrary, that the social meaningfulness of these latter categories accrues in the period precisely through their conceptual attachment to questions of property. What's required of us first of all, then, is an understanding of the logic according to which the idea of property could be meaningfully tethered to kinds and degrees of civic authority.

We are now, as Daniel T. Rodgers has observed, at a scholarly moment that tends to view revolutionary America as neither essentially liberal nor essentially republican in its deepest inclinations, but polyglot, speaking, as it were, in many tongues.[15] But whether we think of late-eighteenth-century America as defined by commercial man or by political man, the question of property remains at the forefront, since, as J. G. A. Pocock insists, "both political man and commercial man were equipped with theories of property as the foundation of political personality which could not be separated from each other." What makes property so compelling, Pocock suggests, is the way it speaks simultaneously to economic and moral states of being, arguing that "the moral quality which only propertied independence could confer, and which became almost indistinguishable from property itself, was known as 'virtue.'"[16] Jacobson helps us specify the nature of this propertied virtue when he describes "one of the throughlines of American political culture": "republicanism," he writes, "would favor or exclude certain peoples on the basis of their 'fitness for self-government.'"[17] By this measure, the virtue that property confers has something to do with one's capacity to regulate the self. Property is moral, then, insofar as it implies a specific kind of self-relation.

But what is the self-relation "virtue" describes, and how does property guarantee it? Few early American texts trace the relays between economic and moral states as vividly—or with such dizzying circularity—as Benjamin Franklin's *Autobiography*. In one particularly famous passage, Franklin outlines graphically a quality of self-relation whose paradoxes he spends much of the rest of the book wittily embodying. Franklin tells us that, when quite young,

> I met with an odd Volume of the Spectator. It was the third. I had never before seen any of them. I bought it, read it over and over, and was much delighted with it. I thought the Writing excellent, and wish'd if possible to imitate it. With that View, I took some of the Papers, and making short Hints of the Sentiment in each Sentence, laid them by a few Day, and then without looking at the Book, try'd to compleat the Papers again, by expressing each hinted Sentiment at length and as fully as it had been express'd before, in any suitable Words, that should come to hand.
>
> Then I compar'd my Spectator with the Original, discover'd some of my Faults and corrected them . . . This was to teach me Method in the Arrangement of Thoughts. By comparing my work afterwards with the original, I discover'd many faults and amended them; but I sometimes had the Pleasure of Fancying that in certain Particulars of small Import, I had been lucky enough to improve the Method or the Language and this encourag'd me to think I might possibly in time come to be a tolerable English Writer, of which I was extreamly ambitious.[18]

Vanity and self-erasure, ambition and self-negation, all fold together here to exemplify the potent eighteenth-century concept of *emulation*, which, as Jay Fliegelman has observed, "permitted the expression of ambition in the context of a larger reverence for the models of the past, an accommodation of authority and liberty, of ancients and moderns."[19] What's underscored so vividly in this act of emulation (wherein Franklin is humble enough to submit himself to the style of Addison and Steele *and* ambitious enough to want to improve it) is the strange instrumentality of Franklin's self-relation—the partition of his self into possessed and possessing agencies. Though Franklin seemingly disappears in his effort to be "like," there is yet another, simultaneous Franklin there to operate and oversee that gesture of self-negation. As it is staged here, the essential republican gesture of self-abstraction or self-bracketing—the self-negation that underscores disinterestedness, another key vector of republican virtue—seems to depend absolutely upon *a prior position of self-possession*. If I have an inadequate possession over my self to begin with—if, say, other people share in the possession of that self—then any gesture of self-renunciation on my part must be meaningless, because what is not wholly mine to possess I cannot properly renounce. Or again, if self-negation—what Michael Warner calls the "principle of negativity"—is one prerequisite for such authority in the early American republic, then only those persons who enjoy a sole proprietorship over themselves can attain to public authority, because that proprietorship alone gives meaning to the gesture of self-negation.[20] The dependent person—the unpropertied laborer, the wife, the child, the slave—is in this way *insufficiently self-possessed*. The wage-laborer, for instance, owes allegiance to too many proprietors, and so cannot be said to have an autonomous voice with which to speak in public. Autonomous proprietorship over the self is the condition for authority in republican civic life, then, because dependence—the partial possession of the property in a person by several parties—makes impossible the self-renunciation of abstract representativeness. This is the moral tenor of republican property.

The relations among property, virtue, and dependence may thus seem clear enough, at least to Franklin. But the lived realities of race in fact play havoc with the social epistemology of early America. For, as Jacobson notes, "race has been central to American conceptions of property (who can own property and who can *be* property, for example)," which is why "republican notions of 'independence' had both racial and economic valences."[21] But if it seems to answer any uncertainties about race and possession brutally and finally, the practice of slavery actually makes their resolution all but impossible and brings into view a troubling incoherence within republican ideology. Simply put, the absolute dependence of slaves must, and yet in theory must *not*, read as a realization of innate racial properties. Other constituencies made more conceptual sense: children, for example, were clearly dependent on their parents, as wage-laborers were clearly bound to the interests of their employers, as women were clearly tied to the interests of husbands and fathers (which is why, in some states, propertied widowed women voted after the Revolution).[22] But what about Africans in America? Slaves were most certainly subject to a different order of dependence than laborers or married women or (lyrical accounts of slaveholding aside) children: in theory and in law, slaves were beings possessed entirely and comprehensively by a master.[23] But how, then, could republican ideology presume to comprehend the *free* black? If blackness describes an innate failure to be self-possessed, then the free black citizen could not exist in America, as, in fact, he did. This is why, in early America, "*free* blacks, not enslaved blacks, represented the greater political anomaly."[24] If, on the other hand, blackness does not signify a constitutional incapacity to govern the self, then slavery can be regarded as nothing short of a national abomination before God and the world. (State legislatures tended to come down anywhere between these two positions: all Northern states began processes of gradual emancipation after the Revolutionary War, some extended the franchise to propertied free black men, and Southern states responded with their first explicit defenses of the peculiar institution.)[25] The conceptual instability of race in the slaveholding republican nation may begin to explain why, in the words of one exasperated historian of suffrage, "the federal constitution contains no definition of citizenship whatever," and why neither whiteness nor non-whiteness, however socially meaningful, could yet operate in and of itself as a fully reliable index of civic status.[26]

What is clear, then, is that the relation of the social category called "race" to property and to possessive states of self-relation is profoundly unsettled in late-eighteenth-century America. Jacobson is surely right to note that "whiteness was tacitly but irretrievably written into republican ideology," and written largely in contrast to the African and native people whose widely presumed incapacity for self-possession marked them, in turn, as unfit for self-government. But the article of law that Jacobson takes as his point of departure—the Naturalization Act passed by Congress in 1790, which limits naturalized citizenship to "free white persons"—is perhaps less conclusive than he allows. Jacobson reads the Act as a codified exclusion of non-white people from the republic, and as clear evidence of an "untroubled republican equation of whiteness with a fitness for self-government."[27] But it is only partially that. In fact, the Act does nothing to validate the civic status of white subjects (many of the unpropertied did not have the right to vote), nor does it preclude the citizenship of non-white subjects already in the nation (some free blacks *did* have the right to vote). The yoking of non-whiteness to an unfitness for self-government was undoubtedly in discursive circulation, as was the equation of whiteness with self-possession, but neither was fully codified nor written unmovingly into the strictures and institutions of the early republic.

It may be, finally, that this inability to make the fact of race fully comprehensible in the political semiotics of republicanism accounts to some degree for the almost universal refusal on the part of white republican thinkers to conceive of themselves—to conceive of *white men*—in manifestly racial terms. As Jacobson himself notes, "the salient feature of whiteness before the 1840s had been its powerful political and cultural contrast to nonwhiteness."[28] Whiteness, that is, was less a set of attributes to be claimed than a set of moral and civic maladies from which one could claim dissociation. Operating ambiguously in the republican calculus of self-relation, "race" itself could only trouble a citizen's claim to civic status; better, evidently, to presume for oneself an irreproachable racelessness. In this way, whiteness comes to line up with maleness and property in republican ideology, as still another particular interest to which no semblance of partiality is imagined to adhere. Some of the privilege that accrues to white republican men thus resides in the presumption that, whatever histories or affinities they shared, they had no race.[29]

NATURALIST NATIONALISM:
JEFFERSON'S *NOTES ON THE STATE OF VIRGINIA*

Few texts inhabit the conflicted conceptual terrain of race and republicanism as curiously as Thomas Jefferson's *Notes on the State of Virginia*. Written in 1781 and 1782, during the darker days of the war with Britain, Jefferson's monograph was intended to circulate only among a small clique of his Parisian friends. Only after his notes had traveled so widely that an unauthorized French edition seemed soon to appear did Jefferson, in 1787, grudgingly agree to make public a document he had written semiprivately.[30] That Jefferson had imagined his notes would appear in none but familiar and friendly hands begins to explain why in them he disrupts his otherwise scrupulously maintained public silence on matters as potentially divisive as slavery and racialism; but, more plainly, it may explain as well why a number of the disquisitions into which this typically mannered, perspicuous, and formally exacting author launches himself are so conflicted, incoherent, and irreducibly odd.

Composed, as the author remarks in an appendix, "in answer
to certain queries proposed to me by Mons. de Marbois, then sec-
retary of the French legation in the United States" (*Notes*, 229),
Jefferson's little book reads something like the touring notes of
a schizophrenic naturalist: one can never be sure whether the
nature on display, or the commentaries on it, mean really to refer
to qualities of national character, or whether the aggrandizing
observations of national wildlife mean simply to be dry anthro-
pological accounts. Nowhere is this unsettling hybridity of tone
more pronounced than in "Query VI: Productions Mineral, Vegetable, and Animal," a chapter that has to be counted among the
most peculiar documents a future president would ever later avow.
Here Jefferson takes on Comte Georges-Louis Leclerc de Buffon,
a French naturalist of great distinction (Franklin mentions him
approvingly in the *Autobiography*), who has made bold to allege
"that there is something in the soil, climate, and other circumstances of America, which occasions animal nature to degenerate,
not excepting even the man, native or adoptive, physical or moral"
(*Notes*, 230). Jefferson responds to these affronting claims about
the degeneration of American nature with a number of observations, the first of which concerns the discovery, in America, of the
skeleton of a creature, possibly a mammoth, which "bespeaks an
animal of six times the cubic volume of the elephant, as Mons.
de Buffon has admitted" (*Notes*, 45). In tones that are downright
Melvillean, Jefferson's attack rises to its first conclusion: "But to
whatever animal we ascribe these remains, it is certain such a one
had existed in America, and that it has been the largest of all ter-
restrial beings" (*Notes*, 46–47). When Whitman wrote in the 1855
preface to *Leaves of Grass* of "the largeness of the nature of the
nation," he probably had in mind something other than the ex-
humed skeleton of a putative American mammoth; but Jefferson's
account clearly participates in the kind of unbridled and com-
bative nationalism Whitman would go on to champion. Against
assertions of a state of natural degeneration in America, Jefferson
insists on the quite remarkable heft of American wildlife (he
appends a two-column chart: "A Comparative View of the Quadrupeds of Europe and America"), because that heft lends a certain
dignity and grandeur to American nature. And for the practicing
naturalist, such natural grandeur becomes, in turn, a kind of em-
pirical support for any of the claims to be made about the qualities
and potentialities of the national character. American nationalism

thus gets filtered through the lens of an oddly polemical naturalism, and the very real struggle between Europe and America is
transformed into a scientistic confrontation between competing
natures.

But Jefferson has not yet begun to fight, having only discussed
the mammoth and various quadrupeds. "Hitherto I have considered [Buffon's] hypothesis as applied to brute animals only, and
not in its extension to the man of America, whether aboriginal or
transplanted" (*Notes*, 58). Here the real invective begins, since
Buffon has had the gall to assert "'the general fact that all living
nature has become smaller on that continent.'" Jefferson quotes
at length a racist diatribe of Buffon's, in which the Frenchman
unstintingly defames the "savage" of America, concluding that
"'Nature, by refusing him the power of love, has treated him worse
and lowered him deeper than any animal'" (*Notes*, 58–59). Jefferson mockingly counters that Buffon's accusations are "just as true
as the fables of Aesop" and goes on for several fascinating, and oft-
quoted, pages to defend and exalt "the Indian of North America."
What remains terribly ambiguous, though, is the tenor of which
this defense is the vehicle. Is it enlightened anti-racism? Or
nationalistic naturalism? We're given something of a hint by Jefferson's preface to the human section of the naturalist's argument:
despite the fact that all of Buffon's injurious comments are directed at the "savage" of America, Jefferson will consider the problem "in its extension to the man of America, *whether aboriginal or
transplanted*" (*Notes*, 58, emphasis added). The qualification here
makes literal the turn of thought that Jefferson evidently fears is
being made by Buffon only implicitly, and so all the more un-
kindly: that the taxonomic category "man of America" includes
under its rubric *both* Native and Anglo-Americans, such that the
natives and the Anglos are understood to share in some natural—
and naturally American—traits. (We'll have more to say in a
moment about the exclusion of African Americans from either category.) Buffon's attack on the "savages" of North American instills
in Jefferson a particular ire because it works quietly to defame
the *national* nature of which the revolutionary from Virginia, and
future president, cannot but feel himself a part. As Jared Gardner
writes, Buffon's prediction was essentially that "the American
environment would one day turn white Americans into something
resembling the Indian—savage, puny, impotent, and cowardly."[31]
Defending the nobility of the "Indians" from such unscrupulous

attacks, Jefferson at the same time contests a slander directed only slightly less explicitly at the American nation proper.

The ensuing "defense" of the American natives proves to be as eerie as it is fascinating. It is, of course, standard fare in the imperial world after Rousseau for the nation actively destroying an indigenous people to look on the prospect of their eradication with a kind of baleful melancholy.[32] But it is a rather different thing for the conquering nation to coax from these decimated peoples emblems of its own unjustly embattled nobility, and to somehow translate its own genocidal campaigns into figures of deceitful foreign hostility. The unsettling quality of this palimpsestic figure— of the noble savage, speaking through himself the elevation of the nation destroying him—is nowhere more tangible than in the famous speech of Logan, "a chief celebrated in peace and war, and long distinguished as the friend of the whites," who has waged a losing war against the whites in reprisal for an attack in which his family was "unfortunately" killed. Having lost the war, Logan's men sue for peace, but, "unwilling to be seen among the suppliants," Logan sends a message in which he recounts his fairness to the white man, the injustice with which he has been treated, and he concludes:

> There runs not a drop of my blood in the veins of any living creature. This called on me for revenge. I have sought it; I have killed many: I have fully glutted my vengeance. For my country, I rejoice at the beams of peace. But do not harbour a thought that mine is the joy of fear. Logan never felt fear. He will not turn on his heel to save his life. Who is there to mourn for Logan?—Not one. (*Notes*, 63)

Refusing to let his private grief go unavenged, or disrupt the peace his country seeks, Logan appears here both as national hero (he exalts for "my country") and as perfect republican martyr: he will not be servile to or dependent on the whites whom he refuses to fear, nor will he allow his private affairs, however lacerating, to interrupt whatever process serves the good of his nation. That the figure Logan cuts here corresponds perhaps too exactly to an idealized vision of republican civic virtue was a point not lost on Jefferson's detractors, who would in time accuse him of having forged the speech, the better to prove his point about the natural dignity and eloquence of the Native Americans. But Jefferson's canny response to these accusations pointedly reminds his opponents that his aim in the *Notes* was not to exonerate the "Indian" per se but to redeem an unjustly slandered America. "But wherefore the forgery?" he writes. "Whether Logan's or mine, it would still have been American" (*Notes*, 230).[33] Speaking as the idealized republican hero, the noble native attests to the natural dignity and elevation of "the man of American, whether aboriginal or transplanted," even as he describes the annihilation of one group by the other.

Jefferson's famous satire of racialism follows hard on this passage. "I do not mean to deny," he writes,

> that there are varieties in the race of man, distinguished by their powers both of body and mind . . . I only mean to suggest a doubt, whether the bulk and faculties of animals depends on the side of the Atlantic on which their food happens to grow, or which furnishes the elements of which they are composed? (*Notes*, 63)

Jefferson believes in the fact of races—to do otherwise might suggest his incompetence as a naturalist—but in this instance he refuses to deduce moral faculties from them, if only because Buffon's Euro-American racialist division threatens the Anglo-American with a sort of racial degradation by association with the non-Anglo-Americans, the Native Americans. In opposition to this schema, Jefferson insists that the bedrock for "genius" is provided not by "race" and its spurious determinations but by *nations*. Accordingly, he brings to a close his argument against Buffon with a ringingly nationalistic peroration, listing the many homegrown geniuses American has already produced, and prophesying the inevitable decline of England, who "herself seems passing to that awful dissolution, whose issue is not given human foresight to scan" (*Notes*, 65). To account for "Indians" racially, as Buffon does, is thus to forget that they, too, belong to distinct nations, "each of which," Jefferson observes in the "Aborigines" section, "in a long course of time, had separated into so many little societies" (*Notes*, 92–93). Racialism, Jefferson seems finally to conclude, is the Old World's way of *not* talking about the actual social forms and attachments that distinguish groups of people, and by which they might rationally be judged. These forms and attachments, for Jefferson the Enlightenment thinker, form the only real basis on which a rational evaluation of different populations can proceed.

Such anti-racialist nationalism does not, however, disqualify a uniquely American racism: for between whites and blacks, Jefferson would famously observe, "the difference is fixed in nature, and is as real as if its seat and cause were better known to us" (*Notes*,

138). Unlike the "Indians," blacks cannot be said to bear any elemental relation to American nature as Jefferson conceives it, since
they were stolen away from a place neither America nor Europe.
As a result of this theft, moreover, blacks stand before Jefferson in
a pitiable state of social dispersal—of *nationlessness*—which makes
them susceptible to precisely those reductions and degradations
from which Jefferson had so studiously shielded Native and Anglo-
Americans. The relations of nationality, in his account, protect a
population from the stigma of racialization; in the absence of any
recognized inherited social formation—of any perceived nationality—Africans in America form, instead, a race.[34] This is why the
crux of the difference fixed in nature is posed not as a difference
between black and white natures but as the difference broached,
in Jefferson's weirdly tautological phrase, by *"the black of the
negro."* It is the difference, that is, between a people with, and a
people without, race.

Jefferson's meditation on "the real distinctions which nature
has made" between blacks and whites comes in the midst of a pro-
posal to amend some of Virginia's current laws. Among Jefferson's
suggestions: "To emancipate all slaves born after the passing of
the act," an emancipation after which "they shall be colonized to
such place as the time should render most proper, sending them
out with arms . . . seeds, pairs of the useful domestic animals, etc.,
to declare them a free and independent people" (*Notes*, 138). The
question to which Jefferson must address himself in making this
recommendation is fairly plain: are black people, whom whites
have enslaved, morally deficient by nature, or has their enslavement corrupted them? If they are not inferior beings by nature,
and are therefore adequate to the demands of civic life, how can
the American nation understand its civic duties with respect to
the newly emancipated black person, to the black citizen? Is such
a being even conceivable in a republican civic and economic
framework? The answer Jefferson returns to this latter question
is, simply, no[35]—indeed, it seems that the only setting in which
Jefferson can conceive not just a free but "a free *and independent*"
black person is a colony, as untouched as the world Noah lit upon
(with his various pairs of animals), and located, presumably, at a
safe distance from the shores of America.

But not without conflict or contradiction does Jefferson come to
this understanding. After listing in gruesome detail the many qualities that mark the black person as debased and inferior (among

these is "the preference of the Oran-ootan for the black woman over those of his own species"), and after allowing that "it will be right to make great allowances for the difference of condition," Jefferson offers his conclusion with a great flurry of qualification, hesitation, and, to use his word, "diffidence": "I advance it therefore as a suspicion only, that blacks, whether originally a distinct race, or made distinct by time and circumstances, are inferior to the whites in the endowments both of body and mind" (*Notes*, 143). Part of Jefferson's diffidence surely derives from the reticence with which he had by this time learned to speak at all about Africans in America. The revisions of his draft of the Declaration of Independence, which consisted for the most part in the deletion of all his remarks on slavery—"mutilations," he would later ruefully call them—had reminded him with ample pointedness that a nation wishing to remain united would have to tread softly indeed around matters as potentially divisive as slavery. Still, it's worth wondering why, given such evident misgiving, Jefferson soldiers on to the conclusion, which can only have been foregone, that blacks are so different, so degraded, so constitutionally inferior to whites that social coexistence is impossible. If the "evidence" to hand is so inconclusive, what manner of compulsion necessitates the conclusion?[36]

Exactly what sort of threat, in other words, do blacks pose to the healthy functioning of American nationality? The most convincing answer to this question returns us, I think, to questions of dependence and self-possession. For Jefferson's most barbed statements in the *Notes* on the moral and political health of the nation come not in his discussions of race but in the tiny, almost incidental chapter entitled "Manufactures." Here Jefferson pauses to give hearty thanks that, in America, manufacture has not been an industry of much importance at all, there being "an immensity of land courting the industry of the husbandman" (*Notes*, 164). The availability of land in the nation is praiseworthy because

> Corruption of morals in the mass of cultivators is a phenomenon of which no age nor nation has furnished an example. It is the mark set on those, who not looking up to heaven, to their own soil and industry, as does the husbandman, for their subsistence, depend for it on the casualties and caprice of customers. Dependence begets subservience and venality, suffocates the germ of virtue, and prepares fit tools for the designs of ambition. (*Notes*, 165)

Here again is the Jeffersonian rhetorical sweep, deployed in this instance to damn unreservedly any who depend on "the casualties and caprice of customers"—"carpenters, masons, and smiths," he will go on to assert, make up this unhappy lot. Again, "corruption," "venality," "subservience" all describe the citizen who has bartered on the commercial market his first and most precious possession: his body and its energies. The product, as we have seen, is a citizen insufficiently self-possessed, and so unfit for the rigors of republican self-renunciation and disinterestedness.[37] Too many of these people—who are not simply victim to but bear the "mark" of their corruption—and the nation will dissipate: "generally speaking, the proportion which the aggregate of the other classes of citizens bears in any state to that of its husbandmen, is the proportion of its unsound to its healthy parts, and is a good-enough barometer whereby to measure its degree of corruption" (*Notes*, 165). Nonagrarian labor threatens to infect the otherwise healthy agrarian nation with the illness of dependence, of corruptibility. Jefferson finishes the point by completing the viral metaphor: "The mobs of great cities add just so much to the support of pure government, as do sores to the strength of the human body."

What begins to come into view here, in the inflation of rhetoric and in the sudden figural density, is the stake Jefferson might have in the positing of an ineradicable black inferiority; or rather, Jefferson's thoughts on dependence seem to specify where that ineffable something—that impossible-to-discover "black of the negro"—might actually reside. For slavery, as we have seen, mandates a relation of dependence unlike any other: the sustained brutality of its coercions is "justified" not with any recourse to contracts or to markets, but only by the positing of an absolutely inadequate self-relation on the part of the slave, *an insufficiency of self-possession that must precede the moment of enslavement.* The "moral" logic of slavery turns, that is, on an imagined constitutional black dependence.[38] (This is why Jefferson thinks it only right to provide emancipated blacks with *skills*—which, presumably, they otherwise lack—before sending them out to their own independent state.) The free black, regardless of circumstance, can in Jefferson's sight never be free of the stigma of innate dependence, because the mere fact of his blackness will always announce it—it is the ineradicable "mark" of his corruption. And since the dependent citizen is an infection, a sore on the healthy body of the virtuously republican nation, it makes a tortured kind of sense for Jefferson to banish all blacks from the republic, as though they were Plato's poets. The inscrutable "black of the negro" finally resides for Jefferson in this unforgettable fact of his, or of his kind's, having been enslaved and so dependent for life itself— and, conversely, unto death—on the will of another.

For Jefferson, then, the fact of slavery mandates a kind of racial determinism with respect to blacks in America: whether free or unfree, laborer or farmer, the black person appears before Jefferson with the horror of dependence stamped into the very surface of his or her dark body. As such, the idea of a post-emancipation black citizenry is simply unthinkable, and this is why—hesitantly, diffidently—Jefferson sanctions the deportation of all black persons. Not strictly for this policy, though, did Jefferson's relatively few writings on race and slavery become, as Winthrop Jordan notes, "a fixed and central point of reference and influence" after the Revolution.[39] I would suggest that what marks Jefferson's text as influential—indeed, prophetic—are not its legislative proposals but rather its stammering, convoluted effort to make race and states of possessiveness somehow communicable. Jefferson's must be counted among the first sustained efforts to present the determinations of race in terms that might allow racial discriminations to fit more comfortably into a civic structure whose principle moral coordinates are those of property. This yoking of race to possessive states of self-relation distinguishes Jefferson's text as, in its way, revolutionary. The vehement racialism of the antebellum nation, however distant it seems from Jefferson's "diffident" speculations, would turn on an extensive and ever more precise unfolding of exactly this conceptual coordination.[40]

REPUBLICANISM REDUX

> . . . the system of wage labour is a system of slavery.
> KARL MARX, "CRITIQUE OF THE GOTHA SYSTEM"[41]

In 1842, in the small-sized state of Rhode Island, there occurred what one bemused historian would later describe as "a small-sized revolution."[42] In his capacity as founder of the Rhode Island Suffrage Association, one Thomas Dorr led a movement of white workers—shoemakers, carpenters, blacksmiths—who called for an expansion of suffrage via the abolition of Rhode Island's property requirements. "In April of 1841," Kirk Harold Porter tells us, "a huge mass meeting was held in Providence to start the machinery for calling a constitutional convention. The meeting was a great success."[43] Alarmed, the state assembly promised to call a convention, but the Rhode Island Suffrage Association, and the masses that had gathered around it, would not be postponed. In the fall of 1841 they held their own convention—The People's Convention—and there they drew up their own constitution, "The People's Constitution." This they presented to the Rhode Island electorate, who approved the document overwhelmingly. The official state assembly responded with a "Landholder's Constitution," which quite liberally offered a universal white male suffrage only slightly qualified with residence requirements;[44] but on March 1, 1842, the measure was defeated at the polls. Dorr, who under the People's Constitution was elected governor, decided that the legitimate government had fallen, and, being governor himself, began organizing a government of his own. Here the actual revolution began. The events unfold as follows:

> On May 18 [Dorr] undertook to seize the arsenal as a first step in his warlike program of ousting the legitimate government and establishing his own. He had a goodly following and marched up to the arsenal boldly enough. He ordered the defenders to surrender, which they refused to do. He had brought an old cannon with him and now ordered the men to shoot it. But, as has been well said, "The men who followed Mr. Dorr to the field, it appeared, had not gone there to fight, but to witness the fulfillment of his prediction that the arsenal would be surrendered without firing a gun." He tried to fire the cannon himself, but it would not go off. The attack was then given up for the time being. The government treated the affair with great indulgence. Dorr was permitted to escape from the state, but a month later he returned and issued various proclamations as governor of Rhode Island, calling the people to arms.[45]

Federal troops were sent in, Dorr fled, and his party dispersed; but by that time the constitutional convention had approved universal manhood suffrage, without property or taxpaying requirements, and without any exclusion directed at free black men.[46]

Thomas Dorr, though in some ways absolutely singular, is in fact one among many white men who in the several decades before the Civil War set themselves to the task of elaborating and implementing what recent historians have called a labor republicanism.[47]

Part of the historical allure of Dorr's decidedly "small-sized" revolution would appear to lie, then, in the concision with which it brings into contact two vastly more grand social upheavals. On the one hand, Dorr's unsubstantiated proclamations and ineffectual assaults all but beg us to read his rebellion, in perfectly Marxian style, as a somewhat farcical reenactment of the republican revolution against England in which the American nation came into being. On the other, the disputes over property and citizenship at their core makes the incidents in Providence seem little more than ripples in the aftermath of the period's truly great socioeconomic wave, the *market* revolution. Sketching the years between these two epoch-making revolutions—between these two Thomases—one would certainly mention as salient occurrences the rise of mechanical invention, massive economic growth, an influx of immigrant labor, a widespread transition from subsistence farming to wage labor, and, as a consequence of this latter development, an increasingly vocal demand for universal manhood suffrage.[48] It may not be in any way wrong, then, to presume that these and similar events, taken together, describe the unfolding of a new and decisively economic civic dispensation, one defined in form and in structure by the demands of the market. But occurring simultaneously with these upheavals, and bearing with respect to them a relation that is both intimate and ambiguous enough to warrant our sustained attention, is an equally striking transformation in the social meaningfulness of race.

Kirk Harold Porter's almost tipsy account of the mock-epic events in Rhode Island, for instance, fails quite conspicuously to mention that a great deal of the animosity surrounding the People's Convention developed in and around Dorr's vexed relation to abolitionism and the question of free black enfranchisement. Dorr himself was a lifelong abolitionist and argued during the People's Convention that the convened Suffrage Association lend its support to the cause of black suffrage. But when the association voted to exclude black voters, Dorr remained loyal to its wishes, and by doing so incurred the disfavor of the region's many abolitionists (including, notably, William Lloyd Garrison and Frederick Douglass).[49] In fact, the Dorr Rebellion met its most indomitable adversary in the Law and Order Party, which in 1842 countered the Dorr offensive by "offer[ing] to grant the vote to black men on the same terms as whites . . . in return for their support against the Dorrites."[50] After the rebellion had been successfully quelled, the

Law and Order Party made good on their promise and extended to black men (as Dorr's party would not) all the voting rights of native-born white men.

The imbrication of race, property, and national citizenship as vectors across which an individual's civic status might be adjudicated is made clear enough in the peculiar saga of Thomas Dorr, as is the ease with which the points of stress between abolitionist and labor claims to civic enfranchisement might be violently exacerbated. But what the example of Rhode Island curiously occludes is the positively assaultive force with which the very possibility of black citizenship is refused in the period. While the free black men of Rhode Island in 1842 found their serviceability within a local political contest rewarded with the right to vote, free blacks elsewhere in the nation had since the 1820s seen their broader social utility expressed again and again in voting reforms that singled them out for exclusion. As Noel Ignatiev tersely notes: "Everywhere, the movement that expanded the franchise for whites curtailed it for persons of color."[51] From the purview of these reforms, Jefferson's conflicted adumbrations seem patently academic: "race" has by this time acquired a new potency in the social epistemology of American life and has acquired about it as well a degree of self-evidence to which Jefferson plainly felt unable to defer. By 1842, that is, the conceptual nexus called "race" has arrived at its position as perhaps the single most decisive quadrant of being in an individual's relation to the American state. How do we account for such an upheaval in American polity, as it unfolds alongside a broad economic transformation? What occurs in the years between Thomas Jefferson and Thomas Dorr to make them such starkly different revolutionaries?

"I think our governments will remain virtuous for many centuries," wrote Thomas Jefferson to James Madison in 1787, after receiving a draft of the Constitution; "as long as they are chiefly agricultural."[52] We have seen already the intensity of Jefferson's fear of a nation in which too great a proportion of men are dependent for their very livelihood on "the casualties and caprice of customers." By the time Andrew Jackson stepped into the White House in 1829, those "mobs" from the "great cities" Jefferson had wished away were very much a reality; complicating matters, many of them were immigrants, whose racial status was not yet entirely secure. The presence of so many wage laborers created a particular kind of social and political problem, which one historian has aptly described as "the anomaly of dependence in a society in which self-employment was the moral norm."[53] To be a laborer in the 1830s and 1840s, just as in the 1780s, was to be dependent for one's existence on the caprices of another, and to have, in effect, "rented out" the proprietorship of one's self. The crucial difference between the two eras, though, is that by the 1830s this "renting out" was a vastly more common procedure. If republicanism designates a government for the common good by disinterested *and therefore nondependent* citizens, why would wage laborers of the mid-nineteenth century, who seem to be dependent by definition, turn to it as a promising ideological form? What could a labor republicanism even look like?

It would, in all events, be white. Among the many social scandals of an industrializing America is the suddenly available equation of white wage laborers with Southern slaves, an equation whose painful instability is marked by the popular emergence, and the subsequent disavowal, of the terms *white slavery* and *wage slave*.[54] On the one hand, slavery provides the new masses of white workers with a lexicon to describe the coercive brutality of a world organized by market relations—the underpaid laborer identifies his exploitation with that of the unpaid laborer and becomes a "wage slave." On the other hand, though, the difference between wage labor and slavery offers white workers a way to distinguish themselves as, precisely, in-dependent, as freemen. That is, the merely *partial* dependence of the wage laborer recedes almost to invisibility when juxtaposed with the absolutely dependent relations of slavery. The white worker can be rented out and purchased piecemeal but cannot ever be reduced to a single unit of property. Race is of tremendous consequence to labor republicans, then, because what lawfully protects the wage laborer from ever being sold or bought outright—from becoming a slave—is whiteness.

There is of course something specious in the idea that partial or impermanent possession is not dependence. Marx would have nothing to do with such a notion (which Carole Pateman has called "the fiction of labour power") and so considered wage labor to be slave labor by other means: a buying and a selling not of labor power but of the persons who possess such power.[55] For white workers in the antebellum nation, though, some meaningfully substantiated version of the fiction of labor power was, in effect, necessitated by their anxious proximity to the laboring relations of slavery, by the haziness of their separation from civically degraded, "socially dead" slave laborers.[56] C. B. Macpherson gives clear shape to this fiction in the premise to possessive individualism: "that a man's energy and skill are his own, *yet are not regarded as integral parts of his personality*."[57] By this premise, all of the individual's labor power is alienable in its transformation into a commodity, but the whole of the person is not—a wholly alienated person, a human commodity, is, properly speaking, not a laborer but a slave. If labor power is thus separable from persons—if the laboring "personality" is given consistency by a property in the self that cannot be alienated—then wage labor can be recuperated as a contractual relation that in no way broaches or constrains the "integral" self of the laborer. The laborer, by this account, retains an essence of self into which market relations simply cannot penetrate.

It is precisely this fiction that whiteness substantiates. By law, since only African Americans can be legally enslaved, whiteness protects the wage laborer from becoming a slave, as we have seen. By extension, though, whiteness reads *as* the magical kernel of self that is inalienable in the individual's commodification of his or her labor power. That is, *whiteness realizes and concretizes the fiction of an inalienable property in the self*.[58] Fashioned as a property beyond the extractions of any market, the wage laborer's whiteness erases the stain of dependence by ensuring a self-possession that cannot be unsettled. By this calculus, simply being white guarantees an unfailingly possessive self-relation, and guarantees as well a certain degree of innate civic virtue. Universal white male suffrage makes sense as a manner of labor republicanism, then, because the nature of "dependence" and "self-possession" has been radically redefined; or rather, a racial whiteness has been installed in the very bodies of laborers that precludes the possibility of white male dependence. Whiteness emerges—and a cast of phrenologists, ethnologists, philologists, and literary nationalists are waiting just offstage—as an ineradicable, because constitutional and embodied, self-possession.

It's true as well that, as an unprecedented number of immigrants flooded the antebellum nation, whiteness itself became less monolithic, and more amply variegated: something one possessed in degrees, rather than outright. As Matthew Frye Jacobson contends, the tremendous influx of immigrants "generated a new perception of some Europeans' *un*fitness for self-government, now rendered racially in a series of subcategorical white groupings—

Celt, Slav, Hebrew, Iberic, Mediterranean, and so on—white Others of a supreme Anglo-Saxondom." It's important to recall, though, that alongside this partitioning of whiteness into subtly graded degrees of social acceptability, there unfolded as well an increasing *political* consolidation of whiteness of whatever kind, a new assurance of a degree of institutional civic status— the right of the franchise, for instance—that color had not previously guaranteed. Jacobson may be perfectly correct, then, in his appraisal of a shift "from the unquestioned hegemony of a unified race of 'white persons' to a contest over political 'fitness' among a now fragmented, hierarchically arranged series of distinct 'white races.'"[59] But whatever the unfitness for self-government Irishness suggested at midcentury, it was of a different order than that of non-white people, and not grave enough finally to preclude any number of civil rights and responsibilities. For whiteness now conferred a quality of self-relation that, however much it might vary among white ethnicities, was nevertheless widely recognized for its unique civic aptitudes.

No less dramatically, labor republicanism transforms the meaningfulness of "race" as it pertains to African Americans as well. In the first place, there is no more dallying over the circumstantial or innate location of the "black of the negro": by midcentury, blackness is increasingly understood to signify in its every occurrence an insufficiency of self-possession, and black people, free or otherwise, to be *"filled with a spirit of dependence."*[60] Black persons thus appear within labor-republican ideology not as noncitizens but, in David Roediger's trenchant phrase, "as *anticitizens"*—as subjects innately dependent, and so innately unfit for national citizenship.[61] But this increasingly presumed deficiency in self-relation has other, more grave consequence as well; for that capacity (or incapacity) for self-relation comes more and more to be translated into the terms of a capacity for relation *to others*, a capacity for attachment. "The Negro has no family," Alexis de Tocqueville would write, "woman is merely the temporary companion of his pleasures, and his children are on an equality with himself from the moment of their birth."[62] To be black, then, is to be judged deficient not only in self-relation ("The Negro has lost all property in his own person," says Tocqueville, "and cannot dispose of his existence without committing a kind of fraud") but in the capacity *for* relation: communities, families, nations, histories, all are effaced in a regime that recognizes the racialized subject as fundamentally deficient in the capacity for attachment. Without that elemental human aptitude for relation, the black subject appears in the latter-day republicanism of the antebellum nation as being alarmingly dispensable, an entity around which nothing like an ethics can or need be formed.[63]

Though by no means a labor republican, the Southern philosopher and sociologist George Fitzhugh provides some of the most striking commentary on the pressures and dilemmas to which labor republicans address themselves. Like Jefferson's *Notes*, Fitzhugh's 1857 polemic, *Cannibals All! or, Slaves without Masters*, impresses with the force of its sheer perversity: Southern slavery, he vehemently argues, is not merely the natural, not merely the inevitable, but the altogether preferable and indeed the only moral mode of human social arrangement. The grave enemy, for Fitzhugh as much as his foreign contemporaries Marx and Engels, is industrial capitalism, and the energy that appears to drive this rather repetitive but inexhaustibly argumentative text comes from Fitzhugh's earnest horror at the presence, in the North, of demeaned white men—of men scorned, exploited, for all intents and purposes possessed, but not cared for in the least. Slavery compares favorably to wage labor in his account because the master is self-interestedly concerned with the well-being of his slave, while the employer takes possession of an individual in his employ but refuses any responsibility for his health, happiness, or survival. "You, with the command over labor which your capital gives you," Fitzhugh intones, "are a slave owner—a master without the obligation of a master. They who work for you, who create your income, are slaves, without the rights of slaves. Slaves without a master!" No one is more contemptible, in Fitzhugh's social cosmology, than the man who employs, without protecting entirely, the person of his employee:

> "Property in man" is what all are struggling to obtain. Why should they not be obliged to take care of man, their property, as they do of their horses and their hounds, their cattle and their sheep.
> Now, under the delusive name of liberty, you work him "from morn to dewy eve"—from infancy to old age—then turn him out to starve. You treat your horses and hounds better. Capital is a cruel master. The free slave trade, the commonest, yet cruelest of trades.[64]

The more than occasional purpleness of prose means, perhaps, to distract us from the fact, so nicely framed by Peter Kolchin, that "every stage of master-slave relations depended either directly or indirectly on physical coercion."[65] But, lyrical and rather blandly generic accounts of the bucolic nature of slave life aside, Fitzhugh's text is remarkably unconcerned with slaves or the material conditions of slavery itself (though he does pause to mention the innate servility of black people, remarking that their enslavement is "really necessary to the protection and government of themselves" [77]). He proceeds largely in the abstract, dipping down into physical particulars only to underline, once again, the insupportably brutal nature, not of slavery, but of capitalism and wage labor. Part of the perversity of Fitzhugh's thought is its unwavering absolutism: "It is contrary to all human customs and legal analogies," he writes, "that those who are dependent . . . should not be controlled. The duty of protecting the weak involves the necessity of enslaving them" (28). We may well balk at the untenably quick slide from "dependence" of whatever sort to "the necessity of enslaving" those who are dependent; but one of the things such absolutism insinuates is an ardent disbelief in the fiction of labor power. Not unlike Marx, Fitzhugh refuses to believe in the noncoincidence of the laboring body, its energies and skills, and the person of the laborer—he merely amends Marx by noting that, if there must be dependence, it should take the form of the complete possession of the dependent individual by a person who, out of rational self-interest, will protect and care for him or her. Fitzhugh returns to this point with an almost hypnotizing doggedness: "Public opinion unites with self-interest, domestic affection, and municipal law to protect the slave" (25); "The master is under obligation, legally, theoretically, and practically to labor for [his slaves]" (80); "Your freemen at the North do the same work and fill the same offices. The only difference is, we love our slaves" (220). Because he forces the laborer into a relation of dependence, the capitalist is a slave-driver; but because the convenient fiction of a nonintegral labor power allows him to refuse to his dependents any form of protection or care beyond the meager wage he pays them, the capitalist escapes entirely the responsibilities of the master. And because the transformation of their labor power into a commodity can only read to Fitzhugh as a commodification of the whole of the person, the unfortunate white laborers—unprotected, exploited, and despised by those on whom they must depend—become slaves without masters.

Late in the book, Fitzhugh claims for himself the task of

vindicating slavery "in the abstract," by which he means, without reference to the exigencies of race (199). But from its first sentence—"We are all, North and South, engaged in the White Slave Trade"—to the smallest of its logical assumptions, the book depends intimately and absolutely on a calculated epistemology of race; and depends, I think, somewhat less on the presumed innate servility of the African race than on what he terms "the personal liberty of all whites," which industrial capitalism everywhere perverts. We can mark Fitzhugh's difference from labor republicans in his refusal to believe in the noncoincidence of the laboring body and the person of the laborer. Like them, though, he relies on an understanding of whiteness as a kind of embodied autonomy, an inherently sufficient self-relation. He observes, in his chapter on "Negro Slavery," that "from inferiority, or rather peculiarity, of race, almost all negroes require masters, whilst only the children, the women, the very weak, poor, ignorant, &c., among the whites need some protective and governing relation of this kind" (201). Exactly here, in this racist kernel of his argument, does Fitzhugh's abstractness venture into a kind of white idealism, or willful social arealism: given that dependence of any sort necessitates enslavement for Fitzhugh, the world he conjures here, in which among white men only "the very weak, poor, ignorant" would be of necessity enslaved, seems pure social fantasy. It supposes an economic world —by 1857 long, long gone—in which no free white man would of necessity seek employment for wages. We can only read this as Fitzhugh's vision of the edenic and fully racialized state of nature, in which vision capitalism, by forcing white men into positions of dependence, gets to play the serpent. Labor republicans regard their whiteness as a kind of inalienable property because material circumstances force them to alienate their labor power for pay; Fitzhugh simply will not believe in the necessity of that condition and turns again and again to the fact that the innate property of whiteness can be, but by its nature ought never to be, violated and demeaned by the bartering, in the commodity market, of white bodies and the power to labor they possess.

In either account, the matter is self-possession—or rather, a sufficiently possessive self-relation. For Thomas Dorr and men like him, a racial white masculinity secures a property in the self that, because it is inalienable, guarantees a definitionally virtuous, self-possessed citizen; for Fitzhugh, white masculinity designates a similarly innate and ineradicable self-possession, which, to his

unrestrained horror, market capitalism continually and exploita-
tively violates. According to either paradigm, whiteness is now
something securely in and of the body: it gives miraculously back
to the laborer the integrity of the body whose lesser components—
its skills and energies—he has bartered for pay. And blackness,
too, acquires new properties: it signifies a no longer circumstantial and remediable degradation but a constitutionally deficient
self-relation so unbecoming to moral agency that the "freedom"
of free black persons can read only as an affront to truly free and
virtuous citizenship. The phrenologists, the ethnologists, the nationalists all set to their particular tasks like bureaucrats in an
amazingly coordinated system of racial dissemination; and it is
with no slight amazement that Reginald Horsman writes, "By the
early 1850s, the inherent inequality of races was simply accepted
as scientific fact in America."[66] What had seemed to white citizens
in the revolutionary era merely the stuff of arcane debates in the
rarefied fields of international naturalism and political philosophy
has by midcentury become the simple material of day-to-day life
in America.

CONCLUSION: RACE AND AFFILIATION

"The government of the United States, its institutions and its
privileges, belong by right wholly and exclusively to white men;
for they were purchased, not by the blood of the negroes, but by
that of our fathers."[67] So wrote James K. Paulding in *Slavery in
the United States*, a volume published not quite fifty years after
Jefferson had opined, in his letter to Madison, that the health of
American institutions would depend chiefly on its leaders' intimate relation to the land. For Jefferson and his fellow republicans,
the matter of defining, as legitimate, an individual's relation to
property was, as we have seen, a rather shifty affair, unsettled in
particular by the prominence of social categories (like gender and
race) whose possessive meanings were by no means static or secure.
For Paulding, by contrast, the question of legitimacy is dramatically less opaque. Indeed, his terse social epistemology has about
it what Hortense Spillers describes as "a manichean overtness":
by Paulding's terms, there are quite simply two possessions—
whiteness and maleness—without either of which a person cannot
be sanctioned as a political agent.[68] Part of the much-remarked
"populism" of the new white male republic might be said to reside,

then, in the immediate legibility of its authorizing social codes. So conclusively has white masculinity been identified with the self-authorizing rigors of possession—with a civically compelling self-relation—that by the 1830s and 1840s the puzzling and arcane requirements of real estate property can simply pass away, to be replaced by a social semiotic whose utter transparency is one mark of its broad "democratic" appeal.

But this transparency is far from unruffled. For if Paulding presumes with a certain blitheness that whiteness confers a particular quality of self-relation (such that government is an exclusively white and male affair), he also insinuates that in whiteness one finds a range of different, yet similarly relational meanings. Consider, for instance, Paulding's remarks about those whites who would countenance the "project for intermarrying with blacks." Such persons, Paulding tells us, are not merely perverse and unnatural but "are traitors to the white skin"—a phrase that identifies whiteness with a kind of nationhood, and sexual deviancy with national betrayal. The stridency of Paulding's emphasis on the traitorousness of racial mixture suggests that race acts as no mere socionorm here but possesses a specifically affective reality: it is the name he gives to a quality of bond between persons that is so powerful, and so intimate, that it is susceptible to no less violation than betrayal. If on the one hand whiteness designates a quality of self-relation for Paulding, it suggests to him as well a far-reaching and deeply felt relation to others, to the distant fellow citizens of the nation.

Small wonder, then, that Paulding's defense of slavery proceeds in the name of a passionate nationalism, one that places the imperatives of national cohesion literally above all else. The premise guiding his book, he writes in the introduction, is as simple as it is sweeping: *"That no beneficial consequences to any class of mankind, or to the whole universe, can counterbalance the evils that will result for the people of the United States from the dissolution of the Union"*—for it is this Union, he claims, "which all good citizens believe to be the great palladium of their present happiness, and that of their posterity."[69] Even in his *Letters from the South*, a more moderate book of 1835, Paulding places the highest of premiums on national coherence, which he believes will be aided by a greater sense of connectedness between the dispersed and mutually anonymous citizenry. "I think it is much to be wished," he writes, "that the people of the various divisions of the United

States were a little more acquainted with each other, for, I am satisfied, they would be the better friends for it."[70] In the slavery tract of the following year, what has begun to emerge—though as yet as only a flickering possibility, momentarily glimpsed—is the notion that whiteness might be the ideal vehicle for that longed-for cohesion-through-affective-connectedness that would solidify the Union. Coming together in Paulding's remarks, however fleetingly, are a nationalist discourse and a racialist discourse, both still inchoate but sharing in a unique emphasis on attachment, affiliation, the relational.

Over the next several decades, this conjunction of social languages would grow increasingly prominent, flowering now in the rhetoric of Free-Soil campaigners, now in the manifestos of American expansionism, and now in the literary exhortations of Young America and in the *Democratic Review*. For as whiteness and blackness came to designate ever more socially determinate states of self-relation, the progressive translation of those states of self-relation into qualities of relation to others paved the way for the use of race in a language of nationality that envisioned "America" not in terms of the state or its decrees but as a state of *being-related*, a somehow intimate attachment among citizens who have never met. Importantly, this kind of racialized nation-language insinuates a version of how race means that is somewhat afield of most of our critical models; in these terms, race acquires its most consequential meaning not as an identity-category, nor even as an arbiter of social positionalities, but as a way of being attached—to the past, to a dispersed community, to nationality itself.

The broad movement we have seen, then, is from the idea that property confers a politically meaningful quality of self-relation, to the installation of whiteness *as* a form of inalienable property in the self, which results in turn in the idea that race itself confers both a quality of self-relation and, by gradual extension, a capacity for relation to others, for affiliation. By the start of the 1840s—at which time an explosion of literary production, later called the American Renaissance, was just getting underway—the elements were in place for the bonding of an affective, affiliative language of race to an affective, affiliative language of nation. But with the ascension of this particular style of affective racial nationalism, in which the whiteness shared by dispersed Americans becomes the tissue of their affiliation, comes another, more intricate set of processes. "To identity *as*," Eve Sedgwick writes, "must always include multiple processes of identification *with*."[71] But the reverse is also true: sometimes to identify *with* requires that one identify *as*, in potentially new and untried ways. Inasmuch as American nationality was understood as a precipitate of the whiteness bonding together the far-flung citizenry into a coherent affective collectivity, then to exactly that degree would the effort to identify oneself with the nation and the national public—to imagine oneself included in the embrace of the American collective—inescapably involve an identification of oneself *as* white. Whiteness, that is, was coming less and less to be the privileged expansively nondetermining attribute it was for Jefferson, whose rewards were made available to republican men not because they claimed their whiteness or identified themselves with it but because it alone allowed them to claim for themselves the signal virtue of racelessness. With the rise of racial nationalism, whiteness begins to emerge instead as a form of identification one was significantly less free to disclaim—at least not if one wished to imagine oneself safely within the affective circuit of national belonging. Of course, the compulsion to identify is not the gravest of afflictions. (Far graver, as we have seen, are those inflicted by the new racial dispensation on persons who were not *permitted* to identify as white, especially those who yet wished to seek justice or solace or some more ample, more congenial future in the expansive promise of the idea of America.)[72] Indeed, for some the opportunity to identify as white was welcome, since it would allow them entrée into a national public from which they might otherwise have been excluded. Particularly for members of the nonpropertied laboring classes, these were the very wages of whiteness.

But this is not the whole of the story. Alongside these transformations, so ably documented for us in so much new historiography, is another, smaller, more intimate drama. For the call to identify as white was not responded to, even by white subjects, with any kind of uniformity—and certainly not with uniform enthusiasm. What is more, one need not have been a crusader for racial justice, or even much of an anti-racist, to feel a certain uneasiness before the new national imperative to identify as white, and so make oneself a part of the affective collectivity of the nation. To be sure, some antebellum citizens found the aggrandizements of whiteness like Paulding's both absurd and unjust, and on these grounds considered it an unlikely form of self-identification. For others, though, the uneasiness was bound up with a distaste for the promiscuous class-mixing such strictly racial affiliation implied; while for others the idea of an intimate affective proximity to persons whom one did not know—the nationalist ideal for which whiteness was a vehicle—was itself too potentially unsettling, of too many codes of social and physical propriety, to be enthusiastically embraced. And it was possible, too, to wish to hesitate the seamless identification of the amplitude of one's self with the mere fact of one's race, one's whiteness. None of these latter hesitancies necessarily implies a heroic white anti-racism, or even an exhaustive disidentification with whiteness. They do suggest, however, that the call to identify as white, precisely because it was so bound up with the range of one's other relations, affiliations, and identifications, was less likely to produce a monolithic sort of "subjectivity"—what Nelson calls "white manhood"—than a varied series of partial attachments and ambivalent self-nominations.[73]

The variety and complexity of such fractured identifications is perhaps nowhere more distinct than in the colloquy of voices surrounding the ideal of an America given coherence not by the state, not by an inherited aristocratic order, but by the quality of affective mutuality that traversed its far-flung citizenry. Because it drew so heavily on the fantasy of an expansive white affiliation, without necessarily acceding to it, the dream of an intimate nationality became one prominent site for the negotiation of exactly these tenuous enthusiasms and wrought ambivalences. Addressing themselves to an idea of America, however obliquely or forthrightly, antebellum authors simultaneously addressed their own relation both to a whiteness that had become newly nationalized and to a model of nation-ness that had grown increasingly racialized. So I want to turn now from the larger story of racial transformation we have been observing in this chapter to look closely at some of the contours of that smaller, more intimate drama, of allegiances, identifications, disidentifications. The particular, idiosyncratic relations of three prominent authors, each white and male, to these nation-languages—to their identificatory demands, as well as to their broader vexations and affordances—are the subject of the chapters that follow.

CHAPTER 2

The Melancholy of Little Girls: Poe, Pedophilia, and the Logic of Slavery

The median age of pubescence for girls has been found
to be thirteen years and nine months in New York and
Chicago. The age varies for individuals from ten, or
earlier, to seventeen. Virginia was not quite fourteen when
Harry Edgar possessed her. He gave her lessons in
algebra. Je m'imagine cela. They spent their honeymoon
at Petersburg, Fla. "Monsieur Poe-Poe," as that boy in
one of Monsieur Humbert Humbert's classes in Paris
called the poet-poet.

VLADIMIR NABOKOV, *LOLITA* (1955)

Tucked in among the many other curiosities surrounding the life and work of Edgar Allan Poe is the following fact: more than any other major figure in the American literary canon, and certainly more than any author of the American Renaissance, Poe is read to, and read by, children. Indeed, it's difficult to think of a so-called serious writer, from any nation or era, to whom American schoolchildren are likely to be introduced before they encounter Poe. (It is in just this vein that Leslie Fielder, thinking particularly of Poe, writes that "our classic literature is a literature of horror for boys.")[1] The brevity, vividness, and morality-play concision of many of Poe's tales explains in part why parents and teachers and other guardians of youth should think it a reasonable idea to hand Poe over to, say, a nine-year-old—or rather it almost explains it. There yet remains a kind of dissonance, a residue of sheer perversity, that no strictly formal rationale can fully obviate. In exactly what sense, one wonders, is something as morbid as "The

Black Cat," or as vengeful as "The Cask of Amontillado," or as sexually piquant as "Ligeia" or "The Fall of the House of Usher" or any number of other Poe tales "suitable material for minors," as the school psychologists might say? In what terms could anybody justify such a weird, though apparently common, infliction? To put this as censoriously as possible: who says Poe is safe for children?

If the ritual of offering Poe to children is an inherited practice—a tradition of sorts—it finds an odd form of substantiation, and perhaps even a source, in the accumulated criticism of Poe's work. For one prominent motif in the work of many of Poe's critics (and especially of his detractors) is an impulse to return in their nominally aesthetic appraisals of Poe to a thematics of unripeness, immaturity, and—here's the rub—adolescence. Henry James wrote famously that "an enthusiasm for Poe is the mark of a decidedly primitive stage of reflection," and T. S. Eliot only sharpened the point by designating Poe's intellect "that of a highly gifted young person before puberty."[2] But as my epigraph suggests, there is today no possible way for us to read such remarks as innocently as they may, or may not, have been intended. What has intervened most pressingly between ourselves and these older critics, and what lends to the word "puberty" such uncommonly lubricious resonance, is of course Vladimir Nabokov's *Lolita*, a novel that labors with single-minded determination to recall to us the intricacies and peculiarities of Poe's vision of sexual intimacy. When, in the Stanley Kubrick version of *Lolita*, James Mason's Humbert seduces Sue Lyons's Lo onto his lap by reading to her from the hypnotic "Ulalume," we might wonder afresh at the unlikeliness of Poe as a figure to be included in the otherwise sanitized canon of grade-school literatures.[3]

But Poe's unlikeliness is, of course, chronic: if the undisguised sexual vexations of his work make Poe an especially improbable figure in the grade-school canon, he is a figure no less unlikely in the Americanist canon itself, and particularly in the canon of explicitly *nationalist* antebellum authors. Teresa Goddu is probably correct in her assertion that Poe is admitted into the canon, when he is, largely as a kind of straw man, "an excused aberration [who] becomes the representative of a number of problems that the American literary tradition recognizes but refuses to claim."[4] Through Poe, she claims, the American canon gets to have, and then disown, popular literatures, literatures of gothic excess, problematically racist literatures, and so forth. But however mercenary or opportunist this kind of critical use of Poe may be, those critics who read him as a figure somewhat marginal to antebellum nationalist endeavor have done so not without reason or provocation. Poe himself, at given moments, was not at all shy about expressing his contempt for the very notion of a "national literature," and for Americanism more generally—a contempt F. O. Matthiessen would immortalize when, in an early footnote in *American Renaissance*, he described Poe as "bitterly hostile to democracy." For Matthiessen, Poe was clearly ill-suited to stand among those who dreamed of a literature adequate to the expansive, untold promise of American itself, and Poe's apparent disdain for that idea, for that positively messianic vision of unity and destiny, marked him as aristocratic, anti-nationalist, and, finally, "bitterly hostile" to America's democratic potentialities.[5]

Poe may have been exactly that. But in this chapter I want to suggest that Poe's writing, in the very grain of its apparent antinationalism, nevertheless gives us a unique purchase on the peculiar nature of antebellum nationalist endeavor: on its ambitions, its presumptions, and especially on its operative fantasies of intimacy, mutuality, and belonging. Whatever his posturings, Poe was very clearly not unfamiliar with, or even necessarily averse to, the idea of an American literature; two of his books were brought out, after all, as part of Wiley and Putnam's Library of American Books, a "distinctively American" series and chief venue for the ardent literary nationalism of the Young America coterie.[6] Poe's nationalist ambivalences, which are real, derived instead from the particular form of nation-ness such literary ambitions tended to imply, a form of collectivity and mutual attachment that Poe's work, for a variety of reasons, could not countenance. I want to argue, more exactly, that it is in fact the near-impossibility of any intimacy in Poe, of any human proximity that is not eventually terrorizing, that makes the very notion of *national belonging*—of an attachment among the mutually anonymous—virtually unthinkable for Poe. Inasmuch as nationality is inseparable, for Poe, from an idea of attachment or intimacy, he cannot assent to it, since for him the idea of intimacy is inseparable, in turn, from every variety of horror.

Poe's uneasiness with nationalist literary pursuit returns us, then, to the point where we began, the point so many critics and writers and biographers have chosen to dwell on: the vexations of intimacy in Poe, particularly as they are expressed in the prevalence of pedophiliac erotics and investments. In this chapter, I want to tell a story about how sexual intimacy does and does not work in Poe, and the question I use as an angle into these problems is a simple one: why is that only little girls seem suitable objects, in Poe, for sustained erotic attachment? Of course, the question of pedophilia in Poe is itself in no way a simple one and cannot be "solved" by a turn to what Jacques Derrida has called "psychobiographism." (It will not do, in other words, to read every nuance and opacity of Poe's writing through the revealed truth of pedophilia, as though all of the former were merely symptoms of the latter.)[7] As a textual problem, the matter of intimacy and its disturbances in Poe is in fact terrifically complicated, and by a number of factors, as we will see: by the idiosyncrasies of Poe's narrative style; by the anxieties of racial distinction into which his morbidly acute narrators seem always to propel themselves; and by the violent contortions of femininity that are used, in turn, to deflect and contain those racial anxieties. Each of these matters bears careful explication, and none, I think, is separable from any other—which suggests, among other things, that the story of *how* the pedophilic dynamics of Poe's work actually operate requires from us a good deal more than a knowledge of Virginia Clemm's age on the day of her wedding.

This complicated story of the fate of intimacy in Poe is important to tell, for several reasons. Most immediately, doing so helps us to think together aspects of Poe's writing that have seemed to many critics crucial but difficult to bring into dialogue: his work's involvement with the racial logic of his day *and* its affective and sexual idiosyncrasies. For the most part, psychoanalytic criticism has been invested in the latter—as in the volume built around Derrida and Lacan's readings of Poe, *The Purloined Poe*—to the exclusion of the former. Newer work on Poe and race, which has been salutary and welcome (and has tended to follow from Toni Morrison's work on whiteness and Africanism in her 1993 collection *Playing in the Dark*), has likewise suffered from one-sidedness. Even in the fine essays collected in *Romancing the Shadow: Poe and Race*, the desire to describe Poe's engagement with the racial imperatives and discourses of the antebellum republic results in a thoroughgoing disregard for the sexual investments and erotic peculiarities that so vividly mark Poe's text—it is a matter that none of the nine essays takes up in a sustained way.[8] Looking closely at Poe's relation to the ideal of an intimate nationality has seemed to me one way to find rapport between these divided critical impulses, and so allow for a fuller vision of Poe's work: through close attention to the matter of intimacy, that is, we might discover both how to do justice to the racial dynamics of Poe's work without simply forgetting the sexual vexations on equally prominent display there, *and* how to talk about the erotic peculiarities in Poe without inadvertently removing him, implicitly or otherwise, from the turbulence of antebellum national life.

Most crucially, though, this complicated story of how intimacy does and does not work is, for Poe, also the story of how and why the very idea of American nation-ness, of a vast network of anonymous affective bonds, does not and cannot work. As we will see in the conclusion, Poe was willing to believe many things of whiteness in his work—he believed particularly that it ought to secure a definitive separateness from the corporeal volatility involved in non-whiteness—but not that it was an aspect of self through which he was somehow affiliated, in a quite intimate way, with persons unknown to him. The path toward this larger point is a circuitous one and involves us in the examination of many of the more local entanglements of Poe's writing (with morbidity, with slavery, with femininity). But such circuitousness is also instructive, inasmuch as it serves to remind us that Poe's writerly obliquities and idiosyncrasies are not merely the mark of his aberrance, and much less of his removal from what is commonly understood as "history"; on the contrary, if we are willing to read them patiently and in close detail, they describe for us his *relation* to some of the most consequential ideals and imperatives of his moment. Matthiessen was perhaps right, then, to describe Poe as a "revelatory contrast" to the likes of Whitman and Melville, since what his resistances reveal are the intimate contours of the nationalisms they would, in their different ways, more unhesitatingly endorse. More haunted than solaced by the idea of human intimacy, Poe offers a gothic that both glimpses, and adamantly refuses, an America made of affective, intimate ties among strangers.

THE IDIOM OF THE ANIMATE CORPSE

Disturbances in the realm of intimacy are of course a standard feature of the gothic, a genre not noted for its happy marriages, lighthearted couplings, or long and untroubled friendly allegiances. At the same time, it is fair to say that there is nothing at all standard or routine about Poe's gothic—it is, to the contrary, as idiosyncratic, and as unyieldingly particular, as the absolutely singular style in which he realizes it. Indeed, few idioms of the antebellum era are more immediately identifiable than those employed in the fictions of Edgar Allan Poe. That what we identify in Poe is his idiom, even more than his personae, is an important point to recall. For, despite what his detractors may wish to claim, the distinctive thing about Poe is not that his narrators are nearly all murderous, or delusional, or in some other extremity of psychosis.[9] Such habits of character distinguish Poe's writing with no more subtlety or refinement than a caricature (and Poe has, over the years, been subject to many a caricature, pictorial and otherwise). But if, by contrast, a master stylist like Vladimir Nabokov is right—if his *Lolita* is any indication—then Poe's uniqueness as a writer is not thematic but fundamentally *rhetorical* in constitution. Humbert Humbert's baroque first-person monologue argues quite vividly that if Poe's narrators share any one thing, it is not derangement as such, but rather an ability to experience and, especially, to record their every inward sensation, physical or emotional, with phenomenal, hyper-real acuteness. What they share, in other words, is not a single pathology but a single rhetoric—a single style—of self-perception.

Accordingly, the surest way to begin unraveling the many imbricated strands of Poe's idiosyncratic work is to look closely at the mechanics of that style, to see what it does and how it works. "The Fall of the House of Usher" seems particularly well suited to such inquiry, if only because its narrator happens to be neither a murderer nor a dissipating invalid nor the victim of a premature interment—although, like these other Poe narrators, he too seems burdened by a self-consciousness that is perhaps too finely tuned. Here is the opening paragraph in its entirety, in which that quality of hyper-real meticulousness, so common in Poe, is particularly evident:

> During the whole of a dull, dark, soundless day in the autumn of the year, when the clouds hung oppressively low in the heavens, I had been passing alone, on horseback, through a singularly dreary tract of country; and at length found myself, as the shades of the evening drew on, within view of the melancholy House of Usher. I know not how it was—but, with the first glimpse of the building, a sense of insufferable gloom pervaded my spirit. I say insufferable; for the feeling was unrelieved by any of that half-pleasurable, because poetic, sentiment, with which the mind usually receives even

the sternest natural images of the desolate or terrible. I looked upon the scene before me—upon the mere house, and the simple landscape features of the domain—upon the bleak walls—upon the vacant eye-like windows—upon a few rank sedges—and upon a few white trunks of decayed trees—with an utter depression of soul which I can compare to no earthly sensation more properly than to the after-dream of the reveller upon opium—the bitter lapse into everyday life—the hideous dropping off of the veil. There was an iciness, a sinking, a sickening of the heart—an unredeemed dreariness of thought which no goading of the imagination could torture into aught of the sublime. What was it—I paused to think—what was it that so unnerved me in the contemplation of the House of Usher? It was a mystery all insoluble; nor could I grapple with the shadowy fancies that crowded upon me as I pondered. I was forced to fall back upon the unsatisfactory conclusion, that while, beyond doubt, there *are* combinations of very simple natural objects which have the power of thus affecting us, still the analysis of this power lies among considerations beyond our depth. It was possible, I reflected, that a mere different arrangement of the particulars of the scene, of the details of the picture, would be sufficient to modify, or perhaps to annihilate its capacity for sorrowful impression; and, acting upon this idea, I reined my horse to the precipitous brink of a black and lurid tarn that lay in unruffled lustre by the dwelling, and gazed down—but with a shudder even more thrilling than before—upon the remodelled and inverted images of the gray sedge, and the ghastly tree-stems, and the vacant and eye-like windows.[10]

Part of the pleasure that comes from reading a passage like this has to do with a particular kind of recognition: though you may never have read this tale before, if you've read any Poe at all you will probably be able to place this one, since it too is suffused with a handful of absolutely distinctive verbal tics, with patterns of idiom and syntactical arrangement that are, in effect, Poe's signature. We recognize a piece of Poe's exposition, perhaps first of all, by its conspicuous fastidiousness: by its pile-up of detail, its successive dependent clauses and fussy adjectival qualifications (as in the phrase "I reined my horse to the *precipitous* brink of a *black and lurid* tarn that lay *in unruffled lustre* by the dwelling"). We recognize Poe as well as by his often exaggerated erudition, his willingness to adopt stuffy, cold, or quasi-academic locutions to describe states of passion and emotional extremity (as in the turn that begins with the professorial "*I say insufferable*," after which follows a discriminating exposition on the different registers of "gloom"). These are the stylistic markers, first and foremost, of a narrative consciousness that is not at all shy about performing its determination to get every description, every utterance, exactly right. Such flourishes constitute, I think, a kind of boasting—as though, with the insertion of every additional modifying clause, the author were asking us to note just how exaggeratedly meticulous he is willing to be. And this stylistic bravado or gamesmanship begins to explain, in turn, that odd indeterminacy of tone in Poe: to explain, that is, why even the most grisly or horrible of Poe's narrations can seem pitched just this side of the comic; why his mournful tragedies can read like parody; and why you can never quite be sure, when treading on the taut surfaces of Poe's prose, of the degree to which he is, or is not, putting you on.[11]

Working in tandem with Poe's self-conscious verbal exactitude, and just as clearly on display in the opening of "Usher," is also a strategy involving what we might call the micromanagement of narrative sequence. We notice, for instance, how densely this paragraph is populated with phrases and locutions that act almost entirely as temporal place-markers or connectives: "during the whole of," "I had been passing," "at length," "as the shadows of the evening drew," "with the first glimpse," then later, "I paused to think," "I reflected," "and, acting upon this idea." Very little occurs here that is not situated, by virtue of this multiplication of hypotactic figures, within a meticulously plotted linear sequence. The highest of premiums is thus placed by this style on the regulation, and legibility, of narrative time. Indeed, the very adjectives Poe applies to the objects on display here bring to those objects a variety of temporal specifications: trees are *decayed*, the tarn is *unruffled*, images in it are both inverted and *remodelled*. These past-participial adjectives (holdovers from Poe's Southern classicist education in Latin) etch the passage of time *into* the objects to which they are attached, so that time itself is seen both to have coursed over and scarred the landscape, and to have been brought under an almost diagrammatic narrative control. Like Poe's descriptive fastidiousness, this obsessively sequential mode provides for a kind of boasting as well. For when Poe levels the gaze of his acutely temporalizing narrative style at the world, what he tends to see are not objects or even events but *processes*, whose minute increments, because they can be separated out each from each, are therefore infinitely susceptible to obsessive ordering and pains-taking sequential arrangement: in short, to narrative. Among the principal illusions Poe's style works to foster is thus that of a nar-rative consciousness that can account exhaustively, and with abso-lute precision, for every instant of its unfolding—a consciousness upon which, to modify James, not so much as a heartbeat is lost. This is why the narrator of "The Fall of the House of Usher" pauses in his exposition to *say* that he paused to think: that little parenthetical quip, and the temporally regulated analysis that follows it, call clear attention to the fact that even cognition, once held in the unyielding grip of Poe's sequentializing style, can be anatomized down to its least tremors and tiniest operations.

For all that, "The Fall of the House of Usher" is yet among the very least exaggerated versions of this style we can find in Poe's work. For what the famed nineteenth-century orator Martin Fahquhar Tupper described as Poe's "microscopic power of analy-sis" involves not only this ability to break down into minute and progressive stages the activities of *cognition* (as in the famous tales of "ratiocination") but also, and more vividly, the activities of *embodiment*.[12] Here, for instance, is a not at all untypical piece of first-person narrative exposition, which appears near the close of "The Premature Burial":

> There arrived an epoch . . . in which I found myself emerging from total unconsciousness into the first feeble and indefinite sense of existence. Slowly—with a tortoise gradation—approached the faint gray dawn of the psychal day. A torpid uneasiness. An apathetic endurance of dull pain. No care—no hope—no effort. Then, after a long interval, a ringing in the ears; then, after a lapse still longer, a pricking or tingling sensation in the extremi-ties; then a seemingly eternal period of pleasurable quiescence, during which the awakening feelings are struggling into thought; then a brief re-sinking into non-entity; then a sudden recovery. At length the slight quivering of an eyelid, and immediately thereupon, an electric shock of a terror, deadly and indefinite, which sends the blood in torrents from the temples to the heart. And now the first positive effort to think. (676–77)

The alternation of physical and "pyschal" details, strung together by a chain of uniformly temporal connectives ("then," "after a long interval," "at length," "and now"), make the passage a perfect example of what we might call Poe's style of phenomenological hypotaxis. Among the primary effects of such a discursive form is the radical temporalization of being in the body: living embodiment, that is, reveals itself under such stylistic scrutiny to be an ever-unfolding sequence of microprocesses, whose "tortoise gradations" are thus available to infinite, infinitely specifying, narrative description. Given this style, it is of course small wonder that the simple fact of having a body, in Poe, habitually induces upheaval, transformation, and continual uncertainty; the very nature of Poe's verbal imagination disposes him, again and again, to exactly these turns.

It may be, however, that talk about syntax and idiom and sequence is just a particularly involved way of describing an effect that is, in truth, quite straightforward, or, at the very least, quite immediate, particularly to those readers who appreciate Poe for no grander reason than that he writes an honest-to-god scary story. For what Poe's distinctive brand of horror depends on, for its chief effects, is precisely the thrilling nonagreement between the lunacy of his narrators, on the one hand, and the exquisite clarity of their narrative perceptions, on the other. In these tales of murder and mania, we find ourselves confronted again and again with narrators who are avowedly deranged, yet whose accounts of that derangement are eerily calm, detached, and painstaking: it is derangement, then, but derangement possessed of a downright clinical acuity. (And it is this narrative conceit, far more than the sonorous names or the atmosphere of artistic melancholy, that seems most to enable Nabokov in the sentence-by-sentence assembly of *Lolita*, whose narrator describes his own semi-deranged ardor for young Dolly Haze in a language that is at once heartstoppingly mellifluous and, at moments, hyper-real in its detached precision.) These effects of style are, as I say, immediate enough; yet the acute sensitivity of Poe's narrative personae—their tendency to perceive all phenomena as gradually occurring microprocesses—produces as well a number of other, rather more complicated effects.

Consider, for instance, some of the conclusions that arise when Poe's narrative gaze turns, as it often does, to the problem of Life, Death, and their difference from one another. "The boundaries which divide Life from Death," he writes at the outset of "The Premature Burial,"

> are at best shadowy and vague. Who shall say where the one ends, and where the other begins? We know that there are diseases in

which occur total cessations of all the apparent functions of vitality, and yet in which these cessations are merely suspensions, properly so called. They are only temporary pauses in the incomprehensible mechanism. (666)

It's certainly not unusual to think of vitality, of life, as an elaborate system of processes and microevents; this kind of "vitalism" is indeed perfectly commonplace in a variety of nineteenth-century writings. But so intent is the quality of Poe's narrative scrutiny that, under its gaze, *death too becomes its own kind of process*, distributed in time, and always torturously slow to complete itself. Rather than unchanging states, in other words, for Poe death and life are both—are equivalently—processes of corporeal transformation, and as such their respective operations can often appear disconcertingly similar. Thus we find in Poe, as nowhere else in American literature, such sentences as: "No one suspected, or indeed had reason to suspect, that she was not actually dead" (667); "Yet not for a moment did I suppose myself actually dead" (494); and, of course, "'For God's sake!—quick!—quick!—put me to sleep—or, quick!—waken me!—quick!—*I say to you that I am dead!*'" (841).[13]

Actually dead: only in Poe can we find qualifications that so bizarrely hesitate the supposedly absolute difference between vitality and quiescence, life and its absence. What such qualifications make clear, though, is the fact that death is meaningful for Poe not merely as the absence or cancellation of life: only rarely does death simply descend in his tales, as though it were a lightning bolt from the heavens. Far more frequently, death unfolds, in maddeningly partial and progressive stages. And to say that death unfolds is of course to intimate that death, properly conceived, actually *lives* in the bodies of Poe's creations, and has therefore an unnervingly animate presence in the body that in most instances cannot be readily distinguished from the functions of life—which is one reason why what are taken for corpses in Poe tend not to stay dead.[14] But this mortal uncertainty works the other way as well: so thoroughly do the processes of death inhabit those of healthy life, that any one of Poe's clear-eyed narrators may well discover, in his frenzy of self-scrutiny, that he is himself actively dying, or, to put this another way, *insufficiently alive*. Equipped with such high-powered stylistic tools of self-perception, Poe's narrators seem always to find themselves riveted by the faintest echoes of a death that ticks away inside themselves. We tend to call this nervous condition, for want of any better word, morbidity.[15]

To find that one's self is always already partially dead, or that it is involved in the ongoing processes of dying, is disturbing in any circumstance. But for Poe, and for Poe's America, that disturbance had a very particular edge to it. Listen to Henry David Thoreau, who in 1854 brought his address "Slavery in Massachusetts" to a remarkable conclusion. "Slavery and servility," he writes,

> have produced no sweet-scented flower annually to charm the senses of men, for they have no real life: they are merely a decaying and a death, offensive to all healthy nostrils. We do not complain that they *live*, but that they do not *get buried*. Let the living bury them: even they are good for manure.[16]

Were it not for the cozy naturalist metaphor bookending them, Thoreau's pronouncements might well impress us with the force of their curious gothicism. What lends Thoreau's homespun wit its notable bite in this passage is the very thing that makes for anxiousness and volatility in Poe's tales: Thoreau trades here on the uncertain aliveness of the slave—on its status as animate property, as a marginally sentient thing—and uses that troubling indeterminacy as a figure with which to condemn not slaves but the institution of slavery. Hence, the national practice of slavery appears in Thoreau's sight as, precisely, a monstrously reanimate corpse, whose ghastly presence haunts the civic landscape. Thoreau thus provides us with a concise and particularly vivid example—and we might think too of Harriet Beecher Stowe's initial title for *Uncle Tom's Cabin*, "The Man That Was a Thing"—but we need not have left Poe's own corpus to be reminded of the salience of slavery with respect to figures of ambiguous animation.[17]

The racial meanings of uncertain vitality are just as clear, for example, in a tale of Poe's called "The Man That Was Used Up," which features a certain "Brevet Brigadier General John A. B. C. Smith," an Indian-fighter and man of some social renown (Poe's narrator describes him as a hero of "the late Bugaboo and Kickapoo campaign"). Throughout the tale, Poe's narrator attempts to solve the mystery of this famous personage, to find what it is about him that so intrigues and beguiles his society. After a series of frustrated investigations, each of which is interrupted just as the narrator is about to be told the General's secret, he finally seeks the great man out at his home. "It was early when I called," he writes,

and the general was dressing; but I pleaded urgent business, and
was shown at once in his bed-room by an old negro valet, who
remained in attendance during my visit. As I entered the chamber,
I looked about, of course, for the occupant, but did not immediately
perceive him. There was a large and exceedingly odd looking
bundle of something which lay close by my feet on the floor, and,
as I was not in the best humor in the world, I gave it a kick out
of the way.

    "Hem! ahem! rather civil that, I should say!" said the bundle,
in one of the smallest, and altogether the funniest little voices,
between a squeak and a whistle, that I ever head in all the days
of my existence. (314)

As it turns out, this "exceedingly odd looking bundle of something"
becomes recognizably the General—becomes recognizably human—
only after his "old negro valet," whose name is Pompey, screws in,
joins, and mechanically attaches a series of prosthetic arms, legs,
shoulders, as well as the General's bosom, teeth, eye, and palate
(314–16). "I now began very clearly to perceive," the narrator
writes, "that the object before me was nothing more nor less than
my new acquaintance, Brevet Brigadier General John A. B. C.
Smith. The manipulations of Pompey had made, I must confess, a
very striking difference" (316). Even more cartoonish in its execution than I have made it appear (featuring such characters as
"Reverend Doctor Drummummupp," "Misses Arabella and Miranda
Cognoscenti," and "Mrs. Pirouette"), the story means of course to
be comedy, and its parodic lightness of tone is everywhere evident.
But simply to get the joke of the story, to understand the exact
nature of its laugh at the General's expense, one must recognize
how perfectly the quasi-animate white crusader is doubled by the
person of Pompey, his servant and, as someone who is black, a
figure of no less corporeal ambiguity, a figure no less unclearly
human. By the story's logic, that is, the ridiculousness of the General's fame and pretense to social elevation ("Now, you nigger, my
teeth!" he imperiously commands) reveals itself not so much in his
clear dependence on Pompey but rather in the fact that for the
story's purposes these two men of wildly different social standing
are both, in an equivalent and symmetrical way, only partially
alive.[18]

    The racial logic in which "The Man That Was Used Up" thus
roots its satire quickly becomes a great deal less light-hearted—

becomes, indeed, quite grave—when placed in the context of Poe's general rhetorical practice. For, as we have seen, the very idiom in which Poe casts his acutely sensitive white male narrators seems designed for no other purpose than to disclose, again and again, the deathliness that has imperceptibly begun to pervade their living bodies. Poe's signature style, in other words, produces almost as a rule narrators who are forever discovering themselves to be only quasi-animate—narrators who are forever in danger, then, of succumbing to a state of deathliness or morbidity, through whose bodily symptoms they become alarmingly slavelike, alarmingly *less white*.[19] It makes sense, then, that Poe's is a decidedly volatile figural economy, wherein seemingly antipathetic conventions and generic modes (such as the sentimental and the gothic) tend to collide with one another, often to notably violent effect.[20] The problem that fuels such violence, at its most basic, is this: everything about Poe's verbal and stylistic imagination propels him headlong into figures that are intolerably fraught with racial meaning and racial anxiousness.

THE HEROINE, UNDEAD

We are moving gradually nearer the matter of Poe's uneasy relation to the forms of American nationalism, and the ideals of intimate national belonging, that were developing around him. The racial anxieties surrounding morbidity take us one step further into the frayings and malfunctions of intimacy that characterize Poe's writing, although they do so somewhat obliquely. For the prevalence of such strains of morbidity is not a matter to which Poe's writing is inattentive, and it is the peculiar nature of his response to that morbidity—his careful apportioning of its terrors—that returns us to questions of intimacy and attachment. How exactly, then, does Poe presume to manage the racial anxiousness into which his pervasively morbid narrators and narratives threaten to be dissolved? Once again, "The Fall of the House of Usher" helps us begin to unpack these complicated questions. For one of the most striking things about this tale, along with its hypermeticulous idiom, is the suddenly high premium placed on *gender* in a world potentially overrun with gothic morbidity. The inseparability of Madeline Usher's femininity from her morbidity invites us to wonder exactly where sexual difference fits within an economy of racial meaning. How, we might ask, do the imperatives of racial distinction inflect the meaningfulness, for Poe, of gender? What can we say about the utility of sexual difference within a figural economy whose vexations seem more urgently racial?

Though it features both a dissipating heroine and a reanimate corpse, "The Fall of the House of Usher" might yet seem like exactly the wrong place to begin looking for the effects of sexual difference, since it is the disconcerting elision of that difference—its subsumption by a greater similarity—that marks the story's principle cross-gender relationship. Roderick Usher, the old friend whom the narrator visits in his gloomy manor, the House of Usher, is not the gothic doppelgänger of the tale's narrator, as we might reasonably expect him to be. Instead, he is, literally, the double of his sister and twin, Madeline, and what they share is no mere family resemblance. More deeply and more disturbingly, they partake in a common susceptibility to a condition of nervous illness, bodily wasting, and a more general kind of uncertain animateness: the condition, that is, of morbidity. Of Roderick's appearance, the narrator writes:

> A cadaverousness of complexion; an eye large, liquid, and luminous beyond comparison; lips somewhat thin and very pallid but of a surpassingly beautiful curve . . . The now ghastly pallor of the skin, and the now miraculous lustre of the eye, above all things startled and even awed me. The silken hair, too, had been suffered to grow all unheeded, and as, in its wild gossamer texture, it floated rather than fell about the face, I could not, even with effort, connect its Arabesque expression with any idea of simple humanity. (321)

Of Roderick's equally cadaverous sister, and of her mortifying illness, we are told, "A settled apathy, a gradual wasting away of the person, and frequent although transient affections of a cataleptical character were the unusual diagnosis" (322). Unusual indeed: for what appears to live in these twin bodies are, precisely, the slowly unfurling processes of death and degeneration. In the peculiar stasis of their lives in the tomblike manor, in their pallid cadaverousness and their unwavering morbidity, they give living expression to death; or, put differently, they *are* death, expressed in the form of life. No "simple humanity" attaches to them because they are, as far as the narrator can see, so possessed of the unhuman-ness of death. Indeed, so tenuously alive do Madeline and Roderick appear throughout the tale—so almost-already-dead—that the narrator comes to recognize the "striking similitude between the brother and the sister" only after Madeline has died, as he gazes into her unsealed coffin (329). The point of the narrator's observation, at this particular moment, is fairly plain: what similitude obtains is that between a soon-to-be-animate corpse and its all-but-inanimate living brother.

A thematics of encroachment, doubling, and self-erosion is, of course, the stuff and substance of the gothic.[21] In "The Fall of the House of Usher," however, the paranoia that more typically attends the eerily telepathic encroachment on a male protagonist by a male villain discloses itself instead in the unsettlingly porous relationship of the animate to the inanimate. Not at all coincidentally, this relationship proves to be among the topics on which the morbid Roderick exercises his pertinacious intellect. Midway through the tale, he engages our narrator in a heated argument about "the sentience of all vegetable things." Usher's thesis, which he maintains so earnestly, accomplishes more than the concretization of the narrator's initial impressions of the weird "mystic vapor" that enshrouds the manor; and it does more than scientistically literalize the figurative linking of family and domicile in the appellation "House of Usher." Above all, Roderick's disquisition suggests the communicability of the animate and the inanimate through the mediating term of *sentience*. "The evidence of the sentience" of the stones, according to Roderick,

> was to be seen . . . in the gradual yet certain condensation of an atmosphere of their own about the waters and the walls. The result was discoverable, he added, in that silent yet importunate and terrible influence which for centuries had moulded the destinies of his family, and which made *him* what I now saw him—what he was. (327–28)

Due to that "silent yet importunate and terrible influence" that eats away within him, what Roderick has become by this point, and what his sister in her illness had long been, is a sentient creature verging on the inanimate, just as the manor and its profusions of "leaden-hued" gloom are, to Roderick, sentient entities verging on the animate. Life and death, the narrator is beginning to learn, are states by no means opposed in the forbidding House of Usher; instead, they are threaded together by a quality of sentience that extends equally to sisters, to brothers, and to stones.

The narrator observes these goings-on with palpable apprehension, and what unsettles him in particular is less the permeability of the animate and the inanimate than the apparent contagiousness of the Ushers' morbidity. "It was no wonder," he writes late in the tale, "that [Roderick's] condition terrified—that it infected me. I felt creeping upon me, by slow yet certain degrees, the wild influences of his own fantastic yet impressive superstitions" (330). It seems the Ushers' deathliness can be contracted, caught from them like a virus or flu—and this is what terrifies the narrator more and more as the tale progresses. But the narrator does not contract this morbidity unto death, as do Madeline and, eventually, her brother. For all his nervousness, the narrator is, after a fashion, spared. If the terrifying contagiousness of the Ushers' morbidity thus has an antidote in the story, it appears to arrive in the person of none other than Madeline Usher herself. For Madeline returns from her grave not as a haunting spirit but as an enfleshed monstrosity, and her very monstrousness—the particular form it takes—does a great deal to steady the narrator's vertiginous panic before the prospect of a wandering, infectious morbidity.

By the end of the tale, Roderick has grown, in the narrator's eyes, more completely unhinged: "there was a species of mad hilarity in his eyes," we are told, "an evidently restrained *hysteria* in his whole demeanor" (331). More specifically, the narrator surmises that Roderick's "unceasingly agitated mind was laboring with some oppressive secret" (330)—as though some monstrous sin were devouring him in progressive stages from within. The suggestion of a sin both undisclosed and monstrous (again, the very meat of the gothic) finds a particularly grisly analogue, however, in the tale's climactic moment. In his final monologue, Roderick speaks in "a low, hurried, and gibbering murmur," but what he says is clear enough to the narrator:

> "Not hear it?—yes, I hear it, *have* heard it. Long—long—long—many minutes, many hours, many days, have I heard it—yet I dared not—oh pity me, miserable wretch that I am!—I dared not—I *dared* not speak! *We have put her living in the tomb!* Said I not that my senses were acute? I *now* tell you that I heard her first feeble movements in the hollow coffin . . . Do I not distinguish that heave and horrible beating of her heart? Madman!"—here he sprang furiously to his feet, and shrieked out his syllables, as if in the effort he were giving up his soul—"*Madman! I tell you that she now stands without the door!*"
>
> As if in the superhuman energy of his utterance there had been found the potency of a spell—the huge antique pannels to which the

speaker pointed, threw slowly back, upon the instant, their ponder-
ous and ebony jaws. It was the work of the rushing gust—but then
without those doors there *did* stand the lofty and enshrouded
figure of the lady Madeline of Usher. There was blood upon her
white robes, and the evidence of some bitter struggle upon every
portion of her emaciated frame. For a moment she remained trem-
bling and reeling to and fro upon the threshold—then, with a low
moaning cry, fell heavily inward upon the person of her brother,
and in her violent and now final death-agonies, bore him to the floor
a corpse, and a victim to the terrors he had anticipated. (334–35)

In a way that's as striking as it is eerie, death returns Madeline
emphatically to her gender. "There was blood upon her white
robes," we are told, "and the evidence of some bitter struggle upon
every portion of her emaciated frame." This is all the physical
description of the undead Madeline the narrator will hazard, which
makes the evident sexualization of her violation by the deathliness of the tomb all the more resonant and chilling. One mordant
suggestion here is that Roderick's mania is the symptom of this
sin—that *he* has been the violator of his sister's tombal virginity.
But it is, in any case, the fact of Madeline's having been violated,
as in "some bitter struggle," that comes to the foreground in this
moment. For if Madeline emerges here as the very emblem of morbidity's terror—as death-living, the reanimate corpse—the passage, by thus figuring death's animate presence in life as a kind of
rape, rewrites morbid degeneration as a function of the particular
vulnerabilities of virginal femininity. Elisabeth Bronfen has something of this dynamic in mind when, considering Poe, she writes
of "Woman as the agency that heals the wound of death's presence
in life."[22] By writing the terrors of morbidity as a function of specifically feminine vulnerabilities (as Poe will do again and again in
his stories of reanimate wives such as Lady Ligeia and Berenice),
the tale intimates that femininity itself is the proper living carrier
of death: the pervasive deathliness of life in the House of Usher is
here translated, in other words, into the deathliness of a violable
femininity, and translated with an impressive seamlessness. What
sense of reprieve the narrator may then be allowed to feel from
the threat of morbidity thus derives not least from the security of
his distinction from her *as a man*.[23] For the disease of morbid infection, sexual difference, it turns out, is a kind of cure.

In an odd way, then, "The Fall of the House of Usher" describes with real vividness the entanglements, in Poe, of gender and race—and it does so despite featuring neither slaves, nor any black characters, nor any prominent figures of ruthless tyranny or subservience. It is in the terrors of morbidity, though, that these two strands of social meaning begin to ratify one another. We need only recall, in this vein, how morbidity's chief emblem, the animate corpse, figures a too-porous distinction between life and death, animate and inanimate, person and thing: where morbidity offers these uncertainties, its disavowal will draw much of its urgency, as we have seen, from the need for the embodiment of white men to be of an absolutely different order than that of black slaves. What "The Fall of the House of Usher" makes graphically clear is how sexual difference might provide a terrifically powerful lever for such anxious disavowals; in this tale, white femininity functions essentially as the place where morbidity can be sequestered. Through Madeline's emphatically gendered mostrousness, whatever symptoms of bodily indeterminacy might have unnerved Poe's hyperconscious narrator are effectively enclosed within the province of femininity. Figuring femininity as morbidity's proper vehicle, the tale distances the terrors of morbid degeneration from the white men whose overwrought nervousness and acuity seem also to invite them. Insofar as the distinction between the sexes in Poe remains absolute and unbreachable, then, his nervous white men will have perpetually to hand a way to displace—and so to shield themselves from—threats to their own racial distinction. Sexual difference becomes a vehicle, an alibi, for the racial distinctiveness of white men.

THE USES OF A CHILD BRIDE

The malfunctions of intimacy in Poe now begin to come into sharper focus, and these, as we will see, are at the heart of his wary regard for antebellum nationalist endeavor. For if a certain strain of absolutism with respect to gender promises to ease a number of dire figural double binds in Poe, it also broaches a number of its own problems. Among these is, in short, the terror, even the impossibility of sex—or rather, the impossibility of sexual intimacy across the great and unbridgeable chasm of gender. The sequestering of deathliness and corporeal volatility in the bodies of women may indeed allow Poe's morbid narrators to cast anxieties about racial indistinction in the terms of an apparently less porous sexual difference, as "Usher" so graphically suggests; but a femininity so habitually overrun by the ghastly degenerations of morbidity, whatever its figural utility, is at the same time plainly not amenable to the sexual investments of men. So very emphatic—and emphatically grotesque—is the imagined difference of women from men in Poe that mere desire is rarely capable of traversing its distance. There most certainly are sexes in Poe's world—but is there, in turn, heterosexuality?

An exceptionally compact, exceptionally perverse little tale called "Morella" takes up just these problems. It is the story of a relationship between a man and a woman—a marriage, in fact—whose peculiarities are evident from the first words:

> With a feeling of deep yet most singular affection I regarded my friend Morella. Thrown by accident into her society many years ago, my soul, from our first meeting, burned with fires it had never known before; but the fires were not of Eros, and bitter and tormenting to my spirit was the gradual conviction that I could in no manner define their unusual meaning, or regulate their vague intensity. Yet we met; and fate bound us together at the altar; and I never spoke of passion, nor thought of love. She, however, shunned society, and, attaching herself to me alone, rendered me happy. It is a happiness to wonder;—it is a happiness to dream. (234)

What sustains them in this "fateful" bond of seemingly incommensurate affections are Morella's curious studies—"her powers of mind," the narrator is quick to inform us, "were gigantic" (234). Soon enough, though, even these chaste attachments sour: "I could no longer bear the touch of her wan fingers," he writes, "nor the low tone of her musical language, nor the lustre of her melancholy eye" (235). Indeed, so powerful are the narrator's feelings of repulsion that Morella's obdurate refusal to die, even after many long months of dissipation, drives him to the point of frenzy:

> Shall I then say that I longed with an earnest and consuming desire for the moment of Morella's decease? I did; but the fragile spirit clung to its tenement of clay for many days—for many weeks and irksome months—until my tortured nerves obtained the mastery over my mind, and I grew furious through delay, and, with the heart of a fiend, cursed the days, and the hours, and the bitter moments, which seemed to lengthen and lengthen as her gentle life declined—like shadows in the dying of the day. (236)

The usually complacent narrator (who had "never spoke of passion, nor thought of love") suddenly longs with a remarkably passionate fervor, "with an earnest and consuming desire," for Morella's death. He desires its arrival as he has never desired the person of his wife.

Or has he? In what must be the weirdest turn of this self-consciously strange tale, Morella lays on her unloving husband a deathbed curse and summarily dies—*but not before giving birth to a child*. This revelation comes quite literally out of nowhere and is voiced not by the narrator himself, but by Morella, in her death-bed soliloquy:

> "I repeat that I am dying. But within me is a pledge of that affection—ah, how little!—which thou didst feel for me, Morella. And when my spirit departs shall the child live—thy child and mine, Morella's. But thy days shall be days of sorrow—that sorrow which is the most lasting of impressions, as the cypress is the most enduring of trees." (236)

The narrator's unblinking refusal to remark until the last possible instant the pregnancy that resulted (we are given only to assume) from some past moment of erotic consummation seems to register as forcefully as any other of the story's details the depth of his distaste for the idea of sexual commerce with his wife: such an event may perhaps be evidenced but is apparently too repugnant to him to be adumbrated or even passingly recalled. The pain of such connubial revulsion is not lost on Morella. Her curse, in fact, is a particularly ingenious one, insofar as it seizes on her dispassionate husband's stalled desire and turns its lacerating effects back on him.

Of his new and unnamed daughter, the narrator tells us "she grew strangely in stature and intellect, and was the perfect resemblance of her who had departed, and I loved her with a love more fervent than I had believed it possible to feel for any denizen of the earth" (237). Again, given the tepidity of his affections for Morella, this new "fervor" cannot but strike us as remarkable. But the "perfect resemblance" between daughter and wife quickly causes that ardent, "pure affection" to resonate to a substantially different chord:

> I said the child grew strangely in stature and intelligence. Strange, indeed, was her rapid increase in bodily size—but terrible, oh! terrible were the tumultuous thoughts which crowded upon me

while watching the development of her mental being! Could it be
otherwise, when I daily discovered in the conceptions of the child
the adult powers and faculties of the woman?—when the lessons
of experience fell from the lips of infancy? and when the wisdom
or the passions of maturity I found hourly gleaming from its full
and speculative eye? When, I say, all this became evident to my
appalled senses—when I could no longer hide it from my soul, nor
throw it off from those perceptions which trembled to receive it—
is it to be wondered at that suspicions, of a nature fearful and
exciting, crept in upon my spirit, or that my thoughts fell back
aghast upon the wild tales and thrilling theories of the entombed
Morella? (237)

Fearful and exciting indeed are the thoughts that might crowd in
upon the guardian of a child who, in his fervor of affection, notices
particularly in her "the adult powers and faculties of the woman,"
"the lessons of experience," and above all *the passions of maturity.*" The sexualization both of the child and of the father's atten-
tions could not be more clear, and the pleasure with which Poe
leans upon suggestively ambiguous phrasing is equally evident.
With "an agonizing anxiety," the narrator informs us, "I gazed, day
after day, upon her holy, and mild, and eloquent face, and poured
over her maturing form . . . discover[ing] new points of resemblance in the child to her mother." What horrifies him, he says, is
the "too perfect *identity*" of the child's resemblance to her mother.
But if that identity means to disclose the horror of a soul that will
not die, it presents as its nearly indistinguishable twin the horror
of an identity between a sexually available (if undesired) wife, and
a sexually prohibited (if, perhaps, achingly desired) daughter.[24]
    As it turns out, the child has been possessed by the mother.
We discover as much when the narrator at long last baptizes his
daughter, unwisely names her Morella, whereupon she convulses,
pronounces "I am here!" and dies. Just as his uncherished wife had
predicted, the narrator spends the remainder of his days pining
for the love he has lost:

> The winds of the firmament breathed but one sound within my
> ears, and the ripples upon the sea murmured evermore—Morella.
> But she died; and with my own hands I bore her to the tomb; and
> I laughed, with a long and bitter laugh as I found no traces of the
> first, in the charnel where I laid the second, Morella. (239)

The success of Morella's curse is evident, and seems to lie not merely in her ability to somehow sustain and, in fact, bequeath herself after her own death; its cunning efficacy appears instead in the pangs of desire and refusal that her inattentive widower is made to suffer. By the workings of her curse, the narrator's failures of erotic attachment to his wife return upon him in the form of a specifically Oedipal prohibition: having cruelly withheld sexual attention from his long-suffering wife, he is compelled in turn to withhold, from himself, the sexual satisfactions seemingly offered by his eerily "mature" and "experienced" young daughter. In both cases, heterosexuality is defined in the tale by the form and contours of its impossibility.

Criticism has not wanted for accounts of Poe's sex life and its imagined effect upon his writing. Over the years, any number of critics have painstakingly followed the trail of Poe's clearly melancholic but somehow elusive sexual character. In readings of his poetry, of his prose, and especially of his marriage to the barely pubescent Virginia Clemm, Poe has been pegged as everything from impotent and repressed to neurotic and, perhaps inevitably, mother-fixated. Here are just a few extracts from this uncommonly salacious critical archive:

> There is good reason to believe that this amorous young man avoided all his life the sexual connection with any woman.[25]

> Virginia was Poe's first cousin, and it may be that, on account of this, he had scruples about consummating the marriage.[26]

> [Virginia's] illness, which forbade any direct consummation of erotic desire, inspired those texts in which the fascination for a woman is dependent precisely on her unattainability.[27]

The notion of Poe's sexually obsessive asexuality is a strikingly obstinate piece of folk wisdom, the unmitigated speculativeness of which has become, it seems, no serious cause for diffidence or hesitation. If there is any true consensus among the varied mythographers of Poe, it seems to be that, in life as in his writing, he preferred the melancholy of a foreclosed sexual relation to the erotics of an extant one.

Yet Poe's writing, for all that, is clearly not without a persistent erotic strain. Hence, *Lolita*: on its opening pages, Nabokov lends to Humbert Humbert a sexual initiation whose narrative fleshes out—luridly, hilariously—the erotic details pointedly withheld from

Poe's mournful song of adolescent love and death, "Annabel Lee."
Humbert's ill-fated tryst with that "certain initial girl-child" (a
certain "Annabel Leigh") matches so perfectly the contours of Poe's
poem that we are not likely to miss the joke: Humbert's "problem,"
the novel winkingly suggests, has less to do with any easily schema-
tized psychosexual pathology than it does with his devotion, his
incurable addiction, to the forms and figures of Western love
poetry in general, and of Poe in particular. Among *Lolita's* many
rewards, then, is the riotous candor with which it realizes how
very thoroughly we are haunted in our understanding of Poe by
the many ghostly traces of pedophilia.[28] Like the purloined letter,
Nabokov suggests, those traces are there in plain sight, and his
novel, whatever else it does, invests with new drama and energy
lines as potentially unremarkable as those from "Annabel Lee,"
where Poe writes of his ill-fated child bride, "*She* was a child, and
I was a child, / In this kingdom by the sea" (102).

What the trajectory of our discussion of Poe has made it possible to see, though, is that the erotic charge around figures like
Morella the child and Annabel Lee—the erotic charge to which
Nabokov is brilliantly responsive—is neither inexplicable nor so
patently reducible to the familial oddities and presumed pathologies of Edgar Allan Poe. For in a figural world where adult women
suffer so routinely from the grotesque depredations of morbidity,
*pedophilia affords to heterosexuality what is perhaps its only func-
tional logic.* As we've thus far seen, the strain of sentimental ado-
ration in Poe is never sufficient to insulate living adult women
from the sudden gothic horror of degeneration and gruesome death:
more often than not, Morella the Beloved becomes, in a flash,
Morella the Undead. Such is the unenviable fate of femininity
in Poe's gothic fictive world. Within this world, only very young
girls, who are not yet encumbered by the revulsions of adult femininity, seem capable of providing a site for stable heterosexual
male desire in Poe, since only they do not appear liable at any
moment to mutate into some quasi-animate monstrosity. Thus
the transitoriness Poe finds so very poignant in his women-about-
to-be-monsters is replaced in his pedophilic moments by the erotics
of a similarly fragile moment of suspension that, in the adolescent
girl, precedes the fall into full feminine embodiment, and its re-
pulsions. Morella the child and Annabel Lee inhabit bodies only
marginally capable of sexual attachment, but that marginality, it

seems, is vastly preferable to the volatile morbidity of which adult women are the unfortunate carriers. Though it is not without its own kind of pathos and melancholy—young girls grow up—pedophilia nevertheless exists in Poe to make possible the idea of a sexually available woman.

It's worth noting again that we are at at least one remove, here, from readings that refer the pedophilic erotics of Poe's work securely back to the personal idiosyncrasies of a nineteenth-century magazine writer who married a teenager.[29] What pressures and informs these figures is a relation to the logic of slavery that compels Poe's obsessive white male narrators to make violent use of the distinctions of gender, the better to substantiate the distinctions of race. And that gendered violence in turn unsettles the possibilities of intimacy and of intimate exchange. Nor should we imagine that Poe's move to make gender ratify race is particularly outlandish, still another of this peculiar author's beguiling idiosyncrasies. We might recall, in this regard, the "populist" movement for the full enfranchisement of free white men that gathered momentum across the 1830s and 1840s, a movement that coupled the opening of the franchise to white men with specific exclusions, not only of all African Americans but of *women*—despite the fact that women had only ever voted in two states, and then under special circumstances.[30] The logic of this strangely reiterated disenfranchisement of white women, which becomes clearer from our readings of Poe, is that, as women are incontestably and absolutely different from men, so are whites absolutely different from blacks: the putatively self-evident distinction between the sexes is called on, here under the law, to ratify and, in essence, to clarify the hard difference between the races. For reasons similarly entrenched in the unstable racial logics of his day, Poe's writing clings to exactly that fantasy of absolute sexual distinction above all others—even if it means finally that intimacy remains forever a kind of terror, and heterosexuality a kind of child's play.

Conclusion: Gothic Anti-Nationalism

These vexed intimacies, these foreclosed or terrorized attachments, take us finally into the matter of Poe's unsettled, at times vitriolic relation to the idea of a distinctively American literature, and to midcentury American nationalism more generally. As I suggested at the outset, it is by now taken as a matter of course that Poe's place in the American canon is an odd one, that he sits somewhat uncomfortably among the other prominent antebellum authors, and that his work cuts rather sharply against the grain of the period's stridently nationalist ambitions and endeavors. Matthiessen's opinion of Poe as, again, "bitterly hostile to democracy" has been qualified and specified (often with reference to the many forms of his chronic "outsider-ness")[31] but not contravened. As J. Gerald Kennedy and Liliane Weissberg appraise the matter: "Excluded from the so-called American Renaissance and from most nationalist critical paradigms from F. O. Matthiessen to Sacvan Bercovitch, Poe has occupied an anomalous position in both the old and new canons of antebellum American writing. Evincing little sustained interest in the frontier, the natural landscape, the Puritan past, the settlement of the colonies, the Revolution, or democracy itself, he seems in many ways the most un-American of our early writers."[32] One great irony here is that Poe's involvement, his thorough entanglement, with the both the purveyors and the ideals of literary nationalism was long-standing and complex. But perhaps the more crucial point, which such presumption about Poe's hostilities tends to bracket, concerns the precise nature of Poe's uneasiness with respect to American nationalism. What we have seen thus far about the fate of intimacy in his work suggests, in fact, that Poe's feelings about "democracy," whatever they might have been, were less at issue in his apparent anti-nationalism than Matthiessen would have us believe. There were after all many less than democratic versions of American nationalism in the air, especially in the 1830s and 1840s, and Poe's reluctance to subscribe to them—even to those for which his work, his politics, and his literary allegiances seem ideally suited— tells us a great deal about the nature of nationalist imagining at midcentury.

The disparagements of Poe's nationalist resolve do, of course, make a kind of sense. That Poe's work was ill-matched to the demands of American particularity—that Poe himself opposed Americanisms in whatever form—is not difficult to prove. It's certainly true, in the first place, that at various points in his career Poe went out of his way to speak ill of prominent national literary figures (such as Longfellow), of avowedly national*ist* authors (such as Young America's Cornelius Matthews), and of the boosterism of literary nationalism generally. Little ambiguity clouds the intent

of acerbic lines like these, written by Poe in 1842 for an install-
ment of *Graham's Magazine*:

> Time was when we imported our critical decisions from the mother
> country. For many years we enacted a perfect farce of subserviency
> to the *dicta* of Great Britain. At last a revulsion of feeling, with self-
> disgust, necessarily ensued. Urged by these, we plunged into the
> opposite extreme. In throwing *totally* off that "authority," whose
> voice had so long been so sacred, we even surpassed, and by much,
> our original folly. But the watchword now was, "a national litera-
> ture!"—as if any true literature *could be* "national"—as if the world
> at large were not the only proper stage for the literary *historio*. We
> became, suddenly, the merest and maddest *partizans* in letters . . .
> A foreign substance, at this epoch, was a weight more than enough
> to drag down into the very depths of critical damnation the finest
> writer owning nativity in these States; while, on the reverse, we
> found ourselves daily in the paradoxical dilemma of liking, or pre-
> tending to like, a stupid book the better because (sure enough) its
> stupidity was of our own growth, and discussed our own affairs.[33]

In addition to such vitriol as this, there is, moreover, a wealth of
textual evidence. Poe's settings are very often foreign (France is a
favorite locale, though an unspecified European-ness does the job
in a pinch). His periods, likewise, tend to be arcane (as in, for
instance, "The Pit and the Pendulum," a tale of the Spanish Inqui-
sition). Only very rarely does he populate his tales with the flora
and fauna of native soil, such as those "Woods, Cataracts, Rivers,
Pinnacles, Steeps, and Lakes" whose formulaic presence in a poem
of Cornelius Matthews's Poe is pleased to belittle (*Essays and
Reviews*, 824). This kind of topological recipe for Americanism has
no appeal to Poe, nor do America's lexical flora and fauna (words
like "pine-knot" and "grimy," which so tickle the sensibility of a
writer like Melville) find in Poe much welcome. Indeed, if one powerful index of any poem's "American-ness" is the deftness with
which it balances the earthy, monosyllabic Anglo-Saxon and Germanic roots of the language against the courtly elegance of Latinate polysyllabics, then Poe's verse is a conspicuous anomaly.[34]
Not much of, say, Whitman's rough-hewn exposition can be pulled
out of lines like

> The skies they were ashen and sober;
>> The leaves they were crispéd and sere—
>> The leaves they were withering and sere;

It was night, in the lonesome October
Of my most immemorial year.
(89)

or

And neither the angels in Heaven above
Nor the demons down under the sea
~~Can ever dissever my soul from the soul~~
Of the beautiful Annabel Lee.
(103)

Impatient with the plodding, neo-Wordsworthian pentameters of Longfellow, Poe writes poetry as though he wished English could be Latin—or rather, as if English *were* Latin, with all its tripping anapests. And through all of this—through his Old World locales, his antiquated settings, his de-Anglicized idiom—Poe never seems to have anything particularly good to say, or much of anything to say at all, about an entity called America.

Even here, though, the evidence is perhaps more ambiguous than at first it seems. For, despite all this, Poe was yet capable of allegiances that brought him well within the circle of nationalist literary endeavor, and, in fact, into the very bosom of Young America itself. As Perry Miller reminds us, Poe enjoyed for some time the generous favor of Evert Duyckinck, prominent New York editor, card-carrying Democrat, and staunch advocate of the platform of literary nationalism (of whom we will hear more in the next chapter).[35] Through Duyckinck's politic maneuvering, Poe was for a time styled as, precisely, an American original, a native genius; at Duyckinck's behest, Poe wrote a *favorable* review of a novel by nationalist zealot Cornelius Matthews, praising it as "an ingenious, an original, and altogether an excellent book—a book especially well adapted to a series which is distinctively American" (*Essays and Reviews,* 837). Perhaps most importantly, two of Poe's *own* books, *Tales* and *The Raven and Other Poems*, were brought out as a part of the very same "distinctively American" series of books, Wiley and Putnam's Library of American Books—a series that, as Meredith L. McGill has observed, was "Young America's flagship publishing venture."[36] Terence Whalen may confuse matters somewhat when in his meticulous work on Poe and mass culture he describes Poe's desire for a wide and lucrative "national audience" as a kind of "nationalism"—American literary nationalism, as

Melville would point out so acerbically in "Hawthorne and His Mosses," was anything but mass-marketable in the 1840s and 1850s—but his broader point remains crucial: Poe's relations in and among the literary factions of his day were complicated enough, in their hopelessly overlapping loyalties and debts, to make claims about his uncontoured anti-nationalism seem a bit hasty.[37]

But there is more than this. Poe's Europhilic manner and style, his milieu, and many of his literary and political allegiances, far from disqualifying him, in fact seem to fit him perfectly for a particular brand of antebellum nationalism, which Reginald Horsman concisely describes as "romantic racial nationalism." Drawn rather haphazardly from the scientific racialism of the 1820s, and from the notions of racial unity, distinctiveness, and destiny inherited largely from German romanticism, as well as from the immensely popular writings of Sir Walter Scott, romantic racial nationalism in America rejected "eighteenth-century reason and universalism in favor of intuition and particularism," imagined Americans to be the inheritors of a racially encoded tradition of freedom and expansion, and whiteness to be the repository of these world-altering aptitudes.[38] As Horsman notes, such nationalism was particularly popular in the South, where Scott's influence was most prominent, and where chivalric and courtly social traditions made the influence of European thought far less a matter for anxiousness than in the North. One of the avatars of the movement was William Gilmore Simms, an author who, like Poe, furnished the *Southern Literary Messenger* with a great deal of his work, and who, like Poe, "for a time was aligned with the nationalistic Young America group," until his allegiances to Southern institutions proved too great a strain on his relation with the New York literati.[39] For Simms, who shared with Poe also a penchant for both European mannerism and gothicism, the abiding fascination was with what Horsman calls "the conquering mission of his race." Indeed, sharing pages of Young America's *Democratic Review* with Poe, in 1846, Simms would in a long poem of linked sonnets called "Progress in America" urge Americans toward expansion and implore them above all to "obey our destiny and our blood":

> The race must have expansion—we must grow
> Though every forward footstep be withstood,
> And every inch of ground presents its foe!
> We have, thank Heaven! a most prolific brood;

Look at the census, if you aim to know—
And then, the foreign influx, bad and good;
All helps new lands to clear—new seed to sow.
We must obey our destiny and blood,
Though Europe show her bill, and strike blow![40]

Simms presents a vision of "the race" (the "good old Norman stock," he calls it, "with blood well-temprered") expanding outward but also assimilating into itself the "the foreign influx," bringing foreign strains into the fold of the distinctively American race, which, according to the poem, shares a common, heroic destiny.

Here, then, is a nationalism in which all the familiar disqualifications of Poe do not apply: it is not exclusively Northern or of New England, like Matthiessen's retrospective construction; it is not vehemently opposed to foreign influence or "foreign influx," like so much of Young America's; it does not contravene Poe's putative allegiance to Southern customs and institutions (not least among which is slavery); and, in its strident emphasis on racial inequality and domination, it is certainly not unduly "democratic." What's remarkable, then, is that this too should be a nationalism Poe would refuse to endorse, either critically or in the more varied terrain of his fiction and poetry. His opinions and manners are in several ways cognate with Simms's, but the imaginative cosmology his *work* creates describes entirely different fascinations and imperatives. And a good deal of what makes for that difference is Poe's protracted refusal to take up Americanism, the cause of American nationality, or fully to embrace his whiteness, in such a way that he might, with Simms, "obey our destiny and our blood."[41]

What our readings of intimacy in Poe have allowed us to see is that, from Poe's perspective, the problem Simms shares with Duyckinck, the common problem of all these nationalisms, lies precisely in the idea of *our* destiny, *our* blood. Simms's nationalism, no less than Young America's, presumes that, in sharing a destiny, Americans at the same time share in a kind of relation with one another, a kind of bond that effectively forms them into a "we," which could then say, and understand the consequence of, "our." To partake in a shared destiny, for Simms, implies a particularly intimate relation with the anonymous others who share one's nation and one's race, such that to refuse live up to that destiny would be to adulterate that bond, to act not only against history but, more pressingly, against a series of endowed affective ties. Poe is no racial progressive, but in his work he refuses the sort of triumphalist identification as white that Simms champions. And he does so, I would argue, because the nationalist context in which whiteness found itself invests such an identification with specifi- · cally affiliative meaning—with suggestions of an intimacy between anonymous others—that Poe would not abide.

In this way, our readings of the fate of intimacy in Poe return him to the "history" by which he was surrounded: from this perspective, that is, we see in full detail why Poe's writing would be so ineptly disposed to the rigors of literary nationalism, why his relation to the idea of American nationality could only be suspicious and reluctant. For, in tale after tale, Poe's writing traces nothing other than the tenuousness, instability, and violent horror of the very idea of intimacy. Gothicist that he is, Poe has no register in which to describe any bond between persons—let alone a bond extending mysteriously between unsuspecting strangers— that is not fundamentally terrifying. As we've seen in "The Fall of the House of Usher," where *relations* are fairly indistinguishable from *infections*, any human proximity in Poe stands ready to become encroachment, just as every intimacy threatens to be irreparably self-dispossessing. (It is, again, exactly these dramas that are played out, repeatedly, in Poe's tales of wives who dissipate, die, but refuse to disappear.) If the thread that ties together the great variety of nationalisms surrounding Poe is indeed a belief in the capacity of anonymous citizens to sustain far-flung attachments and intimacies with one another, then Poe himself can have no purchase whatsoever on such a pursuit, since for him the prospect of an intimate relatedness between persons is not the stuff of utopian exhilaration but of horror: the nation consisting of a vast network of intimate relations would be, by Poe's cosmology, the scene of unending panics and dissolutions. These panics, as I have tried to show, derive their force from Poe's entanglements with American social life and its endemic forms of meaning, and in particular from the cross-wirings of racial, gendered, and sexual imperatives. But it is just this vexed involvement that seems finally to instruct Poe, in turn, that the very idea of "the nation," however it might momentarily provide for critical grandstanding and professional self-positioning, is nevertheless something too horrible to be conceived.

CHAPTER 3

Bowels and Fear: Nationalism, Sodomy, and Whiteness in *Moby-Dick*

Would that all excellent books were foundlings,
without father or mother.
HERMAN MELVILLE, "HAWTHORNE AND HIS MOSSES" (1850)

As Poe's messy entanglements with the literati of antebellum New York suggest, the literary world of the 1840s was one full of contention, suspicion, and not a little hostility. Perry Miller's landmark study *The Raven and Whale* reminds us further that, among the denizens of this world, few platforms were more hotly debated than the call for a program of literary nationalism. Miller maps his study around the career of Evert Duyckinck, a prominent New Yorker, one-time leader of the Young America sect of nationalist Democrats, an author, and all-around *litterateur*. Most importantly, though, Duyckinck was an editor who, along with his coterie of author-editor Democrats, implored the young writers of America throughout the 1840s to have done with imitation and literary servility and to set themselves to the mighty task of American originality. Of just what forms and qualities this uniquely American writing was to consist no one in Young America could say with much precision, though they knew clearly enough what it was *not*. Praising the "genius" of an author named Nathaniel Hawthorne, Duyckinck, in 1841, writes that of all Young Americans in print, Hawthorne is "the most original, the one least indebted to foreign models or literary precedents of any kind."[1] Unindebted originality, which is understood here to mean a freedom from the conceptual invasiveness of any foreign model or source, is for Duyckinck quite naturally the first demand to be made of the American author: for the true distinctiveness of America (a distinctiveness that amounts, for much of Young America, to superiority) would be intolerably distorted if expressed in the forms and idioms of another, lesser culture. Since a properly American literature could emerge only by virtue of its strict severance from the potentially corrupting literary past, the nationalist author must willfully abandon all preceding designs. If an uncompromised American literature were ever to appear, the argument went, it would have to be born, as it were, unparented.[2]

Herman Melville was, for a time, not at all shy in his advocacy of this brand of literary nationalism, and one of the most intriguing documents he produced on the subject is "Hawthorne and His Mosses," a review he wrote for Duyckinck in the summer of 1850, while in the throes of the composition of *Moby-Dick*. As exuberant and self-contradictory as the novel that would follow it, the essay uses Hawthorne's writing as an occasion to adumbrate the broader problems of American literary endeavor—to praise the avatars, scold the small-minded, and above all to speculate about "this matter of a national literature."[3] As Melville sees it, the American scene is dreadfully hampered, in both its critical and creative capacities, by the unabated prominence of foreign models and, in particular, by what he sneeringly calls this "leaven of literary flunkyism towards England" (546). "The great mistake," he writes, "seems to be, that even with those Americans who look forward to the coming of a great literary genius among us, they somehow fancy he will come in the costume of Queen Elizabeth's day—be a writer of dramas founded upon old English history, or the tales of Boccaccio" (543). Like Duyckinck, Melville has had enough of American mimicry—"we want no American Goldsmiths . . . we want no American Miltons" (545)—and desires most that native genius, in whatever unfamiliar form it appears, be fostered and revered. He sums up his polemic with an exhortation whose half-comic naturalist figures Ishmael himself would approve: "Let us boldly contemn all imitation, though it comes to us graceful and fragrant as the morning; and foster all originality, though, at first, it be crabbed and ugly as our own pine knots" (546).

Thus does Melville the literary journalist express his (as it proves, momentary) allegiance with Young America, whose collective disregard for "foreign models or literary precedents" he is eager to corroborate. And yet, for all that eagerness, it seems no exaggeration to say that Melville's *opus Americana* is profoundly unfitted to Young America's definition of nationalist "originality." By no stretch of the imagination a work without precedents, *Moby-Dick* might be described more accurately as a text positively glutted with precedents: a text that boldly announces its indebtedness to narratives, rhetorics, symbols, myths, and idioms, virtually all of which have been pilfered from a vast array of inherited sources. We see this immediately in the "Extracts" that preface the narrative, wherein Melville claims as his literary progenitors everyone from the Apostles and Rabelais, through Spenser, Milton, and Pope, right down to Darwin, Daniel Webster, and, of course, Shakespeare.[4] Nor is the narrative itself any less compulsively referential: it consists in its very texture of innumerable digressions into the literary, legal, metaphysical, commercial, religious, or historical precedent for this or that cetological detail. Though perhaps not founded entirely on Old English history and the tales of Boccaccio, the drama of *Moby-Dick* is nevertheless relentlessly *derived*, and derived from an archive of almost exclusively antique and foreign authors. How, then, do we make square so compulsively citational a novel with those proclamations, endorsed by Melville himself, of literary nationalism? What kind of nationalism is it, whose prerequisite of radical originality is satisfied through so vast an absorption of terrifically heterogeneous sources?

In this chapter, I want to suggest that the model of nationalism *Moby-Dick* proposes is of a peculiarly contentless cast; or, to put this differently, that American nationalism in *Moby-Dick* has no more positive attribute than that quality of ineluctable promise— of unbodied possibility—whose substance is the deliberate disqualification or erasure of any existing forms of content. The bearer of this quasi-Emersonian, oddly nihilistic promise is, of course, Ishmael, whose breezy and cheerfully digressive narrative consumes, then systematically dismisses or dissolves, each and every discursive precedent it lights upon. Looking in detail at the contours of that narrative form, I want to make a series of linked assertions. I want to suggest, first, that in Ishmael, Melville finds a voice with which he can both acknowledge a tremendous archive of inherited sources for America and undermine their accumulated authority. Just as crucially, though, this strangely voided nationalism represents, in turn, Melville's cagey response to a language of American nationalism that had grown to new prominence by 1850, and had done so in alarmingly close proximity to Melville: the thoroughgoing epistemological dislocations of Ishmael's narrative, that is, are part of Melville's prompt reply to the racially inflected expansionist nationalisms—the visions of white nationality—with which the Democratic partisans of Young America had come more and more to associate themselves. In the grain of that reply we see most clearly, I think, the character of the uneasiness with which Melville regards, not the epistemology of "race" per se, but the nationalist investment of whiteness with escalatingly determinate relational and characterological meaning. The novel's relentless negations, I am suggesting, work in large part to rescue the premise of nationalism from the racialist languages in which it was increasingly taken up at midcentury; and it is mainly through the deviousness of Ishmael's narration that Melville attempts to manage and displace the growing coincidence, in Young America's nationalism, between one's identification as "white" and one's identification as "American." Part of what we see in *Moby-Dick*, then, is Melville hammering out the complexities of his relation not only to whiteness but to its *nationalization*, to those new modalities of racial meaning that had begun to gain frightening currency in the antebellum republic, not least in the supremacist languages of Young America itself.

But we will see as well that the task of translating Ishamel's contrary, boisterous, self-corroding, anti-nationalist nationalism into the knotted terms of human *relations*—into the terms of social cohesion and belonging—proves tremendously difficult, even terrorizing, for the novel. To accomplish this complicated task, Melville turns repeatedly to the impious, matrimonial, and always tantalizingly inexplicit intimacy of Ishmael and Queequeg, using it in an attempt to envision a kind of sociality unbeholden to any inherited structures of relation. This is, in a sense, the novel's utopian strain, but it is a utopianism about which Melville feels precious little optimism: in the end, it is the tragic misalignment between abstract belief and human relation, between a hypothetical America and the one lived in the attachments of its citizens, that becomes the increasingly dominant note of the novel, as it speeds with Ahab to its doomstruck conclusion. The immense ambition of *Moby-Dick*, then, is to fabricate an America that defies all the terms with which it could be described; the impossibility of doing so is the story the novel tells.

NATIONALITY AND DISBELIEF

I try all things; I achieve what I can.
"THE PRAIRIE"

Among the many remarkable aspects of Melville's sequence of letters to Nathaniel Hawthorne—the breadth of their literary reference, their rhetorical range, the ardency of attachment they avow—contemporary readers are apt to be most startled by the stinging, sometimes plainly abject quality of Melville's apparent self-regard. Melville writes to his newfound friend for a variety of incidental reasons: to inform Hawthorne of his doings, to share literary ruminations, or to update him on the progress of "my 'Whale'" (557). But most of all, it seems, Melville writes simply to keep open and active the channel that had been established between himself and the older writer, so that if nothing else the mere opportunity to indulge in far-flung literary and metaphysical speculation ("ontological heroics," Melville calls them [561]) might forever remain on hand. It is as though even the loftiest of Melville's divagations were, in truth, essentially phatic, meant to express the pleasures of exchange—the pleasure of his relation to Hawthorne—rather than sustain any one argumentative point.

Melville himself seems to recognize as much, and his writerly self-diagnosis occasions, on the one hand, a familiar brand of comedy-through-hyperbole:

> If the world was entirely made up of Magians, I'll tell you what I should do. I should have a paper-mill established at one end of the house, and so have an endless riband of foolscap rolling in upon my desk; and upon that endless riband I should write a thousand—a million—billion thoughts, all under the form of a letter to you. (567–68)

On the other hand, though, Melville's flattery can very quickly turn corrosive. His eagerness not only to dismiss himself and all his intellectual errancies but to dismiss them *as though he were Hawthorne* is at times painfully evident. Ringing like a refrain through the letters are Melville's preemptive excuses and exonerations for an affront Hawthorne has yet to commit, but which Melville apparently fears is imminent: "This is a long letter, but you are not at all bound to answer it"; and later, in a postscript to the same missive, "Don't think that by writing me a letter, you shall always be bored with an immediate reply" (567–68). Or again:

I am writing to you; I know little about you, but something about myself. So I write about myself—at least to you. Don't trouble yourself, though, about writing; and don't trouble yourself about visiting; and when you *do* visit, don't trouble yourself about talking. I will do all the writing and visiting and talking myself. (558)

It's hard not to be discomfited by Melville's repeated apologies for his own burdensomeness, especially since those self-castigations are offered always in Hawthorne's name, from his perspective as a recipient of these letters; indeed, Melville rather insistently implies that the vantage from which his own foolishness, inadequacy, and pretense are most nakedly apparent belongs to none other than the very person to whom he most wishes to be endeared. Melville's hurry to relieve Hawthorne of every and any sense of responsibility toward him could very well have made the older writer uneasy, since in those overtures he might have read not only well-intentioned flattery but the depth and urgency of Melville's need to be approved of. What would read in another context as merely conventional epistolary self-effacement, in other words, is here seen to propel a rather different drama of writer-reader provocation and dependency: for self-effacement, when crossed with a neediness as evident as Melville's, seems more properly to be called masochism. His comedy, which is unflagging throughout the correspondence, is thus pitched in way that makes it rather difficult for its intended reader to enjoy.

What's starling about the letters, then, is not their continuity but rather their divergence from *Moby-Dick* and its rhetorical postures. Ishmael's comic self-narration, though it employs a very similar kind of perspectival mobility, does so to dramatically different effect—an effect that has more to do with a particular kind of demolition than with the vagaries of self-doubt. Consider, to begin with, the solicitation of the reader that unfolds in the opening chapter, "Loomings," where Ishmael's voice indelibly establishes itself. Here, the comedy works not only by hyperbole but through a distinctive kind of figural juxtaposition. After listing the various forms of ill behavior that harbinger an illness of his spirit (such as "stepping into the street, and methodically knocking people's hats off") Ishmael's self-introduction takes us on a brief detour out of damp, drizzly Manhattan: "With a philosophical flourish Cato throws himself upon his sword; I quietly take to the ship" (3). The turn of mind that would place a classical Roman on narrative center stage, and stand him momentarily beside a down-in-the-mouth American sailor, finds itself more and more indulged as the chapter continues. Pondering the tendency of the contemplative to seek out oceanfronts and sea vistas, Ishmael proposes the figure of Man Thinking as a kind of wind-up divining rod:

> Let the most absent-minded of men be plunged in his deepest reveries—stand that man on his legs, set his feet a-going, and he will infallibly lead you to water, if water there be in all that region. Should you ever be athirst in the great American desert, try this experiment, if your caravan happens to be supplied with a metaphysical professor. (4)

Moving from prairie to desert, automaton to metaphysician to make his point, Ishmael then concludes his tour of the waters with a sequence of globe-spanning puzzles:

> Were Niagara but a cataract of sand, would you travel your thousand miles to see it? Why did the poor poet of Tennessee, upon suddenly receiving two handfuls of silver, deliberate whether to buy him a coat, which he sadly needed, or invest his money in a pedestrian trip to Rockaway Beach? . . . Why did the old Persians hold the sea holy? Why did the Greeks give it a separate deity, and make him the own brother of Jove? Surely all this is not without its meaning. (5)

Whatever meaning these examples may auger, they have the effect of informing us, first of all, that ours is a narrator who has at his command an apparently boundless array of perspectives from which to consider any proposition. (Ishmael's schoolmaster pedantry is clearly part of what's on display here.) Curiously, though, this breadth of perspective does not authenticate the seriousness or veracity of Ishmael's speculations. On the contrary, the multiplicity of rubrics he invokes serves instead to foster a kind of precocious unseriousness, or even anti-seriousness—a foolishness, then, which we are invited not to disparage but to participate in and enjoy.

How, exactly, does that inauthentication work? It's worth looking again, and more closely, at the perspectival juxtapositions of chapter 1. Having offered in a variety of guises his hypothesis that "meditation and water are wedded forever," Ishmael then begins to tell us a bit about himself. "For my part," he confides, "I abominate all honorable respectable toils, trials, and tribulations of every kind whatsoever" (5). He is careful, though, to balance such disreputable irreverence with the fact, offered two sentences later, that "there is no one who will speak more respectfully, not to say reverentially, of a broiled fowl than I will" (5). Abominating labor, revering his lunch, Ishmael pushes forward with the task of limning his character by registering its diverse responses to the world's litany of demands. Of the indignities of a sailor's life, he writes, "The transition is a keen one, I assure you, from a schoolmaster to a sailor, and requires a strong decoction of Seneca and the Stoics to enable you to grin and bear it" (6). Just so, Ishmael reflects philosophically on the abuse he is liable to take from a superior at sea, reasoning that "everybody else is in one way or other served in much the same way—either in a physical or metaphysical point of view, that is; and so the universal thump is passed round, and all hands should rub each other's shoulder-blades, and be content" (6). Able to swing casually between physical and metaphysical points of view—philosophical enough to endure abuse but practical enough to savor the sweetness of remuneration ("But *being paid*,—what will compare with it?")—this narrator seems less concerned to prove his inclinations rational than to show how virtually any inclination, when seen at the proper distance or through the necessary lens, can be made to answer to the demands and standards of rationality. Rationality, in other words, is by Ishmael's account not internal to an act or proposition, but a function of the angle from which it is viewed. (This lesson in interpretive vertigo will be spelled out in detail in a chapter called "The Doubloon.") And in just how ludicrously broad a perspective Ishmael is willing to place his own lifetime's adventures is seen in the "grand programme of Providence" in which he imagines himself listed as a "brief interlude"—"Whaling Voyage By One Ishmael"—sandwiched in between "*Grand Contested Election for the Presidency of the United States*" and "BLOODY BATTLE IN AFGHANISTAN" (7).

The effect of the novel's perspectival mobility in chapter 1 is thus double. On the one hand, Ishmael's comic juxtapositions underline what we might call the indefensible pretense of certainties, showing how they can be established or dismantled not according to inherent qualities but to the interpretive vantage one happens to select. That is, by the range and variousness of interpretive vantages he employs, Ishmael suggests again and again how easily one moment's certainty might become another's nonsense. On the other hand, the puns and alliterative wordplay that the novel's immensity of scope seems to sponsor attest to Melville's determination not to abjure but in fact to savor the many pleasures of speculation offered by a world from which certainty has been banished. That all propositions are uncertifiable means, according to Ishmael's logic, that any proposition is plausible and may therefore be entertained, perhaps for no more serious purpose than to find what verbal felicities it might uncover. ("In New Bedford, fathers, they say, give whales for dowers to their daughters, and portion off their nieces with a few porpoises a-piece" [32].) Ishmael's narrative thus offers us the rare privilege of a disbelieving, beguilingly agnostic form of extended contemplation; it presents us with the opportunity to sever ourselves from the plaster-bound strictures and landlocked certainties by which we are confined and drift for a while among indefinite, unresolving possibilities. If chasing through *Moby-Dick* can sometimes induce a readerly sensation of expansive unconstraint—of a kind of cognitive freeing-up, not at all unlike Ishmael's relief at sea—it is in part an effect of this invitation to sustained disbelief. Something of this drama, I would suggest, invests Ann Douglas's sense of the novel as "a conversion process" in which "Melville plots brilliantly to bring his audience to his side."[5] In a more somber mood, Ishmael will frame his "mortally intolerable truth" in exactly the oceanic terms of chapter 1, whose theme is confinement and release: "all deep, earnest thinking," he says, "is but the intrepid effort of the soul to keep the open independence of her sea; while the wildest winds of heaven and earth conspire to cast her on the treacherous, slavish shore" (107). Ishmael's manner of self-presentation—his will to perspectival variety—thus swears clear allegiance to pleasures of being, as it were, attentively at sea, ever at a distance from the world's slavish certainties.

The stylistic imperative here helps us begin to account for the novel's frenzy of referentiality, what Leo Bersani calls its "cannibalistic encyclopedism."[6] It might appear, for instance, that Melville's appropriation of such an enormous archive of sources testifies to the earnestness of his desire to, as he advises early on, "look at [the] matter in other lights; weight it in all sorts of scales" (109). But the scales themselves are, in their turn, placed under fairly continual assault; or, to put this another way, Melville adumbrates the world through a breathtaking range of interpretive models and schema, but the very proliferation of such models—along with the deviousness of Melville's prose—has the effect of siphoning much of their presumed validity, of hollowing out whatever interpretive authority they might have claimed. In the chapters entitled "The Advocate" and "Postscript," for example, Ishmael "would fain advance naught but substantiated facts" to defend the august nobility of whaling from its uninformed detractors; but what he offers instead is a sequence of increasingly implausible figures and analogies, which nevertheless characteristically retain the grammar and syntax of logical exposition. He tells us that his arguments mean to counter the sad fact that, "among people at large, the business of whaling is not accounted on a level with what are called the liberal professions" (108). A desire to establish whaling as a liberal art, then, is the motive that justifies the learned references that follow (to the Bible, Edmund Burke, Benjamin Franklin, "old English statutory law," and ancient Rome) even as the clear preposterousness of the motive makes a kind of joke of all of them. Repeatedly calling on these sources in this way, Melville in effect suspends or dismisses their accumulated authoritativeness.

This kind of playful agnosticism expresses itself not least at the level of the sentence. "The Advocate" provides a fine instance:

> I freely assert that the cosmopolite philosopher cannot, for his life, point out one single peaceful influence, which within the last sixty years has operated more potentially upon the whole broad world, taken in one aggregate, than the high and mighty business of whaling. One way and another, it has begotten events so remarkable in themselves, and so continuously momentous in their sequential issues, that whaling may well be regarded as that Egyptian mother, who bore offspring themselves pregnant from her womb. (109)

Typical of Ishmael in its mix of erudite neologism and cliché ("cosmopolite" and "the high and mighty business of whaling"), in the mock pedantry of its accretion of dependent clauses, and especially in its deployment of a fabulously extraneous *figure* for the completion of a manifestly exaggerated thought, the passage begs us not to read it straight; or, more to the point, the various stylistic tics we come to associate so strongly with Ishmael and his winkingly ironic persona signal not a principled opposition to the exercise of interpretive thought but rather his refusal to believe conclusively in any of it.[7] What remains behind, then, after swimming in the acid-bath of the novel's satiric prose, are merely the afterimages—the proper names, the famous tropes—of literary sources whose power to confer prestige on Melville's sea-yarn has been a great deal attenuated by the laughable purposes he calls on them to serve.

The matter is not simply that Melville uses Ishmael to abjure the past and its monuments. Clearly, many of the achievements of the past appeal to Melville's verbal imagination in powerful and sometimes overpowering ways. (We need only think of the Shakespearean tenor of Ahab's iambic soliloquies, or of the critical accounts of how profoundly Melville's reading in Shakespeare enabled the epic scope and grandeur he discovered in *Moby-Dick*.) Rather, Melville uses Ishmael's oddly friendly, open-hearted dismissiveness, his acerbic receptivity, as a way to manage his inheritances: to solidify a relation to the past that is neither servile nor reverential but which, at the same time, does not preclude inspiration or acts of appropriation. In its complicated disposition, Ishmael's voice answers remarkably well to the opening strains of Whitman's preface to the initial edition of *Leaves of Grass*, which would be published less than four years later. "America does not repel the past," Whitman writes,

> or what it has produced under its forms or amid other politics or the idea of castes or the old religions . . . accepts the lesson with calmness . . . is not so impatient as has been supposed that the slough still sticks to opinions and manners and literature while the life which served its requirements has passed into the new life of the new forms . . . perceives that the corpse is slowly borne from the eating and sleeping rooms of the house . . . perceives that it waits a little while in the door . . . that it was fittest for its days . . . that its action has descended to the stalwart and wellshaped heir who approaches . . . and that he shall be the fittest for his days.[8]

Like Whitman, Melville's Ishmael is more than willing to salute the past, and to accept its lessons with "calmness"; but his respects, also like Whitman's, are more often than not paid in the rueful, even self-congratulatory or triumphalist tones one might offer to a corpse.

If Ishmael's style describes a relation to the past, it also implies a relation to others, in the present tense, which is a crucial point for us to recall as we begin to unpack the nationalist dimensions of *Moby-Dick*. As Ishmael's adventures before boarding the *Pequod* make clear, the effort to remain thus unmoored from the conventionalities of thought is, for the novel, one of the first prerequisites for ethical social being. At the conclusion of chapter 1, Ishmael provides this summary self-description, in which the disposition of his style seems also to be sketched: "Not ignoring what is good, I am quick to perceive a horror, and could still be social with it— would they let me—since it is but well to be on friendly terms with all the inmates of the place one lodges in" (7). The narrative's kaleidoscopic rotation of perspectives, we might now say, represents not only the satiric edge of Ishmael's wit but the specific labor that underwrites his aspiration to be in this way universally "friendly." Ishmael's style, in other words, anatomizes the kind of cognitive dexterity required to sustain such a prodigious openness of disposition. To recognize this is to see that Ishmael's is in fact a perpetually achieved relation to the world—one that involves the constant projection of the self into different circumstances and locales—and not simply a resigned or despairing passivity.[9] By virtue of being thus wrought, what passivity he sometimes displays seems not only idiosyncratic and distinct, peculiarly his own, but an odd kind of accomplishment.

As a narrator Ishmael may begin with such an accomplished disposition toward the world, but as a narrated character he certainly does not. As it turns out, his mentor in the acquisition of such curious serenity is none other than Queequeq, the "cannibal" harpooner whom he first encounters in New Bedford, and the Spouter Inn is his classroom. Ishmael arrives at this inn full of anxieties and distrustfulness, especially with regard to the stranger with whom he has consented to share a bed. "I could not help it," he writes, "but I began to feel suspicious of this 'dark complexioned' harpooner" (15). His suspicions break out into full panic later in the night, driven on, as Samuel Otter observes, by the innkeeper's deliberate tweaking of his "racial presumptions," as well as his own more sexually coded anxieties over bed sharing; but over time these suspicions become strangely mollified, until finally Ishmael finds that his whole sense of the world has undergone a decisive transformation.[10] Observing Queequeg's manner, he writes,

Here was a man some twenty thousand miles from home, by the way of Cape Horn, that is—which was the only way he could get there—thrown among people as strange to him as though he were in the planet Jupiter; and yet here he seemed entirely at his ease; preserving the utmost serenity; content with his own companionship; always equal to himself. Surely this was a touch of fine philosophy . . .

As I sat there in that now lonely room; the fire burning low,
and in that mild stage when, after its first intensity has warmed
the air, it then only glows to be looked at; the evening shades and
phantoms gathering round the casements, and peering in upon us
silent, solitary, twain; the storm booming without in solemn
swells; I began to be sensible of strange feelings. I felt a melting
in me. No more my splintered heart and maddened hand were
turned against the wolfish world. This soothing savage had
redeemed it. There he sat, his very indifference speaking a nature
in which there lurked no civilized hypocrisies and bland deceits.
Wild he was; a very sight of sights to see; yet I began to feel
myself mysteriously drawn towards him. And those same things
that would have repelled most others, they were the very magnets
that thus drew me. I'll try a pagan friend, thought I, since
Christian kindness has proved but hollow courtesy. (50–51)

The "true philosophy" he imbibes from Queequeg's example is
that of a studied "indifference," an equanimity of regard toward
all the wildly contradictory manners, customs, and systems of
belief of which the world is made. Ishmael's admiring account,
and the quality he admires, have a pleasing reciprocity: his ap-
preciation for Queequeg and his "true philosophy" begins with a
modest act of self-displacement, whereby he ventures to imagine
what it might be like to live, as Queequeg does, "among people as
strange to him as though he were in the planet Jupiter." What he
admires *in* Queequeg, too, is the easiness of comportment that
derives from having taken pains to see from vantages other than
his own—"to learn among the Christians" (56)—if only to develop
in the end a cultivated tolerance for their boisterous rituals and
absurd pretenses. Samuel Otter rightly suggests that Melville
uses these moments, which foreground "the difficult, persistent
desire to understand another racial position," to oppose the drive
to racial knowledge and racial certainty he found around him in
the increasingly prominent "ethnological" discourses of his day.
Just as crucially, though, Ishmael learns from Queequeg himself
this lesson of capacious, if disbelieving, tolerance, and strives in
turn to embody it in an idiom that is at once relentlessly satiric of pretenses to certainty and thoroughly pleased to enter-
tain, at least for a sentence or two, every variety of proposition.
Again, as he would later suggest, the key to unbiased interpretation—the key, more generally, to an ethical bearing of the self—is

to "look at [the] matter in other lights; weight it in all sorts of scales" (109).

This will to perspectival variety, and the sort of absorptive incredulity it inspires—what Bersani calls Ishmael's "invalidating tolerance of the search for meanings"—also provide a particularly seductive interpretive model for the reader, who is liable to be at one point or another overwhelmed by the novel's proliferation of omens, portents, and (to borrow a phrase from Hart Crane) livid hieroglyphs.[11] Even before the *Pequod* has left port, we encounter: an almost inscrutable painting of a breaching whale about to destroy a ship, a sign for "The Try-Pots" that hangs over Ishmael like a gallows, the enigmatic Bulkington, the even more enigmatic Ahab, and finally Elijah, who tantalizes with his hints and unjoined prophecies. At the outset of the voyage, the reader's relation to these puzzles is indeed in perfect alignment with Ishmael's: both are confronted with the harbingers of a meaning yet to coalesce, and this coincidence of interpretive perspectives—this shared unknowingness—gives a special tutelary force to the modes of reading Ishmael endorses. As Ann Douglas succinctly frames the matter, "Ishmael is not only an observer and an actor in the book, he is a model for the reader." When Ishmael shows us how, in states of ignorance and interpretive dismay, he soothes himself, he also promises to soothe our own anxieties about interpretive powerlessness and befuddlement.[12] If we pay him the proper attention, that is, Ishmael will instruct us in interpretive evenhandedness, which for him amounts to the fine art of noncommittal contemplativeness: a reading style that places a very high premium on the extraction of speculative possibilities, and a very low one on the specification of facts, answers, and rigid conclusions. (And it's difficult *not* to pay attention to his lessons in epistemology, since they recur with such insistence in the opening chapters: "Surely all this is not without meaning" [5]; "All these things are not without their meanings" [37]; "What could be more full of meaning?" [40].) We learn from Ishmael's example, in other words, that the readerly strategy to be most rewarded by this narrative involves the sustained adumbration of *potential* meanings that, as they accrue, will propagate along new and expanded lines of signification (the biblical allusions amplifying the Shakespearean themes, and so on and so on)—provided, of course, that no attempt is made to nail down any one sign to any one meaning, since this would be to call halt to the endless multiplication of interpretive possibilities. The exhilarating "comprehensiveness of sweep" often attributed not only to the novel but to the experience of reading the novel seems a function of exactly this narrative solicitation: for to read as Ishmael invites us to read is finally to confirm the fundamental *unreadability* of his narrative, its expansion beyond the parameters of any imaginable interpretive perspective. It is, from a wider angle, to avow the irreducibility—and so, the greatness—of Melville's *Moby-Dick*.

The novel's self-designed irreducibility returns us to the question of its intended exemplarity, not only as a novel but as an *American* novel—to the question, that is, of nationalism and its relation to the form of *Moby-Dick*. As we noted at the outset, the novel's compulsive referentiality sits rather uncomfortably with Melville's demand that the American novel be underived, free of all foreign influence. Thus, for a genre that takes orphanhood as its condition of success, Melville's untiring reiteration of his novel's prestigious literary parentage might well seem a self-defeating kind of boastfulness. But the problem changes its bearings rather dramatically when we recall the oddly dismissive sort of citation Ishmael practices, consuming sources but only to regurgitate them as elements of some ludicrous theorem or mocking proof. His breezy narrative seems in this way to undertake the demolition of as many existing measures of truth, reason, and authority as can be accommodated by the tale he tells. If there is a nationalist tenor to these dislocations and derangements of meaning, it lies in the implicit proposition that all the world's histories—all its literature and statecraft and philosophy and lore—arrive in the novel as mere contributors, inadequate in themselves to describe the grandeur and magnitude of American national life. Rather than herald an inescapable subservience to inherited models, Ishmael's manic referentiality instead conveys the grand assurance of his, and of his nation's, severance from the past. As Bersani suggests, this is the novel's ingenious method of orphaning itself.[13]

It's possible, moreover, to derive from Ishmael's narrative a vision not only of the temporality but of the *form* of American nationality. Again, this may seem a self-defeating sort of task, since Ishmael is himself so cheerfully dismissive of the pieties of religion, law, family, race, and not least of nationalism itself (hence the pointedly multinational crew of the *Pequod*); given this deliberate refusal of virtually all the bases from which the notion of nationality typically proceeds, we might well begin to wonder in just what sense the novel's aspirations deserve to be called "nationalist."[14] In one sense, Ishmael's tacit condemnation of every familiar vestige of nation-ness works in the novel as a kind of preliminary gesture or step. What it propels the novel toward is the conjuring of an America founded precisely on *un*familiar, untried, perhaps even unimaginable bases. Ishmael's consuming incredulity suggests, that is, that America will be surpassingly praiseworthy to him to the degree that it repels any of the terms in which it could possibly be founded, or settled on, or merely described. "America," in these terms, is the name the novel gives to a great terrain of inexpressibility.[15] But the very comprehensiveness of Ishmael's agnosticism also implies the unprecedented scope of his nationalist ambition, since it registers a determination to exhaust every possible analogue or schema around which an America might be constructed—as though it were only in the act of demolishing, one by one, each of the available terms of its definition that anything like the grand America Ishmael has in mind could begin to emerge. The residue of a truly monumental act of negation, American nationality thus subsists in *Moby-Dick* as *pure potential*: as an embracing provisionality, an untiring demurral from conclusiveness. "Any human thing supposed to be complete," Ishmael tells us, "must for that very reason infallibly be faulty" (136). Just as Ishmael's narrative aspires to the status of unresolvable hieroglyph, so too does America exist for Melville as a beautiful thought that must never complete itself.

WHITE AMERICA

> *Yea, while these terrors seize us, let us add, that*
> *even the king of terrors, when personified by*
> *the evangelist, rides on his pallid horse.*
> "THE WHITENESS OF THE WHALE"

This was not a nationalism designed to please many nationalists, especially in 1851. It is not difficult to imagine why readers of "Hawthorne and His Mosses" would have felt somehow cheated by Melville's novel and its oblique, elusive, attenuated visions of an essentially epistemological American nationality. Duyckinck, one of Melville's early advocates, could only review the book tepidly and, as Hershel Parker suggests, rather uncomfortably.[16] At the

Democratic Review, George Sanders was much less generous, or hesitant. It was not Melville's sense of profound national destiny, Sanders asserted, but his profound "vanity" as a writer that animated his disastrous novel. "From this morbid self-esteem, coupled with a most unbounded love of notoriety," Sanders writes, "spring all Mr. Melville's efforts, all his rhetorical contortions, all his declamatory abuse of society, all his inflated sentiment, all his insinuating licentiousness."[17] Whatever allegiance Melville might have enjoyed with the ranks of Young America ended here, though Melville's bitterness would not find full expression until *Pierre* and its vitriolic chapter dedicated to "Young America in Literature."[18]

But Sanders's reaction could not have come as too great a surprise. However passionate Melville's attachment to "this matter of a national literature" might have been throughout the writing of *Moby-Dick*, his novel is by no means an endorsement of the nationalisms proposed by Young America. On the contrary, as Sanders may well have intuited, the novel was in many ways an assault on Young America: an attempt, that is, to borrow Young America's ambition (to fashion a novel that would be adequate to the unwritten and unprecedented grandeur of America), but to do so in a way that would corrode the very terms in which American nationalism was increasingly proclaimed. That Melville's nation-language should take the form that it does—that it should be defined by ceaseless evasion, inconclusiveness, and an all-embracing indeterminacy—tells us a great deal about how Melville read and understood the prominent nationalisms of his day, and about how he was invested in the terms of their elaboration.

What exactly, then, was Melville's nationalism, with its strident emphasis on the unmapped and the undetermined, working to evade? All-embracing indeterminacy has an emblem in the novel, and it is an ironic one. "Is it that by its indefiniteness," Ishmael wonders about whiteness, "it shadows forth the heartless voids and immensities of the universe, and thus stabs us from behind with the thought of annihilation, when beholding the white depths of the milky way?" (195). Critics have rightly looked to this chapter, "The Whiteness of the Whale," as an index of Melville's engagement, even before "Benito Cereno," with racial meaning.[19] The precise nature of that engagement, however, is a matter of some disagreement. That whiteness should, in this moment, be defined by exactly that quality of "indefiniteness" with which the novel attempts to invest its ideal America suggests that racial meaning, for Melville, is never far from the terrain of national meaning, or of national definition. But what makes his use of whiteness as an emblem of indeterminacy particularly ironic, I want to suggest, is the way it takes hold of the racial strains of Young America's nationalism and plays them back in reverse.

That Young America was embroiled in the antebellum struggle over racial meaning, in America and abroad, is indisputable, though it is not a matter that much preoccupies Miller in *The Raven and the Whale*. Miller does remind us of Young America's allegiance to the "liberal" Democratic party (as against the "conservative" Whigs), and we might presume that this liberalism refers, among other things, to the strident Democratic opposition to the expansion of slavery into newly acquired territories of the United States. As a number of historians have taken pains to show, though, such opposition to slavery was decidedly not an endorsement of abolition and was in fact almost always in the service of an aggressive "Anglo-Saxonism."[20] Midcentury Democrats tended to oppose slavery not for the sake of the slaves but on behalf of the unpropertied white laborers whose job security they were imagined to endanger. Playing class anxieties and racial animosities off one another soon became a signature strategy of Democratic candidates in the North.[21] To take only one example: the Free-Soil Democrats (of whom Whitman was one) found an easy accord between antislavery propagandizing and an unvarnished white supremacism. Whitman himself framed the matter with great succinctness: "Shall no one among you dare open his mouth to say he is opposed to slavery, as a man should be, on account of the whites, and wants it abolished for their sake?" Opposition to slavery here means opposition to its deleterious effects on America's "true people, the millions of white citizens," who together comprise what Whitman calls "a different superior race."[22]

In this vein of American nationalism, which had become standard fare by the time Whitman wrote his polemic, America's greatness was to be imagined as a function of its racial distinctiveness—not only of its whiteness, but of a distinctively American strain of whiteness. As Reginald Horsman neatly observes, summarizing an 1848 article from none other than the *Democratic Review*, "The 'American race' was simply the greatest of the white races."[23] Consonant with this mode of Americanist racial supremacism was another strain of nationalism with which the Young Americans at the *Democratic Review* and elsewhere were particularly conversant: the nationalism of unchecked imperial expansion, conquest in the name of freedom, or, as Wai Chee Dimock phrases it, "empire for liberty."[24] It was, after all, none other than John L. O'Sullivan, friend to the Duyckinck circle and editor of the *Democratic Review*, who in 1845 coined the phrase "manifest destiny." Writing in the *Democratic Review*, he chastises those nations who would intervene in America expansionism "for the avowed object of thwarting our policy and hampering our power, limiting our greatness and checking the fulfillment of our manifest destiny to overspread the continent allotted by Providence for the free development of our yearly multiplying millions." He went on to predict the future of distant California:

> The Anglo-Saxon foot is already on its borders. Already the advance
> guard has begun to pour down upon it, armed with the plough
> and the rifle, and marking its trail with schools and colleges,
> courts and representative halls, mills and meeting houses.[25]

These remarks give an important resonance to the nationalist exhortation with which O'Sullivan began the *Democratic Review* in 1837: "Why," O'Sullivan asks, "cannot our literati comprehend the matchless sublimity of our position amongst the nations of the world?"[26] Melville himself echoes this sentiment almost exactly in "Hawthorne and His Mosses," when he writes, "While we are rapidly preparing for that political supremacy among nations, which prophetically awaits us at the close of the present century; in a literary point of view, we are deplorably unprepared for it." In O'Sullivan's formulation of 1837, the literary sublimity to which Melville would thirteen years later express his determination to strive is posited as a function, a necessary extension, of the nation's political supremacy—a supremacy that derives in turn, as O'Sullivan's theory of "manifest destiny" would later make abundantly clear, from a kind of American *racial* vanguardism. The conjoining here of an American exceptionalism with a particular kind of racial supremacism would only escalate through the late 1840s and into the 1850s.[27] The point was clear: to "write like an American," as Melville commanded in the Hawthorne essay, would by this score necessarily be to write like a white man.

Expanding on and revising the readings of *Moby-Dick* offered by D. H. Lawrence and especially Michael Rogin, Toni Morrison claims that it is exactly this white supremacist project that Melville deliberately interrogates and exposes in the grain of its

monomaniacal madness. She argues, moreover, that it was precisely for daring to speak such ambivalences that Melville was
chastised, repudiated, and finally ignored. "To question the very
notion of white progress," she writes,

> the very idea of racial superiority, of whiteness as privileged place
> in the evolutionary ladder of humankind, and to meditate on the
> fraudulent, self-destroying philosophy of that superiority . . . was
> dangerous, solitary, radical work. Especially then. Especially now.
> To be "only a patriot to heaven" is no mean aspiration in Young
> America for a writer—or the captain of a whaling ship.[28]

Melville does indeed relentlessly satirize "the very notion of white
progress," and inasmuch as that notion had become an increasingly prominent part of Young America's nationalism, *Moby-Dick*
can be read as an assault on the principal bearers of American literary nationalism—even as it refuses to surrender the premise of
literary nationalism itself. In a similarly complicated move, though
the novel's opposition to racialism and racial nationalism does not
imply an abandonment of the idea of racial meaning. Melville's
reasons for opposing Young America's racial nationalism, in other
words, are perhaps not as unswervingly straightforward—or necessarily as heavenly—as we tend to imagine.

It's clear, first, that what troubles the novel is not the idea that
"race" bears a somehow meaningful relation to the determinations
of character. While the novel is, on the one hand, quite pleased to
fire dart after dart into the hide of Anglo-Christian piety—"Better
sleep with a sober cannibal than a drunken Christian" (24); "as
though a white man were anything more dignified than a white-
washed negro" (60)—it also clearly depends on the distinctions
of racial "purity" for a number of its most thematically salient
symmetries and motifs. Most obvious of these is the harpooners'
origins in the principal "pagan" cultures of the world. There is
Tashtego, "an unmixed Indian from Gay Head" and "inheritor of
the unvitiated blood of . . . proud warrior hunters" (120); Daggoo,
who "never having been anywhere in the world but in Africa" presents a kingly, "imperial" aspect, making him "an Ahasuerus to
behold" (120);[29] and finally Queequeg, whose "father was a High
Chief, a king; his uncle a High Priest; and on the maternal side he
boasted aunts who were the wives of unconquerable warriors"
(55). Add to their ranks the "hair-turbaned Fedallah"—"such a
creature as civilized domestic people in the temperate zone only

see in their dreams, and that but dimly; but the like of whom now and then glide among the unchanging Asiatic communities" (231)— and the novel's credence with respect to the characterological meaningfulness of "race" becomes clear. And though Melville may indeed vigilantly insist that distinctions such as these in no way authorize the exclusion of anyone from the democratic brotherhood of equality he has proposed—an important qualification, as we will see—he nonetheless believes in them *as* distinctions and is anxious to wring from them all the significances he can.

Whatever the uneasiness with which *Moby-Dick* regards racial nationalism, then, it has only so much to do with the idea that "race" predicates, in the non-white person at least, certain essential and occasionally moral attributes—though, again, the novel's steadfast refusal to derive from those predications any qualitative index of human worth does put it at odds with, say, the *Democratic Review*. What Ishmael seems vastly more discomfited by, instead, is the nationalist imperative to racialize *whiteness*, an imperative that he experiences not only as a demand to identify as white but to *embody his race*. It's instructive here to recall how radically the "Anglo-Saxonism" of the *Democratic Review* departs from the largely unformalized epistemology of race that had operated, more or less continuously, for the nation's first fifty years. In the heyday of republicanism, as we saw in chapter 1, the clear privilege attached to whiteness was in large part derived negatively: rather than signify any innate essence or quality or noble attribute, whiteness conferred privilege by exonerating one from the inflictions and depredations of something called "race." "Race" was imagined by republican discourse to be an indelible form of partiality, an attribute whose in-the-body "weightiness" could not easily be transcended in one's effort to deliberate as a part of the disembodied *res publica*—which is why the idea of, say, free black citizenship was looked on so suspiciously in much of postrevolutionary America. To be white, by contrast, was to enjoy the considerable privilege of racelessness, in the same way that being male and propertied, instead of anchoring one's opinions to a particular locality of interest and intent, gave one the unique right to claim for oneself the negative republican virtues of impartiality and disinterestedness.[30]

The expansionist strain of antebellum nationalism revises these strains quite completely. For as an attribute whose determinations, in individuals and in nations, are now positive (in the Young

American vocabulary these would include "activity," "vigor," and "greatness"), whiteness loses its abstractness and is, quite suddenly, very much *in* the body. For antebellum racialists, whiteness is no longer a kind of aparticularity but is, quite to the contrary, an ineradicable, inalienable attribute of the flesh, out of which moral and political saliencies can be determinately unfolded. Morrison follows out a similar point, I think, when she writes that "Melville is not explaining white *people*, but whiteness idealized."[31] Or, perhaps, he is explaining something like whiteness *realized*— that is, whiteness at once idealized and embodied. Consider Ishmael's entrance into "The Trap," which he mistakes for a New Bedford Inn, where the potential frightfulness of a white racial determinism comes home to him with striking intimacy:

> It seemed the great Black Parliament sitting in a Tophet. A hundred black faces turned round in their rows to peer; and beyond, a black Angel of Doom was beating a book in a pulpit. It was a negro church; and the preacher's text was the blackness of darkness, and the weeping and wailing and teeth-knashing there. Ha, Ishmael, muttered I, backing out, Wretched entertainment at the sign of "The Trap!" (9–10)

What we will later understand as Ishmael's prodigious openness of disposition, his desire to be on friendly terms with all the world, here runs hard into something aggressively resistant to it: he finds himself confronted by a community into whose rituals he cannot think how to fit himself. What unfits him, of course, is the whiteness his body carries, and in which, for an altogether frightening moment, the whole of his being seems concentrated. This sudden reduction of his person to a singular unit of meaning—a unit of race—is precisely how Ishmael experiences the nationalist compulsion to idealize, to realize, and to embody whiteness.

Melville's opposition to the protocols of antebellum racialism is thus, in a curious way, as much about epistemology—about the determinate assignment of meaning—as it is about political morality or national destiny. However else it might fail (and Melville will have much to say about its political failure as the plot advances), racial nationalism appears in the novel as a manner of interpreting the world that, particularly when brought to bear on white people, proves unsound in principle and terrifying in lived effect. The generative problem here is not, or is not entirely, that a species of determinism will infiltrate a novel whose deepest hermeneutic commitments are to the constant unmooring of meaning from received or familiar patterns; indeed, the novel mobilizes several perfectly familiar racial figures to give form to one of its major iconographic symmetries, as we have seen. Rather, it is the potential enclosure of *white* personality, the too determinate reading of whiteness, that seems most intolerable for this novel, and that sponsors its contrary renderings of whiteness and its significance. In this sense, "The Whiteness of the Whale" figures not only the metaphysical crux of the novel (in that yawning blankness toward which all human endeavor may, or may not, incline) but also one of its most unsettling political premises, the one that most powerfully suggests a potential incompatibility between democracy, on the one hand, and novelistic cognition, on the other. For here, whiteness emerges both as metaphysical emblem *and* as narratological imperative: the inexhaustibly interpretable meaninglessness Ishmael perceives in the whiteness of the whale—that "dumb blankness, full of meaning"—becomes his novelistic ideal. (As Nathaniel Vinton observes, "even while the white whale is evil on the dramatic level—and so must be hunted down—nevertheless Melville embraces its anomalousness on the linguistic level for the deformity that it inspires.")[32] He endeavors, that is, to concoct a novel, and through it a form of nationality, that will be similarly invested with impregnable indefiniteness: similarly impervious to determinate claims, and similarly irreducible to its variously perceived characteristics.

It is for this reason that *Moby-Dick* pits itself in at times feverish opposition to the supremacist, but paradoxically reductive interpretive determinism of Young America's racial nationalism, a nationalism that denies the magisterial indeterminacy or "indefiniteness" of whiteness in the effort to aggrandize it. The America *Moby-Dick* aspires to invent might indeed be called a White America as well, but only from the countersupremacist perspective that Melville insists on in "The Whiteness of the Whale"—only if we recognize in such whiteness a steadfast refusal, not of interpretation, but of determination or conclusiveness. The correlate, and profoundly unsettling, suggestion is that the only way a democracy can truly respect the indiscriminate equality of human worth and potential in its citizens—"that great democratic dignity which, on all hands, radiates without end from God himself" (117)—is by protractedly refusing to deduce from the wealth of human *characteristics* any determinations of human *character*.

This is what Samuel Otter has in mind when he writes of Melville's ultimate refusal, especially where race is concerned, "to identify character with characteristics."[33] (The "august dignity" democracy prizes, Melville writes, resides "so far within us, that it remains intact *though all the outer character seem gone*" [117, emphasis added].) It is a principle of agnosticism that broaches, in its farthest repercussions, a vast unloosening from the comforts and conceits of personality.

This is why whiteness is finally an object of unappeasable terror in the novel, why Ishmael would suspect that "there yet lurks an elusive something in the innermost idea of this hue, which strikes more of panic to the soul than that redness which affrights in blood" (189). The novel is forever posing the question: what would it mean actually to *live* a life separated from the past and its legacies, from the parameters of being and of thought it has bequeathed to the present? If Ishmael's seems a mordant but undispirited meditation on just such a possibility, the novel itself produces a vision of immersion in the unknown and unforeclosed that is vastly more harrowing and grim. For to be unmoored from all determinations, and so cut loose from the conventionalities that map out human understanding and human personality—to emerge into a kind of *terra incognita*[34]—is, in the world of *Moby-Dick*, to falter into madness, as both Pip and Ahab bear witness. "The sea had jeeringly kept his finite body up," Ishmael says of Pip's hourslong abandonment to the open sea,

> but drowned the infinite of his soul. Not drowned entirely, though. Rather carried down alive to wondrous depths, where strange shapes of the unwarped primal world glided to and fro before his passive eyes; and the miser-merman, Wisdom, revealed his hoarded heaps; and among the joyous, heartless, ever-juvenile eternities, Pip saw the multitudinous, God-omnipresent, coral insects, that out of the firmament of waters heaved colossal orbs. He saw God's foot upon the treadle of the loom, and spoke it; and therefore his shipmates called him mad. So man's insanity is heaven's sense; and wandering from all mortal reason, man comes at last to that celestial thought, which, to reason, is absurd and frantic; and weal or woe, feels then uncompromised, indifferent as his God. (414)

Here the Emersonian utopia of a consciousness stripped of all worldly misinheritances and confronted finally with the "ever-juvenile eternities" of "the unwarped primal world" is played out as a kind self-annihilating terror. That "celestial thought," the wandering from the comforts of the world's certainties and determination, results in something "absurd and frantic" is as much a problem for Melville's hypothetical America as it is for his doomed characters.

"THIS SUDDEN FLAME OF FRIENDSHIP"

> *It is the easiest thing in the world for a man to*
> *look as if he had a great secret in him.*
> "THE PROPHET"

For all his encrypted assaults, Melville nevertheless shares with the nationalist prophets of Young America both an ambition—to create a great and distinctively American work of art—and a significant dilemma. The troubling question, for both, is this: How is it possible to translate a nationalist premise into the terms of human relations, of social bonds? For Melville, the problem is still more acute, since he must translate an essentially epistemological nationalist premise—one involving the ruthless demolition of all inherited forms of meaning—into the realm of sociality and its varied affective entanglements. As we saw in the introduction and in chapter 1, one of the real attractions of racial nationalism, particularly to literary types who felt an urbane disgust for the pettiness and chicanery of the state, was its aptness to describe a network of social ties that encompassed the whole of the nation but were not contained by or reducible to the state and its institutions. Insofar as one wished nationality to refer not to any subservience to common laws but to a quality of *relatedness* that would obtain even between citizens who had never met, one might find in "race" an exceptionally potent conceptual tool, since the discourse of race provided a particularly adaptive set of terms with which to imagine how such anonymous attachments might proceed. Simply being white, by the racialist account, could mean that one shared not only a form of distinction but a special kind of bond—perhaps even an intimacy—with the dispersed national citizenry one had never encountered personally. (It is this strand of antebellum nationalism Whitman confronts most directly, as we will see in chapter 4.) By deploying race both as an innate quality of character and as a language of attachment, racial nationalism allowed even those who reviled the corruptions of government a way to believe in a unified, incarnate America, one whose substance was not the decrees of state but the affective ties that knit its citizens together into lived cohesion.

Moby-Dick, too, is unquestionably hostile to state decree and its pretenses to justly derived authority—witness the mocking legal meditations of a chapter like "Fast Fish and Loose Fish." And yet the novel's relation to "race," as either a viable substitute paradigm or a form of social tie around which collectivities adhere, is once again vastly more tentative and suspicious than that of Young America. The *Pequod*'s crew is, after all, multinational and polyglot; what attachments sustain their unity are plainly insusceptible to the explanations of race, and perhaps, Ishmael suggests, to any explanations:

> They were nearly all Islanders in the Pequod, *Isolatoes* too, I call such, not acknowledging the common continent of men, but each *Isolato* living on a separate continent of his own. Yet now, federated along one keel, what a set these Isolatoes were! (121)

Here, then, is a collection of men who in their solitude regard as specious all claims of common being, yet who have somehow, miraculously, been "federated" into one "set." The narrative calls a baffled kind of attention to the enigma of their cohesion:

> How it was that they so aboundingly responded to the old man's ire—by what evil magic their souls were possessed, that at times his hate seemed almost theirs; the White Whale as much the insufferable foe as his; how all this came to be—what the White Whale was to them, or how to their unconscious understandings, also, in some dim, unsuspected way, he might have seemed the gliding great demon of the seas of life,—all this to explain, would be to dive deeper than Ishmael can go. (187)

Something irreducibly mysterious, some "evil magic," invests this federation of Isolatoes, such that Ishmael himself, the novel's gamest hypothesizer, can offer no insight whatsoever into the sorts of attachment that structure such improbable cohesiveness; there are, it seems, simply no terms available to him with which he might begin to describe them. Of course such an avowal of the inadequation of language or thought—in this case, with respect to the nature of the crew's compact—invites us to pose the inevitable question: Is the *Pequod*, then, the small-scale expression or approximation of the dreamed-of, indescribable America the novel means to disclose? If so—and it seems a possibility we are meant at least to consider—what are the defining features of its relations? What manner of social bond best embodies a nationalism that is, by the novel's own design, so resistant to embodied realization?

We might best approach these questions by giving close attention to the novel's most sustained, and most teasingly irreducible, figure of intimate attachment. The relationship between Ishmael and Queequeg shares a number of qualities with the affective dynamics of the *Pequod* and is at times called on to emblematize, in miniature, the relations of sailor to sailor more generally. Yet it is, for all that, a relationship about which very little can definitively be said. Indeed, if the bond between the two men has any one identifying trait, it is an indefiniteness or, more suggestively, an *inexplicitness* whose evocation recalls the novel's other strategies of epistemological disorientation. In Ishmael's intermittent and irregular account of his relationship to Queequeg, one figure recurs with the regularity of clockwork:

> Upon waking next morning about daylight, I found Queequeg's arm thrown over me in the most loving and affectionate manner. You had almost thought I had been his wife. (25)

> [Queequeg] seemed to take to me quite as naturally and unbiddenly as I to him; and when our smoke was over, he pressed his forehead against mine, clasped me round the waist, and said that henceforth we were married; meaning, in his country's phrase, that we were bosom friends; he would gladly die for me, if need should be. In a countryman, this sudden flame of friendship would have seemed far too premature, a thing to be much distrusted; but in this simple savage those old rules would not apply. (51)

> How it is I know not; but there is no place like a bed for confidential disclosures between friends. Man and wife, they say, there open the very bottom of their souls to each other; and some old couples often lie and chat over old times till nearly morning. Thus, then, in our hearts' honeymoon, lay I and Queequeg—a cosy, loving pair. (52)

> It was a humorously perilous business for both of us. For, before we proceed further, it must be said that the monkey-rope was fast at both ends; that for better or for worse, we two, for the time, were wedded; and should poor Queequeg sink to rise no more,

then both usage and honor demanded, that instead of cutting the
cord, it should drag me down in his wake. (320)

Such matrimonial trappings seem, at first glance, to fit easily
among the mock-serious, comically extraneous figures the novel
employs. Just as the juxtaposition of sailors with kings (117), a
whale's head with Plato's (344), and a blubber-cutter with an arch-
bishop (420) mean to deflate monarchical, metaphysical, and religious claims to authority, so too, we might surmise, does the novel
ironize the supposed sanctity of marriage by inhabiting its figures
with as unsanctimonious a pair as Ishmael and Queequeg. From
this perspective, their bond offers the novel a shining opportunity
to dismiss, by rhetorical misappropriation, still another of the
world's established pieties.

From a different perspective, though, the "marriage" of Queequeg and Ishmael appears quite distinct, in form and in effect,
from the rest of the novel's rhetorical fabulations. In the first place,
as we have seen, "marriage" is presented not as a provisional description of Ishmael and Queequeg's bond—not as a figure induced
by an alluring pun, or carried out on a gust of rhetoric—but as
the trope by which their relationship is defined, to the degree that
it can or will be. To equate this marriage with the novel's other
undifferentiatedly satiric digressions is, moreover, to diminish the
fact that Ishmael's very conversion to open-hearted agnosticism
(what Andrew Delbanco winningly calls "the expansion and un-
stiffening of Ishmael's mind") is initiated by his mysteriously
powerful attraction to Queequeg.[35] "But see how elastic our stiff
prejudices grow," he writes of his transformation, "when love once
comes to bend them" (54). And finally, as the winking suggestiveness of the previous quotation attests, the figure of an unspecified
sort of "marriage" between two men invites a speculative scrutiny
that is necessarily intensified by the deliberately teasing prospect
of *sexual* revelation. The sexual disclosure the novel both intimates
and withholds, in other words, establishes a drama of readerly ini-
tiative and dependence—a keen desire to know more—that Melville may then manipulate.

This drama unfolds in the novel, moment by narrative moment,
according to a kind of pattern. There is, to begin with, a sort of
rhetorical cat-and-mouse game between connotation and denota-
tion, whereby a figure is deployed that suggests a specifically sexual content, and is then protractedly, even garrulously unclarified.

The first several chapters concerning Ishmael's "marriage" to Queequeg are exemplary in this respect. Chapter 4 begins the morning after their first night as bedmates, when Ishmael wakes to find "Queequeg's arm thrown about me in the most loving and affectionate manner. You had almost thought I had been his wife" (25). The somewhat puzzling pronouns and tense-modulations of the latter sentence (who is this "you"? does Ishmael mean that he *had been* like Queequeg's wife the night before?) do nothing to dispel its connotative force, nor does the qualification "almost" (which in fact raises more questions than it settles, since we are not given to know what about their embrace, exactly, makes it *almost* wifely, rather than simply wifely). At least one of the suggestions afoot here is clearly that the "loving and affectionate" embrace they are sharing is matrimonial because desiring or, more plainly, sexual. But as quickly and as clearly as this suggestion appears before us, just as quickly does the narrative gaze turn its attention elsewhere, onto objects and figures that, rather than focus, seem actually to deflect our view under these covers. In the next sentence, Ishmael notes the design of the counterpane, its similarity to Queequeg's tattooed arm, and at the end of the paragraph once again observes, this time somewhat more equivocally, that "Queequeg was hugging me." The gentle affability implied by the word "hugging" chastens to some degree the couple's "loving and affectionate" clasp; yet it does so without canceling any of the erotic possibilities condensed in the phrase "You had almost thought I had been his wife." What keeps all the possibilities open, in this pile-up of differently inflected connotative suggestions, is above all the narrative's studied reticence with respect to physical details. Ishmael's overproduction of visually unspecifying *figures* allows him to describe a bodily intimacy even as he withholds the physical particulars of which that intimacy is made, and according to which it might be distinguished in kind or type. This is exactly the strategy that gives the closing paragraph of chapter 10 its peculiar charge:

> How it is I know not; but there is no place like a bed for confidential
> disclosures between friends. Man and wife, they say, there open
> the very bottom of their souls to each other; and some old couples
> often lie and chat over old times till nearly morning. Thus, then,
> in our hearts' honeymoon, lay I and Queequeg—a cosy, loving
> pair. (52)

The final sentence proposes a host of sexual interpretations, none of which, however, it will confirm with some more revealing or concrete erotic detail. Ishmael's narrative in this way untiringly confirms the *possibility* of sexual exchange between himself and Queequeg, without ever allowing that the nature of their bond could be described exclusively or exhaustively in sexual terms.

The figure of Ishmael and Queequeg's "marriage" thus describes a form of attachment that is resilient, in its irreducibility, to the very anatomizing terms it invites. This is not to suggest that *Moby-Dick* exemplifies "the peculiarly American form of innocent homosexuality"—an assertion that makes one wonder what exactly distinguishes an innocent homosexuality from, say, a guilty one. If the answer is something like "genital contact" or "sexual exchange," then the drive to exonerate Melville on this score is, to say the least, suspicious (and is more likely purgative, phobic, willfully obtuse).[36] For although the exact tenor—or rather, the physical specifications—of their matrimonial love appears in the novel only in the form of a deliberate inexplicitness, it yet seems an unwarrantable mistake to consign the attachment enjoyed by these two life-mates to a false chastity. We can only do so, of course, by playing dumb—by regarding the accretion of frank innuendo with so vehement a refusal of credulity that we wind up insisting, in effect, on little more than the insulating power of our own apparently ineducable ignorance.[37] If the novel is indeed content to let its sexual intimations remain forever unsubstantiated, this is clearly not because it wishes to affirm Ishmael in his early objection to "the unbecomingness of . . . hugging a fellow male in that matrimonial sort of style" (27). Rather, Ishmael's narrative deliberately *incites* a readerly desire for disclosure and specification—a desire for taxonomic certainty—in order to show, by frustrating that desire, how powerfully averse the bond between Queequeg and Ishmael actually is to specifying claims of any sort. The point of such attenuations is therefore not that sexual exchange could never have taken place between them, but that whatever bonds subsist between them are insusceptible to comprehensive explanation, in terms of *either* the sexual or the merely friendly. The repeated troping of the unclarified figure of marriage works, in other words, to coax into narrative existence a kind of bond, *inclusive of the sexual*, that yet has no place in the available languages of attachment.

With respect to the sexual dimension it thus includes, we might describe this bond as "sodomitical," though it should be understood that the aptness of this term derives not least from its irreducibility—derives, that is, from the plurality of passions, pleasures, investments, exchanges, and acts the term references without specifying. Even the historian B. R. Burg's attempt to narrow the definitional field of sodomy to "homosexual contact between adult males" leaves a great deal to the imagination (what *manner* of contact?). It is this apparently endemic definitional elasticity that prompts Foucault's memorable reference to sodomy as "that utterly confused category."[38] Moreover, few historical moments could be more thoroughly confused than the moment of *Moby-Dick*. For if *Billy Budd*, a text of the 1890s, defines a new moment "after the homosexual," as Eve Sedgwick contends, and Foucault's eighteenth century describes the last long moment before the appearance of the homosexual as a species or characterological type, then Melville's studied attenuations in *Moby-Dick* suggest that the mid-century marks a particularly volatile in-between time, a period of transition between definitional paradigms. More precisely, Melville's deployment of sodomy as an attachment that resists intelligibility seems to define a particular moment in the development of American sexual ideology, a moment unfolding in the space before it was assumed that every individual could and must be assigned either a hetero- or homosexuality, but in which the stirrings of that impulse toward taxonomy could already be felt—in the new medicalized "sciences," such as phrenology, in the newly proliferate tracts on marital and sexual health, and not least in the anti-onanist polemics (most famously, Sylvester Graham's 1848 "Lecture to Young Men") that Melville would parody so joyously in the famous sperm-squeezing chapter, "A Squeeze of the Hand."[39] By this score, the novel plays directly into the encroaching mid-century desire for taxonomic specificity, only so that it might be made to disintegrate in the face of Ishmael's and Queequeg's obdurately unyielding mutual affection. Erotic friendship between men thus appears in Melville as a possible locale in which some form of resistance to a developing regime of sexuality might be sheltered: in an already heated atmosphere of sexual specification that would, over the years, grow only more hostile, these bonds subsist in an as yet uncollapsed space of definitional ambiguity.

This is what makes sodomitical attachments such an ideal expressive model for the peculiarly voided American nationalism that *Moby-Dick* proposes. Accordingly, the sodomitical bond between Ishmael and Queequeg is on several occasions shown to be uniquely expressive of the relations that bind together the crew of the *Pequod*. Consider the narrative of "A Squeeze of the Hand." Here, elbow-deep in coagulated sperm, Ishmael experiences a species of rapture, which leaves him "divinely free from all ill-will, or petulance, or malice, of any sort whatsoever":

> Squeeze! squeeze! squeeze! all morning long; I squeezed that sperm till I myself almost melted into it; I squeezed that sperm till a strange sort of insanity came over me; and I found myself unwittingly squeezing my co-laborers' hands in it, mistaking their hands for the gentle globules. Such an abounding, affectionate, friendly, loving feeling did this avocation beget; that at last I was continually squeezing their hands, and looking up into their eyes sentimentally; as much as to say,—Oh! my dear fellow beings, why should we longer cherish any social acerbities, or know the slightest ill-humor or envy! Come; let us squeeze hands all round; nay, let us all squeeze ourselves into each other; let us squeeze ourselves universally into the very milk and sperm of human kindness. Would that I could keep squeezing that sperm forever! For now, since by many prolonged, repeated experiences, I have perceived that in all cases man must eventually lower, or at least shift, his conceit of attainable felicity; not placing it anywhere in the intellect or the fancy; but in the wife, the heart, the bed, the table, the saddle, the fire-side, the country; now that I have perceived all this, I am ready to squeeze case eternally. In thoughts of the visions of the night, I saw long rows of angels in paradise, each with his hands in a jar of spermaceti. (416)

Ishmael wishes he *could* abide forever in this all-male paradise of masturbatory endearments, for it would relieve him from the unhappy fact that the "attainable felicities" (the wife, the bed, the fire-side, etc.) are but dreary domestications of the high-flown fancies and intellectual aspirations with which one begins in life. The sodomitical attachments that bind the crew together here—figured in this instance as a kind of mutual masturbation—are presented as the antidote to such tepid comforts, and indeed as an antidote to the headlong mania of Ahab's quest. ("I declare to you," Ishmael writes, "that for the time . . . I forgot all about our horrible oath.") The very unseriousness of the passage attests, once again, to the extravagance of this bond, to its capacity to outstrip the languages in which it might be described. These scenes, as Bersani suggests, work to "transform the representation of both friendship and homoeroticism into an inconceivable social bond."[40] And it is finally by this sustained irreducibility—this unresolving inconceivability, provisionality, and indefiniteness—that we recognize sodomitical attachment as a premiere vehicle for the novel's speculative nationalism. Sodomy, that is to say, appears in *Moby-Dick* as the nearest expression, in the realm of human relations, of the America its author wishes to invent.

Again, though, a species of terror hangs irrevocably about this utopianism. The protean sexual energies of the *Pequod*'s crew are on similarly vivid display in the chapter "Midnight, Forecastle," where bawdy sailors pining for "Spanish ladies" dance wildly in one another's arms (173). ("Partners!" the Maltese Sailor cries, "I must have partners!" [174]). But on equally clear display in the chapter is a tendency toward violence and chaos not always capable of being restrained, and which, in the end, erupts into a knife fight, interrupted only by the coming of a squall. Pip's admonishing prayer provides an apt summary: "Oh, though big white God aloft somewhere in yon darkness, have mercy on this small black boy down here; preserve him from all men that have no bowels to feel fear" (178). That the bowels (archaic term for the seat of pity, tenderness, and courage) appear as the site where Pip locates a capacity for fear—that fearfulness *should* strike the crew through their bowels, but does not—is a pun of some consequence, since it seems to magnetize all the sexual suggestions and obliquities that had spotted the narrative up to this point. On the one hand, the moment suggests again that sodomy (which in this case refers more specifically to an anal erotics) is the defining form of attachment on the *Pequod*, that which most fully expresses the sailors' fearlessly dismissive relation to custom, piety, and decorum. On the other hand, that form of attachment is no proof against violence, chaos, and disunity. "(*They scatter*)" is all the description Melville will hazard of the sailors' response to the storms without and onboard, which is not the vision of intimate cohesion an ardently nationalist reader might hope to find.

Moby-Dick's is not, then, a redemptive account of same-sex desire, nor an account of the democratic utopianism inherent to male homosexuality. Sodomitical attachments may figure a kind of sociality that is unbeholden to the past and its inherited hierarchies, a sociality as unmapped as the America *Moby-Dick*, with its disdain for the ideal of a racialized white republic, wishes to dream into being. But it is not, for that, a kind of sociality that provides much in the way of unity, or collectivity, or sustaining mutuality. In "The Candles," when Ahab calls down God's fire and wrath, Ishmael recounts the crew's terrified reaction:

> Overhearing Starbuck, the panic-stricken crew instantly ran to the braces—though not a sail was left aloft. For the moment all the aghast mate's thoughts seemed theirs; they raised a half mutinous cry. But dashing the rattling lightning links to the deck, and snatching the burning harpoon, Ahab waved it like a torch among them; swearing to transfix with it the first sailor that but cast loose a rope's end. Petrified by his aspect, and still more shrinking from the fiery dart that he held, the men fell back in dismay, and Ahab again spoke:—
>
> "All your oaths to hunt the White Whale are as binding as mine; and heart, soul, and body, lungs and life, old Ahab is bound. And that ye may know to what tune this heart beats: look ye here; thus I blow out the last fear!" And with one blast of his breath he extinguished the flame.
>
> As in the hurricane that sweeps the plain, men fly the neighborhood of some lone, gigantic elm, whose very height and strength but render it so much the more unsafe, because so much more a mark for thunderbolts; so at those last words of Ahab's many of the mariners did run from him in a terror of dismay. (508)

Whatever their bond, it is not capable of forging itself into a collective motive, into anything more than a fleeting "*half* mutinous cry." Moreover, in their "terror of dismay," the crew appear incapable of providing virtually anything in the way of resistance or opposition to the most tyrannical forms of authority. Onanistically squeezing hands in sperm, the sailors "forget [their] horrible oath"—but only momentarily. Sodomitical attachments appear as something of an alternative to Ahab's destructive and terror-forged unity in the novel, then, but as an alternative that is, finally, unviable.

That the novel wishes to demolish every variety of certainty—tyrannies of thought, as it were—is clear; but Ishmael's compulsive dismissals, and the sort of voided sociality they aspire toward, seem to render him and his fellows uniquely *susceptible* to tyrannical designs, such as Ahab's. The impious wit he brings to bear on the world is notably powerless to intervene, at any moment, in the *Pequod*'s trajectory toward annihilation—he is in fact willfully complicit in "Ahab's quenchless feud" because it inspires in him what he calls a "wild, mystical, sympathetical feeling" (179). The deliberate disqualification of the world's available terms of being thus results not only in the "ontological comedy" for which Melville is famed but also, where Ishmael is concerned, in a certain blankness of motive: surrendering himself as to the capricious Fates, he is carried along in his devouring agnosticism by the force of contingency and momentary need. If such blankness means, on the one hand, to allow for the emergence of an as yet unimaginable disposition of being and social relatedness, it also responds with frightful equanimity—submissiveness, in fact—to any force that promises to arrogate to itself all the plaguing dilemmas of motive, directedness, and will. What we see here once again is that Ahab's monomania is not the antithesis of Ishmael's agreeable refusal of conclusiveness, but the engine that sustains it.[41]

And the novel is quite clear about the kinds of unanimity and coherence, the models of belonging and of collectivity, that can and will sweep into the space of voided motive, or that might be likely to overtake men unloosed from any inherited structure of order or affiliation. Here is the novel's account of the crew, beginning its second day of giving chase to the white whale:

> The frenzies of the chase had by this time worked them bubblingly up, like old wine worked anew. Whatever pale fears and forebodings some of them might have felt before; these were not only now kept out of sight through the growing awe of Ahab, but they were broken up, and on all sides routed, as timid prairie hares that scatter before the bounding bison. The hand of Fate had snatched all their souls; and by the stirring perils of the previous day; the rack of the past night's suspense; the fixed, unfearing, blind, reckless way in which their wild craft went plunging towards its flying mark; by all these things, their hearts were bowled along. The wind that made great bellies of their sails, and rushed the vessel on by arms invisible as irresistible; this seemed the symbol of that unseen agency which so enslaved them to the race.
>
> They were one man, not thirty. (556-57)

Whatever our doubts about the duplicity of the word "race" as it concludes the paragraph, or about its ramifying significances, the ironic reference to the crew's "enslavement" should, I think, lay them decisively to rest. These are men made one, we are told, by an enslaving dedication to "the race," to the headlong and vengeful pursuit of whiteness even unto death. Here the terrific power of whiteness as a vehicle for unyielding social adhesion is displayed as nakedly as anywhere else in the novel, as is the consequence of such a form of collectivity: the ship, as we know, is speeding toward its destruction. The sodomitical bonds with which the novel had at moments imagined the crew to be joined impiously together are in this climactic moment shown to be wholly insufficient to withstand the force of a form of order and cohesion magnetized by race. *Moby-Dick* may well be a novel about the profound wrongheadedness, the monomaniacal madness of "race" and its nationalization; but it is also about the apparently irresistible lure of such a promise of binding coherence, especially to societies cast out on the seas of history, cut loose from the past and its constraining but also stabilizing forms of order and belonging.

For the novel's purposes, then, there is finally no way to disentangle the vision of a heroically unformed America from the catastrophe of its embodiment, no way to translate the America of unbodied promise and potentiality into the tangled realm of human attachments, of sociality. Melville's consuming, voided nationalism provides a beautiful dream of indescribable, impossibly expansive American possibility—and in doing so, I think, registers Melville's unwillingness to think of the nation, or for that matter himself as author, in the terms of a strictly racial identification. But that dream, as Melville cannot help but demonstrate, will not be made amenable to the demands of relation, of intimate mutuality, which the very idea of nation-ness, in the antebellum republic, carries within itself. And this, for *Moby-Dick*, is the catastrophe of American promise. In this respect, *Moby-Dick* is less a redemptive or utopian text than a novel of violent and unflinching grimness. (Part of what is miraculous about the book is that it manages, even through that abiding grimness, to be unfalteringly high-spirited and funny.) *Moby-Dick*'s America thus seems finally to subsist as a form a desire—*whose* desire, it is difficult to say—that might consume and withstand anything in the world, other than the prospect of its fulfillment.

CHAPTER 4

Loving Strangers: Intimacy and Nationality in Whitman

Here is adhesiveness—it is not previously fashioned—
it is apropos;
Do you know what it is, as you pass, to be loved by
strangers?
Do you know the talk of those turning eye-balls?
WALT WHITMAN, "SONG OF THE OPEN ROAD" (1860)

Or again: *Is it possible to be intimate with someone you haven't met?*
To those already wary of Walt Whitman's hyperbolically grand ambitions, both for himself and for poetry, the importance to his work of this curious question will not be reassuring. For however much forbearance one brings to Whitman's moments of gunslinger bravado, however figuratively one tries to read his boasts about the poet who would be "president" and sole arbiter of national life, one must eventually confront a single stubborn fact: virtually every strand of Whitman's utopian thought devolves upon, and is anchored by, an unwavering belief in the capacity of strangers to recognize, to desire, and to be intimate with one another. Whitman's declarations of aesthetic intent, for instance, all circle back to a quality of intimate affection that he promises to extend to an entire nation of readers who are, to him, perfectly unknown. From the 1876 preface to *Leaves of Grass*:

... while I am about it, I would make a full confession. I also sent out "Leaves of Grass" to arouse and set flowing in men's and

127

women's hearts, young and old, endless streams of living, pulsating
love and friendship, directly from them to myself, now and ever.[1]

Among its other indications, this "full confession" bears the impress
of Whitman's earliest and most lasting formal allegiances. Having
begun his career as an attentive student of the forms and methods of the era's two most prominent national media—print jour-
nalism and oratorical address—Whitman soon resolved to fashion
a revolutionary expressive form that would in effect combine the
two, that would accommodate both the physical immediacy he
revered so much in oratory and the general availability of print.[2]
By 1855, what he has developed is an idiom of self-presentation
that is capable of the most intimate proddings and solicitations,
yet whose often thrilling interpellative effects depend precisely
on the mutual anonymity of author and reader. "This hour I tell
things in confidence," says the narrator of "Song of Myself," "I
might not tell everybody but I will tell you."[3] Tugging flirtatiously
against the merely generic inclusiveness of the anonymous "you"
in these lines is the sly suggestion that we are, each of us, selected
for the poet's confidences. From general anonymity to selective
intimacy: this swift telescoping of address is perhaps the signature motion of the 1855 *Leaves of Grass*, and is certainly the place
where an examination of the coy solicitousness of Whitman's carefully molded persona ought to begin. For here, as elsewhere in
Whitman's corpus, we are offered the strange pleasure of being
solicited by an author who, while admitting that he does not and
cannot "know" any of us, nevertheless pledges himself as an intimate companion, bosom comrade, and secret lover.[4]

   Whitman's fascination with the idea of strangers is of equally
great consequence in the context of antebellum literary nationalism, where so many of his avowedly political ambitions take
root. Like many other nationalist authors of the period (and we
might include here writers as differently inclined as Hawthorne
and Douglass, Melville and Stowe), Whitman's love for America—
which is clearly passionate and in earnest—only barely exceeds
his vitriolic contempt for the state, its institutions, and its agents.
(Lincoln was to be an important, and rare, exception.) "Where is
the real America?" Whitman wonders in the altogether violent
polemic from 1856, *The Eighteenth Presidency!* "Where is the spirit
of the manliness and the common-sense of These States?" Of one
thing he is certain: "It does not appear in the government" (*Poetry*

and Prose, 1334).[5] The problem to which Whitman addresses himself here, as we saw in the introduction, is the problem of the antebellum nationalist author more generally: If the state fails so utterly to account for or to circumscribe or to accommodate true "American-ness," of what, exactly, is nationality made? In what terms ought one to imagine the substance and coherence of that yet rather tenuous imagined collectivity called "America"? In a now-famous passage from the 1876 preface, where he discusses "Calamus" and what he calls its "political significance," Whitman gives his most unequivocal answer:

> In my opinion, it is by a fervent, accepted development of comradeship, the beautiful and sane affection of man for man, latent in all young fellows, north and south, east and west—it is by this, I say, and by what goes directly and indirectly along with it, that the United States of the future, (I cannot too often repeat,) are to be most effectually welded together, intercalated, anneal'd into a living union. (*Poetry and Prose,* 1035)

Whitman cannot too often repeat that the nation is an entity not of institutions and abstract strictures, but of *relation.* To talk of "America" is to talk of the bonds of "beautiful and sane affection of man for man" that "effectually weld[ ] together" a dispersed and mutually anonymous citizenry. The "real America" is not to be found in the government, then, because governments deal only in proclamations and in strictures, to which one's proper relation is that of allegiance or, more pointedly, obedience. For Whitman nationality is something quite different. It consists neither in legal compulsion nor geographical happenstance, but in the specifically affective attachments that somehow tie together people who have never seen one another, who live in different climates and come from different cultures and harbor wildly different needs and aspirations. To be properly American is thus, as Whitman conceives it, to feel oneself related, in a quite intimate way, to a world of people not proximate or even known to oneself. That these "fervent" intimacies might include even sexual desire (and certainly do not preclude it) simply shows the extent of Whitman's belief in the richness and affective depth of which relations between strangers are capable; and from this belief springs his utopian vision of an America given coherence not by the state but by the passionate ties that join together its far-flung citizens.[6]

There may well be some interpretive leverage to be gained, then, in pretending ignorance for a moment of Whitman's other nominations (the Poet of Democracy, the Poet of the Body, the Poet of Nonconformity, etc.) so that we might declare him instead America's great Poet of Attachment. The obverse of Dickinson, whose charmed realms are those of solitude and inwardness, the Whitman we invoke here looks always to represent, to consecrate, and— at his most ambitious—actually to sponsor intimacies, affectionate ties, bonds with and among a world of people who are, to each other and to him, strangers. ("Crossing Brooklyn Ferry" gives the matter its most concise expression, where Whitman asks of his unborn future readers: "What is it then between us?" [*Poetry and Prose*, 310].) In this chapter, I want to explore the contours of this unlikely attachment—this intimacy that bypasses familiarity— and to look in particular at a few of the terms Whitman draws on to corroborate his dream of an intimate nationality. My principal contention is that between 1855 and 1860, in the initial "Song of Myself" and in the "Calamus" poems, Whitman considers and finally adopts, even as he revises and in some respects resists, two conceptual models for the anonymous intimacies of national life. He finds these models in the array of languages surrounding race and sex—more specifically, in the racialist languages of the Free-Soil Democrats, and the emerging sexological languages of phrenology. As we will see, though, Whitman's method is not simply to accede to these public languages but to pressure and, in effect, contort them: to raid their conceptual vocabularies, and to turn them to political purposes at once more expansive and more idiosyncratic than their initial contexts seemed to offer. In both instances, the purposes to which Whitman labors to adapt race and sex are those of a visionary nationalism, structured around the promise of anonymous intimacies.

We are today of course accustomed to thinking of sexuality and race as manifestly political terms to the degree that they describe not intimacies but identity—to the degree that they mark and differentiate *types* of people. Whitman's work is uniquely instructive in this context—more so, I think, than that of any other mid-century author—since it allows us to see with startling clarity how race and sex might acquire political potency in antebellum America not only (and perhaps not even principally) as differential markers of social status and identity but as *languages of attachment*. To Whitman, in other words, both race and sex offer

enormously powerful conceptual models with which to imagine
how persons who have never met might yet enjoy a special kind
of bond with one another, and as such they are to him political
languages, and specifically nationalist languages, of the highest
consequence. Unfolding around Whitman's efforts to wrench these
languages into alignments more exactly suited to his utopian nationalism—as well as to the distinctive stylistics he was bit by bit
assembling—is one of the great uncaptured dramas of the early
poetry.

ANONYMITY AND SYMPATHY

I do not ask who you are . . . that is not important to me,
You can do nothing and be nothing but I will infold you.
"Song of Myself" (1855)

How, then, do Whitman's grand nationalist ambitions actually
work, in the poetry itself? It's wise to begin where Whitman's poetic
career itself auspiciously begins, with "Song of Myself" as it appears
(as yet untitled) in the 1855 *Leaves of Grass*. This poem, it will be
recalled, traces an immense, progressive self-dilation, whereby a
narrative persona called "Walt Whitman, an American" comes to
be the living repository for all the teeming data of American life,
past and future: "I am an acme of things accomplished," the poet
tells us, "and I an encloser of things to be" (48, 77). Part of the
extraordinary, often disarming bravado of the poem lies, first, in
the breeziness of the poet's presumption that absolutely every
corner and crevice of national life falls firmly within his percep-
tual ken. Striving throughout to make good on his claim from the
preface that the true American poet will be in every way "com-
mensurate with a people"—will be, in fact, "the age transfigured"
(6, 21)—Whitman presents a nation whose defining attribute, even
more than its fascinating variousness, seems to be its sheer transparency to the consuming poetic consciousness. The enumerative
catalogue is of course the most remarked-upon rhetorical form
through which Whitman looks to evince this comprehensive mutual
absorption of poet and nation, but it is not the only, or even the
principal, verbal strategy he employs.[7]

Another prominent strategy in the poem—the one whose presence is perhaps most immediately felt—is that of perspectival

fracture and manipulation. In section 2 of "Song of Myself," for instance, Whitman presents himself in a rapid-fire succession of rhetorical forms and stances, each of which implies a different proximity or location with respect to a scene described. In the space of twenty-four lines, the narrative voice jumps through the following modes of address: omniscient descriptive ("Houses and rooms are full of perfumes"), subjective testimonial ("I breathe the fragrance myself, and know it and like it"), fragmentary declarative ("My respiration and inspiration . . . the beating of my heart . . ."), interrogative ("Have you reckoned a thousand acres much?"), imperative ("Stop this day and night with me . . ."), concluding finally in a prophetic second-person address wherein the promise of the poem is summarized: "You shall not look through my eyes either, nor take things from me, / You shall listen to all sides and filter them from yourself" (25–26). By the terrific speed with which he darts and charges through this extended range of rhetorics and modes of self-presentation, the poet attests, first of all, to the vastness of his perspective. The eyes of this poem are not merely Whitman's own, since he himself will filter and encompass all imaginable vantages, "all sides." Speaking paratactically from a multiplicity of angles of view, the poet works to situate himself everywhere—both within and at a distance from an impossibly diverse set of locales.

Remarkably, though, this deliberate self-scattering in no way disperses or depersonalizes the poem's center of consciousness (as it does in, say, the work of a Whitman heir like John Ashbery). For that fractured perspective also remains tangibly Whitman's own— remains in fact quite singular—by virtue of being codified in an idiom whose handful of stylistic idiosyncrasies we are very quickly taught by the poem to recognize as a kind of discursive fingerprint, a signature. Reading Whitman is ever a process of acquisition and acculturation. His grammatical contortions are so aggressive, his rhetorical postures so distinctive, that each verse paragraph, whatever else it describes, also provides us with painstaking instruction in how to distinguish Whitman's perspective from any other. We come to learn, for instance, that rhetorical questions pitched in the second person comprise one of this poet's favorite forms of emphasis, and are among the devices with which he looks to anticipate and actually to conscript the perspectives of his audience ("Have you practiced so long to learn to read?" [26]). We learn as well that sentence fragments consisting mainly of noun clauses will be allowed to follow one after another, often at great length, for the purpose of forming the heterogeneous details of national life into a kind of eternal-present tableau (as in the catalogues of sections 33 and 37). We learn that neologisms—nonce words ("foo-foos," "fatherstuff"), nouns twisted into verbs, verbs congealed into nouns ("It throbs me to gulps of the farthest down horror")—will be cultivated throughout in an effort to dramatize the poet's struggle to expand the descriptive range of the American idiom, and to make it (as he says in the preface) "the medium that shall well nigh express the inexpressible" (23). And we learn further that unlikely figures and word juxtapositions are among this poet's favorite means to unsettle the familiarity of common bits of idiom and to return sharpness and a kind of tactility to figures that have been dulled by overuse (as in phrases like "Echoes, ripples, *buzzed whispers*"—where, rather than *soft* or *muffled*, the whispers are bees—and "Only the lull I like, *the hum of your valved voice*," where the potentially incorporeal voice is transformed into a mechanical, brassy instrument, whose valves are released and depressed in the production of sound [25, 28, my emphasis]). The combination of these handful of tics and devices makes up what we might simply call the poet's "style": Through them, he asserts the presence in his poems of a continuous and deeply particular organizing consciousness.[8] We will return later to these identifying turns of language, and to the impress of particularity they provide, but for now I want only to note that the all-important effect of persona is, in Whitman, essentially rhetorical. By the suffusion of every register of discourse and exposition with these verbal cues—cues that occur at the level of grammar and syntax, of word and phrase—Whitman establishes the center of consciousness in his poems as a kind of character, bristling with arrogance and charm, whose tangible locality anchors the poem's enormity of perspective.

More than anything else, it is our faith in the consistency of that local persona that carries us (*some* of us) through the thronging catalogues of sections 15 and 33 and 37, where Whitman's perspectival position seems to flatten as it expands to cover every inch of the nation. Here, the poet's omnivorous power of perception manifests itself not by rhetorical sleights but by much more plain-faced assertions of identification (assertions that are also a kind of self-disruption or self-evaporation): "I am the hounded slave," "I am the mashed fireman," "I am the old artillerist" (62, 63). Alternating with the poem's moments of tender revelation and hushed awe, these asserted equivalences work to fashion Whitman as a figure whose endearing particularity ("Washes and razors for foofoos . . . for me freckles and a bristling beard" [46]) in no way inhibits the expansive generality of his very being. "Of these one and all tend inward to me," he writes at the conclusion of the poem's first extended catalogue, "and I tend outward to them, / And such as it is to be of these more or less I am" (40). This knitting-together of the uninhibitedly general and the recognizably particular—a conjoining whose success depends intimately on the unbroken rhetorical effect of persona—provides the backbone for the poet's grand project of national representativeness. Thus does Walt Whitman, "one of the roughs," emerge simultaneously as "a kosmos," a universalized self from whose unique affections no one need be excluded.[9] As he proclaims open-endedly in section 22: "I am he attesting sympathy" (46).

Such open-endedness is of course something of a provocation as well. Along with much cheerful adulation, it has over the years provoked recrimination, incredulity, and outright contempt. An indicative case is that of D. H. Lawrence, who angrily indicts the poet for having offered to prostitutes, syphilitics, and slaves a misbegotten, undoubtedly counterfeit affection. His two-line "Retort to Whitman," while it lacks the detail of his critique in *Studies in Classic American Literature*, spares none of its venom. He writes:

> And whoever walks a mile full of false sympathy
> walks to the funeral of the whole human race.[10]

Mean-spirited though it may be, Lawrence's little revision seems nevertheless to capture one distinctive aspect of the experience of reading Whitman. Though we may not all feel as immoderately irked as Lawrence here appears to be—and though we may not any of us find the explanation for his distaste for Whitman's sympathy at all resonant[11]—the quality of exasperated patience he describes will probably be, at the very least, familiar to most of us. It would, after all, be a benumbed reader indeed who could trundle through the whole of *Leaves of Grass* without once feeling even a twinge of exactly Lawrence's kind of irritation. What's exasperating about the ecstatic Whitman—what Lawrence responds so heatedly to—isn't necessarily the inertness of some of the catalogs, their unrelenting loudness, or even the poet's occasional willingness to be tedious. Rather, one can very easily be unsettled by the completely unhesitating manner with which this poet moves to proclaim the transparency of any imaginable occurrence, any possible vantage, to the vastness of his person. Such gestures, while they do provide for a bravado that is not without its appeal, seem also to require a degree of nuance and finesse that not every passage in "Song of Myself" achieves—of which some passages, in fact, are almost affrontively lacking. There is, to put this differently, something embarrassingly immodest about the unflustered confidence with which the poet casts himself in often improbable roles, and about the immediacy with which he identifies himself with the downtrodden, the suffering, the enslaved.[12] Lawrence, for one, was having none of it, and his skepticism, though idiosyncratic to say the least, does point to an unevenness of tone and execution in "Song of Myself" that is accounted for neither by the poet's fondness for an improvisatory roughness in exposition nor by the mutability of his persona.

I want to be perfectly clear about what I mean by "unevenness" and its potentially "affrontive" effects, since I think these terms— which I've used to describe stylistic anomalies and possible reader-responses to them—lead us at the same time into very different, very difficult critical waters. Following the implications of Lawrence's reading, we have begun to ask a very slippery question of Whitman's sympathy: not *Of what is it made?* but *Is it credible?* If the question seems impertinent (to answer it is simply to divulge the standard one has presumed in the asking), it is nevertheless not one we can so easily dispense with, since debates over the credibility of Whitman's sympathy must also be, more intimately, contestations over the location of that credibility, over the proprietary ground of criticism itself. To ask after Whitman's credibility, in other words, is implicitly to define where in the poems one thinks such credibility (or conviction, or intention, or politics, etc.) most meaningfully expresses itself. Lawrence, for instance, seems more than anything else irritated by the simple fact of Whitman's identificatory claims: To assert that one *is* a slave, a syphilitic, a prostitute, he argues, is to offer a forgery of the soul's instinctual inclination toward such beings. Meaning for Lawrence thus resides mainly in "gesture"—in the general impulses to exclude, embrace, champion, or condemn specific historical characters. And in this he is not alone.

Much of even the strongest historicist criticism of Whitman follows from premises remarkably similar to Lawrence's, locating in the poet's various gestures of identification and inclusion a range of cognate ideological positions. The first thing we might note about this approach—the first thing that might make us wary—is the ease with which it accommodates the most diametrically opposed evaluations of the poet, the most valorizing and the most disparaging. For example, the identical poetic "gesture" ("I am the hounded slave," say) can with equal degrees of scrupulousness be shown to indicate (a) a democratic, revolutionary will-to-include, and (b) a self-amplifying and "unearned" expropriation of the suffering of others—the difference depending, in the main, on the historical archive to which the critic has made the poet answerable.[13] In either case, the actual *execution* of those claims, in language, remains oddly superfluous, as though the realm of verbal texture was, to all practical purposes, the last place to look for any leverage on questions of political or historical concern. Though not exactly the equivalent of reading Shakespeare for the plot, this blandly "historical" approach does tend to presume that all but the most rudimentary aspects of this utterly distinctive poet's form and style are null sets, incapable of delivering to a politically attuned sensibility any mother lode of meaning.[14] What results, finally, is the thorough disconnection of the "politics" of Whitman's texts from the basic elements of which they are made, and by which they are distinguished as Whitman's own.

Restoring the link between the broader social content and textual particularity of Whitman's poetry would require, in the first place, learning to read the poet's rhetorical collapses—his formal unevenness—as among the most faithful markers of upheaval and complication in his political ambitions. One way to approach this problem is to recall how central the deployment of persona is to Whitman's political ambitions for poetry, to his desire to achieve in it a fully national representativeness. A renewed attentiveness to the *rhetorical* constitution of Whitman's persona, to its lapses and points of inconsistency, might offer us an angle into a politics that exceeds mere "gesture" or "stance." Now, to ground a politics in the question of persona is to incur an number of interpretive risks. Pertinent here in particular is Michael Warner's cautionary point about the "obsessive" return in Whitman criticism to "a referential language of character," a return that betrays what Warner, following Vincent Crapazano, disparagingly calls "the ideology of self." Undoubtedly, character-attribution has offered a way to refigure any number of the poet's projects of world-revision as efforts in "soul-making," in tutelary self-perfection; such "characterizing" scrutiny, Warner rightly contends, domesticates Whitman's many avowedly public ambitions. Yet the insistence on Whitman's anti-characterizing radicality does seem willingly to ignore what are, in Leo Bersani's apt phrase, "the by no means unfounded and inconsiderable pleasure[s] of recognition"—of *character* recognition—on which most of the intimacy-effects of the poems depend.[15] The poet who shouts lists and enumerations may well understand the affordances of print generality and impersonality, but his is not, for that, a poetry or a poetic perspective we are likely to confuse with that of anyone else; and that recognizable particularity is, as we have seen, very much a part of Whitman's political project. What sustains the appealing familiarity or legibility of the poet's persona, I would emphasize again, are the signature motions of language—in essence, of style—that populate even the most polyglot of Whitman's expositions. That is, Whitman arrays even his most self-displacing claims of identification in an idiom that is unmistakably his own, whose littlest syntactical tic or lexical juxtaposition or word cluster announces the presence of an eminently particular poetic consciousness.

Indeed, the lighter the touch by which the poet twists or pressures an established discursive mode, the more deeply impressed the whole of the passage becomes with the stamp of his particularity. Such is the elegance of the runaway slave passage from section 10:

The runaway slave came to my house and stopped outside,
I heard his motions crackling the twigs of the woodpile,
Through the swung half-door of the kitchen I saw him limpsey
    and weak,
And went where he sat on a log, and led him in and assured him,
And brought water and filled a tub for his sweated body and bruised
    feet,
And gave him a room that entered from my own, and gave him
    some coarse clean clothes,
And remember perfectly well his revolving eyes and his
    awkwardness,
And remember putting plasters on the galls of his neck and ankles;
He staid with me a week before he was recuperated and passed
    north,
I had him sit next me at table . . . my firelock leaned in the corner.
                                                            (33–34)

Whitman's reserve, the intimacy of the details he supplies, his canny manipulation of verb tense and narrative expectation, all are rewarded in the passage's final glance toward the "firelock" leaning in the corner, unused but promising as direct and violent a resistance to the slave-power as Whitman would ever offer. Moreover, the ease with which he accommodates this potentially unwieldy allegory of Christ's ministrations to an idiom not yet completely stripped of his identifying verbal tics and cues (as in the slight grammatical compression of "I saw him limpsey and weak," or in the reference to the slave's "sweated body") asserts the presence in the passage of an organizing consciousness that is strikingly continuous with that of the poem's less heightened episodes. By drawing the more quotidian narrative persona so unobtrusively into this scene of enormous ethical consequence—by underlining rhetorically the unbroken continuity of the "nonchalant" Whitman and the Whitman of great moral action—the poet gathers the accumulated force of *all* the poem's episodes behind his promise of sympathy.[16] We can measure the amplitude and depth of this particular passage's sympathetic "gesture," in other words, in the degree to which its verbal texture allows it to resonate everywhere else in the poem.

We see here, at the very least, that the problem to which Lawrence points lies not in the mere fact of Whitman's assertion of sympathetic bond with strangers quite unlike himself, but in the local expressions of those bonds. For if Whitman is capable of extraordinarily nuanced demonstrations of sympathy, as in the runaway slave passage, he is also prepared to offer much more ambiguous fare. Consider the following two very different verse-paragraphs, separated from each other in section 33 by only a single stanza:

I understand the large hearts of heroes,
The courage of present times and all times;
How the skipper saw the crowded and rudderless wreck of the
    steamship, and death chasing it up and down the storm,
How he knuckled tight and gave not back one inch, and was
    faithful of days and faithful of nights,
And chalked in large letters on a board, Be of good cheer, We will
    not desert you;
How he saved the drifting company at last,
How the lank loose-gowned women looked when boated from the
    side of their prepared graves,

How the silent old-faced infants, and the lifted sick, and the
sharp-lipped unshaved men;
All this I swallow and it tastes good . . . I like it well, and it
becomes mine,
I am the man . . . I suffered . . . I was there.

I am the hounded slave . . . I wince at the bite of the dogs,
Hell and despair are upon me . . . crack and again crack the
marksmen,
I clutch the rails of the fence . . . my gore dribs thinned with the
ooze of my skin,
I fall on the weeds and stones,
The riders spur their unwilling horses and haul close,
They taunt my dizzy ears . . . they beat me violently over the
head with their whip-stocks.

Agonies are one of my changes of garments;
I do not ask the wounded person how he feels . . . I myself become
the wounded person,
My hurt turns livid upon me as I lean on a cane and observe.

(62–63)

Rather than referring to and amplifying the tonalities of the runaway slave episode, this latter passage seems instead to recall the
painful moment in the preface when Whitman writes, "The attitude of great poets is to cheer up slaves and horrify despots" (15).
Part of the reason "Agonies are one of my changes of garments"
reads as infelicitously as it does here is that it follows hard upon
a passage whose realization is so remarkably less surprising and
vivid than the shipwreck stanza that had preceded it. "I wince at
the bite of dogs" has none of the sharpness or canny unpredictability of, for instance, "the silent old-faced infants." While not saddled
with the clear lexical wrongness of "*cheer up* slaves," it nonetheless sounds as though it might have been lifted from something
as saccharine as Longfellow's "The Slave in the Dismal Swamp"
("He saw the fire of the midnight camp, / And heard at times a
horse's tramp / And a bloodhound's distant bay").[17] Nowhere in the
latter passage do the signature flourishes of rhetoric and grammar find room to extend themselves, and this contributes greatly
to the stilted, ventriloquistic quality of the verse.[18] At this crucial
moment of compassionate self-extension, Whitman seems simply

to reproduce, without in the least enlivening, one of the received genres of his day.

Far from the devastating "critique of tepid humanitarianism" Martin Klammer claims it to be, the episode seems to me an instance of exactly the kind of failed sympathy that so exasperates Lawrence. The startling rhetorical slackness of the "hounded slave" passage—its uncontoured derivativeness—confronts us with a moment in which the poet's sympathy fails quite conspicuously to cross the divide of race (which is also the divide between free and unfree), a moment made only more perplexing by the formal achievement of the runaway slave passage that precedes it by more than six hundred lines. Though that earlier passage should alert us to the interpretive dangers of simply ascribing to Whitman an unsavory and untranscended racialist position, I want to suggest nevertheless that these moments of abrupt formal collapse do record something of a tremor in Whitman's geography of sympathy. For what I have deemed the generic, "borrowed" quality of Whitman's testimony to cross-racial sympathy stands in vivid contrast to the force of stylistic particularity with which he is able to invest testimonies not of racial sympathy but of racial *solidarity*. Listen to the voice that speaks through these sentences:

> Who believes that Whites and Blacks can ever amalgamate in
> America? Or who wishes it to happen? Nature has set an
> impassable seal against it. Besides, is not America for the
> Whites? And is it not better so?[19]

Whatever abiding power to dispirit is contained in this oft-quoted passage must derive at least in part from the fact that the rhetorical gestures its author inhabits are so seamlessly, so unmistakably of a piece with those of "Song of Myself," whose differently motivated author writes

> Who has done his day's work and will soonest be through with his
>   supper?
> Who wishes to walk with me?
>
> Will you speak before I am gone? Will you prove already too late?
>
> (85)

There is no pretending that the author of these prose sentences, written in 1858 to praise the state constitution of Oregon for its exclusion of blacks, is anyone but the poet who attests sympathy—

indeed, the two are the same right down to the idiosyncrasies of grammar and syntax by which they evoke their enunciating particularity. And yet the fact that Whitman's voice should find such a comfortable home in this patently exclusionary politicking is in at least one respect not surprising. For the discourse of racial solidarity into which he fits himself is at the same time—like so much of "Song of Myself"—*a discourse of sympathetic attachment*, of intimate relation among strangers. That is, his remarks on Oregon outline a quality of anonymous sympathy that is simply more local than that of "Song of Myself," and more exclusive—a sympathy that travels strictly along the vein of the American citizens' shared whiteness.

To a degree that might astonish acolytes of the ultrademocratic Whitman, the protocols of race in fact answer perfectly to the demands of Whitman's ardent utopianism. This is made particularly clear in his prose from the period. Even in the most nakedly partisan of his Free-Soil Democrat diatribes, Whitman manages to find a visionary strain, and what that strain devolves upon, I would argue, is precisely his ability to see in "race" a way to describe the secret tissue of *relatedness* by which underrepresented citizens might eventually recognize each other and form a coalition. In *The Eighteenth Presidency!*, he writes

> In fifteen of The States the three hundred and fifty thousand masters keep down the true people, the millions of white citizens, mechanics, farmers, boatmen, manufacturers, and the like, excluding them from politics and from office, and punishing by the lash, by tar and feathers, binding fast to rafts on the rivers or trees in the woods, and sometimes by death, all attempts to discuss the evils of slavery in its relations to the whites. (*Poetry and Prose*, 1335)

These "true citizens," Whitman will go on to say, constitute "a new race . . . with resolute tread, soon to confront Presidents, Congresses, and parties" (1336). Whiteness defines the upstart group Whitman sketches here, but not in the familiar way—not as the enabling distinction on which claims to innate superiority rest (the enemies here are white as well).[20] Rather, whiteness appears in Whitman's account as the element within which a variety of laboring identities ("TO BUTCHERS, SAILORS, STEVEDORES, AND DRIVERS OF HORSES—TO PLOUGHMEN, WOOD-CUTTERS, MARKETMEN, CARPENTERS, MASONS, AND LABORERS . . .") from very different localities ("Manhattan Island, Brooklyn, Newark, Boston, Worcester, Hartford, New

Haven, Providence, Portland, Bangor, Augusta, Albany . . .") can experience themselves as attached to one another, related. In Whitman's hands, that is, "race" is immensely useful inasmuch as it gives name and place to a quality of attachment—potentially, of intimacy—between a dispersed and anonymous population. The exactness of conceptual fit ought to startle us: Answering point by point to Whitman's nationalist desire to establish and sustain intimate associations across widespread localities of interest and need, the agency ascribed here to the mere fact of whiteness simply accomplishes those connections and attachments. If Whitman dreamed for a way to describe the unifying intimacies of national life—and dreamed moreover of a way to imagine the coherence of a national citizenry, outside the decrees of the state—whiteness would seem to have been an ideal vehicle.

What is perhaps most surprising, from this vantage, is the fact that the 1855 *Leaves of Grass* steadfastly declines to take up the cause of racial nationalism with any real vigor or seriousness. (Nor, of course, does Whitman make much of a sustained point to object to it, though in fleeting instances he snipes at racialist decorum by promising to "invite" to his table even "the heavy-lipped slave.") The unforesworn presence of such racialism does bubble up, as I've suggested, in moments where the particularity of the poet's rhetorical persona seems suddenly to evaporate: in instances of formal laxity, in passing turns of phrase ("cheer up slaves" is one), and in moments like that in the preface where Whitman refers to America as "the race of races" (6)—a phrase from which it is not at all clear whether the defining attribute of the American race is its plurality (the race of *many* races) or its exclusive superiority (the one *best* race). Still, these moments have none of the avidity of the 1858 column, nor do they link up with one another to form anything like a coherent "position." The language of racial affiliation, though in some ways ideally suited to Whitman's utopia of anonymous intimacies, nevertheless seems palpably to lack some element, some essential quality without which the poet can make little use of it. A generous reading of this refused endorsement would likely contend that the idea of specifically racial intimacies, however it provides for Whitman's utopian nationalism, grievously inhibits the scope of his embrace: because it excludes by definition so many persons to whom he feels inspired (by compassion? desire? arrogance?) to extend his intimacy, the poet, by this account, shrugs off the spurious unities of race.

But what if, by a less credulous reading, Whitman's early career is taken not as an adjudication of one discourse of affiliation but as an adumbration of several at once? What if the language of racial intimacy is, in fact, complicated, entangled, and perhaps finally overruled by a rival model of intimacy and attachment? In this vein we might do well to observe that those comments about interracial "amalgamation" in America comprise what must be the drabbest sex scene Whitman would ever write.

SEX IN PUBLIC

> *Do you think it is so easy to have me become your lover?*
> *Do you think the friendship of me would be unalloyed*
>   *satisfaction?*
> *Do you suppose I am trusty and faithful?*
> "ARE YOU THE NEW PERSON DRAWN TOWARD ME" (1860)

If "Song of Myself" is thus deeply ambivalent toward, though abidingly interested in, "race" as a language of transpersonal attachment, it is vastly less hesitant about the intimacy-effects of sex. Indeed, in a way that recalls some of what we saw in *Moby-Dick*, it's difficult not to read sexuality as a kind of counternarrative to the racial nationalism Whitman sometimes endorses, since sexuality seems most intensely meaningful to him as it expresses a nearly boundless human capacity for relation to others, for affiliation. "The bodies of men and women engirth me," he writes, "and I engirth them, / They will not let me off nor I them till I go with them and respond to them and love them" (*Leaves of Grass*, 116). The 1876 preface draws the connection between sexuality and the anonymous attachments of national life quite unambiguously. No longer does America exist as "the race of races," as in the 1855 preface, but it is given form by the "endless streams of living, pulsating love and friendship," the "terrible, irrepressible yearning" and "never-satisfied appetite for sympathy" that animates its citizenry (*Poetry and Prose*, 1034–35). By this retrospective account, the remarkably sudden depletion, after 1855, of Whitman's interest in racial conflict and meaning makes a peculiar kind of sense.[21]

For by 1860, in the poems of "Calamus," the poet has apparently given himself over completely to an idiom of attachment grounded not in the shaky affective promises of race but in the world-making power of sex.

The transition between these two strains of nationalism is in fact not nearly so tidy. In the first place, both models coexist, in uneasy accord, in the 1855 *Leaves*. (However Christian the allegory, the details of the runaway slave passage from "Song of Myself"—"[I] brought him water and filled a tub for his sweated body and bruised feet . . . / And remember putting plasters on the galls of his neck and ankles"—tremble with an erotic significance whose muteness does nothing to cancel its charge.) What makes for messiness in the shift from one to the other, above all else, is the fact that the languages of sexual attachment available to Whitman are themselves as riddled with complication and incoherence as the available languages of race. This is perhaps the main reason why the "Calamus" poems, though they may well endeavor to describe American nationality in terms of sexual ties, are nevertheless pointedly unforthcoming about where the definitional boundaries of "the sexual" actually lie. I want to suggest, in fact, that Whitman's refusal in "Calamus" to define sex as a quality of attachment fundamentally distinct from any other—his refusal to circumscribe sexuality in any definite set of acts or relations—constitutes what is arguably the most consequential intervention in American sexual ideology he would ever make. And that intervention, as we will see, is as much a committedly nationalist act as it is proof against a nascent homophobia.

The "Calamus" poems, along with the poems of "Children of Adam," have of course long been considered among the most potent, the most deliberately revealing of Whitman's reveries on sex and sexuality. And while the intensity and variety of male-to-male attachments is certainly on prominent display in "Calamus," it is nevertheless true that much if not all of the poems' palpable flirtatiousness depends on an erotics of intimation and concealment, of *secrecy*. Whitman announces his project for "Calamus" in the closing lines of a poem later named "In Paths Untrodden," the section's opening lyric:

> I proceed, for all who are, or have been, young men,
> To tell the secret of my nights and days,
> To celebrate the need of comrades.[22]

"Calamus" thus begins with the positing of a secret, of something so indecorous or titillating it must be withheld. Yet the following line suggests a content for that secret, *"the need of comrades,"* which is itself so exorbitantly inexplicit that we can only read it as an oblique intimation of some content inexpressibly more numinous and supple. Under the pressure of such suggestion, the details leading up to this moment in the poem ("in this secluded spot I can respond as I would not dare elsewhere," for instance) acquire a curious urgency—curious because the "secret" that so invests them remains to the very end unspecified. "Resolved to sing no songs to-day but those of manly attachment," the poet nevertheless demurs from saying just what it is about that attachment that demands such seclusion and such secrecy. At once perfectly ordinary (common to "all who are, or have ever been, young men") and somehow scandalous (part of "the life that does not exhibit itself"), "manly attachment" emerges in the poem as a phenomenon about which the reader's hunger to know something more— something more definitive—will necessarily be keen. But rather than satisfy that epistemological craving, Whitman prefers instead to test out, by those double movements of occlusion and suggestion, the expressive possibilities of nondisclosure, of extended inspecificity.

"Whoever You Are Holding Me Now in Hand" is exemplary in this respect. It begins:

> Whoever you are holding me now in hand,
> Without one thing all will be useless,
> I give you fair warning, before you attempt me further,
> I am not what you supposed, but far different.
>
> (*Leaves of Grass* 1860, 344)

The second line, "Without one thing all will be useless," invites us to follow whatever lead the poet might offer—how difficult can it be, after all, to discover "one thing"?—and every casual warning and leisurely dismissal serves only to incite us, to strengthen our resolve to unearth that one revealing thing. Once again, the poem's avowed secretiveness fairly electrifies each line with the promise of revelatory disclosure, until at last something of an apotheosis is reached:

> But just possibly with you on a high hill—first watching lest any
>   person, for miles around, approach unawares,

Or possibly with you sailing at sea, or on the beach of the sea, or
    some quiet island,
Here to put your lips upon mine I permit you,
With the comrade's long-dwelling kiss, or the new husband's kiss,
For I am the new husband, and I am the comrade.

                                 (345)

This passage delivers us to a kind of interpretive crossroads: Is
the great secret of this poet's nights and days, then, the fact of his
amorous relations with young men—the fact that toward them he
is both comrade and husband, friend and lover? Or, instead, is this
precisely the question the poem all but requires us to ask, only so
that it may then unravel whatever answer we offer? "But these
leaves conning," the poet continues,

                  you con at peril,
For these leaves, and me, you will not understand,
They will elude you at first, and still more afterward—I will
    certainly elude you,
Even while you should think you had unquestionably caught me,
    behold!
Already you see I have escaped from you.

                                 (346)

The penultimate line drives the point home once more, though with
an extra twist of authorial perversity: "For all is useless with that
which you may guess at many times and not hit—that which I
hinted at." Was the new husband's kiss then not a revelation at
all, but merely a suggestion, a *hint*? Of what? If there are, as the
poet here implies, no actual disclosures in the poem, only hints,
then the world it conjures for us is one susceptible only to speculation, inference, "guess." It is a world, in other words, that solicits
innumerable interpretations by canceling the possibility of *an* interpretation. "For it is not for what I put into it that I have written
this book," the poet tells us, "Nor is it by reading it you will acquire
it." Indeed, what Whitman puts into "Calamus" is a deliberate
leaving-out, an expurgation that leaves us finally with the skele-
tal outlines of a secret whose indisputably erotic aura is designed
both to invite and to resist any and all specifying claims about it.

    Among the most curious things about "Whoever You Are . . ." is
how intimately its drama of sexual disclosure is tied to the manipulation of certain readerly identifications and dependencies. The

relation the poem works so diligently to agitate, after all, is not that of the poet to his many comrades (there is little question that *he* knows what they are about) but of the reader—the "you" who seemingly cannot ever know enough—to the knowing poet. For instance, the show of interpretive invulnerability Whitman offers at the end of the poem works also as a particular kind of solicitation. Proclaiming his remoteness from all common modes of apprehension, and proclaiming further that the details of his poems are but feints and proddings, hints, Whitman yet holds out the tantalizing possibility of recognizing him by other means. Indeed, the poem clearly advertises the fact that, to those capable of such ingenious recognitions, an uncommon intimacy with the poet will be the reward, an ability to walk among the beloved cognoscenti: "Nor will the candidates for my love, (*unless at most a very few,*) prove victorious" (346, my emphasis). Given any reader's hunger to be so solaced by such an avowedly devious text, the promise of an alternative form of recognition will as a matter of course be set upon with eager determination. How would one possibly resist the invitation to think of oneself as among those "very few" who get it, who belong?

This irresistible provocation helps us begin to explain, among other things, why merely recognizing the hardly occluded fact of the poet's erotic attachment to other men can often feel (and has felt for a number of critics, for a number of years) like the acquisition of a passport into the "secret" workings of Whitman's poems, and of Whitman himself.[23] The rewards of that recognition—let's call it, for the moment, a gay recognition—are after all difficult to gainsay. First, there is the splendid readiness with which so many of the poems' details yield themselves to the coherence that recognition provides: secluded locales become cruisy erotic safe havens; inexplicitness becomes practiced solicitation; the very silences of the poems seem flirtatious manipulations of the age-old code of *illum crimen horribile quod nominandum est.* Given such exquisite responsiveness, one can feel deeply confirmed in the sense that each minute detail of "Calamus" had been waiting, all the while, for the touch of just this interpretive wand to enliven it, to bring it fully into significance. Moreover, by thus completing by our own recognitions the erotic scene only suggested by the poet, we accomplish a rather dramatic reversal of the relations of readerly dependency from which we began: No longer mere interpreters, we appear rather at the origin of meaning, as collaborators in the work of engineering the poems' revelations. In these ways and in several others, the ability to discern in Whitman's various occlusions the codes and patterns of a different sort of sexual candor can feel very plausibly like the surest mark of one's readerly aptitude, as well as of one's successful entrée into Whitman's prismatic poetic world.

It's just as likely, however, that this sensation of having found one's way in, rather than a readerly achievement, is actually one of what we might call the poems' *intimacy-effects*. That is, the kind of recognition I've sketched above might also be said to function in "Calamus" as a carefully administered antidote to the avowed obscurity of the poet's intentions, an antidote designed to engender a sense of intimacy with the poet that is only more keen for the anxieties of readerly incapacity it works to soothe. So perfectly does the key of gay recognition unlock the encrypted meanings of the poems, so magisterially does it overcome every threatened opacity, that we might well begin to suspect the poet of having offered those occlusions strictly for the purpose of investing our "discoveries" with an added charge of accomplishment. Do we in fact discover anything in "Calamus," other than our own capacity to feel accomplished in the act of discovery? How is it, in other words, that in a sequence of poems that so vocally broadcasts the saliency of male-male desire, the mere recognition of that erotics continues to yield such a powerful sense of having been achieved, having been wrought?

We should note, first, that gay recognition is ever an achievement *as against* a tradition of Whitman scholarship in which the poet's desire for men, when it is not fully ignored or frankly attacked, is subject to more urbane assaults, as in the now-familiar rejoinders: *There's no hard evidence that it happened*, and *If it happened, it has no bearing on the poetry*, and (the cagiest) *Back then it didn't mean what it means now*.[24] Most of these approaches are easy enough to answer. If the playful inexplicitness of much of "Calamus" is the terra firma on which some readers stake their agnosticism about Whitman and the love that dare not speak its name, we need only remind the unbelieving that Whitman's love for his comrades does speak its name, and often in the most indelibly erotic terms. There is, for instance, precious little ambiguity about "City of Orgies" or the gorgeous "When I Heard at the Close of Day," which ends with the poet in bed with "my dear friend, my lover": "And his arm lay lightly around my breast—

And that night I was happy" (*Leaves of Grass* 1860, 357–58). Such moments as these are by no means rare in the poems, and are straightforward enough in the pleasures they display to make the "did he or didn't he" biographical hubbub around Whitman seem, at best, priggish. Against such an unpromising critical backdrop, the insisted-on recognition of the gay content of even these explicit scenes can indeed seem a hard-won victory.

But the world of biographical criticism is not the only source of resistances to be overcome by interpretive pertinacity. Rather, the "Calamus" poems themselves, by their own complicated workings, do a great deal to trouble the security of an erotic recognition which, by the same motions, they invite. We've seen already how the reiterated secretiveness of "Whoever You Are . . . ," while it rewards many aspects of a reading in which the poet's desire for other men simply *is* his secret, nevertheless marks that reading as untenably partial, insufficient. The perfectly direct occlusions of that poem ("these leaves, and me, you will not understand") find their analogues in the more delicate maneuvers of encryption and concealment that operate elsewhere in the sequence, and these are worth looking at in some detail.

If the "Calamus" poems unfold according to any one "pattern" of disclosure—as, for instance, the pattern of observation-meditation-resolution defines the romantic lyric—it works something like this (with examples culled from the poem later titled "Behold This Swarthy Face"): (1) a question or problem is broached ("Mind you the timid models of the rest, the majority?"); (2) that question is dropped or rerouted as the poet avows his greater interest in a particular attachment, the intensity of which more or less directly suggests sexual exchange ("Yet comes one, a Manhattanese, and ever at parting, kisses me lightly on the lips with robust love"); (3) there follows a description or summary that neither refutes nor confirms the sexual connotation but, far more pointedly, dilates over its opacity ("We are those two natural and nonchalant persons") (*Leaves of Grass* 1860, 364). Neither a denial nor an avowal of any one sexual recognition results from these maneuvers, but an unresting affirmation of the possibility of such recognitions. Consider again the conclusion of "When I Heard at the Close of Day," which I have already cited as exemplary for its sexual candor:

For the one I love most lay sleeping by me under the same cover
in the cool night,

In the stillness, in the autumn moonbeams, his face was inclined
toward me,
And his arm lay lightly around my breast—And that night I was
happy.

(358)

Though there is nothing at all that one could call unclear about
this passage, one notices still a flicker of deviousness about the
phrase "And that night I was happy," which after so much concrete
erotic detail presents itself as almost winkingly inexplicit. Indeed,
the more potentially revelatory the scene, the greater the pleasure
Whitman seems to take in withdrawing just enough into abstraction to infuse the whole proceeding with the tantalizing shimmer
of ambiguity. If a sexually specifying reading feels to the reader
like something she must continually and heroically accomplish, it
is thus in large part because the poet invests even the frankest of
his disclosures with a degree of attenuation so fine, so precisely
dosed, as to border on the cunning. (This is what Eve Sedgwick
seems to have in mind when she writes of "the play of calculation
and haplessness" that constitutes "the erotic surface" of Whitman's
persona.)[25] Nothing at all is foreclosed by these attenuations;
rather, they serve to raise the simplest acts of connotative interpretation to the status of an achieved confidence, a hard-won intimacy with a poet whose secrets one comes, by one's own efforts,
to share.

"Calamus" may thus have a secret, but it is one that, from the
first, everybody is welcome to know. By deploying the rhetorical
mechanisms of secrecy, Whitman simply gives a sweet taste—the
taste of accomplishment—to the reader's discovery of what was
never hidden. To argue that what I have called a gay recognition
is thus a provided structure in the poems, a lever for their calculated intimacy-effects, is not, however, to say that same-sex attachments are salient for Whitman only as they orchestrate a drama
of reader-author solicitation. But to begin to explore the breadth of
meaning these attachments might provide, we would need, first of
all, to move past the routinized exercises of "discovery" in which
readings of the poems (and of this poet) can so quickly become
stalled.[26] If, in other words, it can at this point be little more than
self-congratulation to claim to have "discovered" the secret of Whitman's desire for men, then perhaps we ought to look to the poems'
peculiar forms of emphasis (inexplicitness, occlusion, encryptment)

for different kinds of revelation. We might wonder, for instance, how the poems' epistemological dislocations give inflection to the broader notion of attachment itself, under whose conceptual arc all the vexations surrounding sexual definition can be said to occur, and which also figures so prominently in Whitman's 1876 description of the nationalist ambitions of "Calamus."

To open up the question of attachment cogently, we need to recognize, first, that neither modesty nor shame is a plausible motive for the poet's occlusions, as is sometimes suggested.[27] The poet's inexplicitness with respect to the "manly attachments" he describes does absolutely nothing to chasten their sexual aura, as we have seen—quite to the contrary, it seems in fact to propagate in every poetic detail a potentially homoerotic suggestiveness. Yet the ambiguity Whitman cultivates, while it does not disallow most any form of sexual recognition, nevertheless builds into the passionate attachments of men to men a resilient irreducibility. No amount of rereading "Calamus" can produce what "Whoever You Are . . ." calls the "one thing" necessary to, as it were, "prove" that the attachments figured in the poem are sexual attachments, that the scenes of affectionate exchange are scenes of sexual exchange; though it is difficult to imagine what that "one thing" would be, it is at any rate explicitly defined in "Calamus" as that which is withheld. What is withheld from us is of course not the ability to recognize the sexual piquancy of any scene of male bonding—such recognition continues to abound—but the ability to name or to classify those bonds, or any bonds, as *simply* affectionate, simply sexual, simply anything. A kind of enforced agnosticism with respect to the taxonomic certainty of any attachment is the most immediate result of the poems' fine-tuned attenuations. If we are excluded here from any one vantage or form of interpretive power, it is thus *the power to decide which bonds count as sexual and which do not.*

The power to recognize and to name sexuality in the field of human relations—the power of *sexual knowledge*—would of course come by roughly the end of the century to dominate almost every ritual of identity, filiation, and truth in European and American cultures, and to do so with an increasingly terrorizing effect on sexually deviant populations. According to this now-familiar sexual calendar, it seems noteworthy—it seems odd—that in 1860 Whitman should be so concerned with the mechanisms of sexual knowledge.[28] (It goes rather strongly against David Reynolds's breezy description of the antebellum state of sexual affairs: "Gender roles," he writes, "were fluid, elastic, shifting in a time when sexual types had not yet solidified.")[29] Yet I am inclined to agree with Michael Warner, who argues in an essay about Thoreau that critics who look too dogmatically "to the late nineteenth century as the period in which sexuality was recodified in Western culture" are apt to overlook the operative codes of sexual definition that had begun to coalesce several generations earlier.[30] One such standardized code was particularly important to Whitman, supplying him with both a conceptual framework within which to maneuver and, just as crucially, a lexicon to invade and re-deploy. Though it sounds like it might be, the keyword *adhesiveness* is not one of Whitman's neologisms. It comes directly from the annals of a science called phrenology.

Although its principal object of study was the human cranium and the various "faculties" contained in its neatly patterned regions or "zones"—and although it is most famous for its white-supremacist conclusions about human aptitudes and capacities— phrenology had for several years been preparing the way for the ascension of a particular brand of sexual taxonomy.[31] (Nationally renowned "practical phrenologists" Lorenzo and Orson Fowler both went on to write, when such things were in vogue, tracts on marriage and sexual health.) The sexological relevance of phrenology is in fact evident in its most basic tenets. For instance, by the phrenological account, "attachment" is a sharply differentiated phenomenon, the origins of which are to be found in the five "affective faculties" of the human brain. Whitman is of course most fond of "adhesiveness," which is the organ responsible, in Lorenzo Fowler's words, for "friendship, attachment, sociability . . . manifested regardless of sex." The other four "affective faculties" are: Philoprogenitiveness (the love of children), Inhabitiveness (the love of home), Concentrativeness (which unifies thought and feeling), and Amativeness, which according to Fowler refers specifically to a reproductive "love between the sexes."[32] What's notable about this mapping of the human affective world, first, is how readily the correlations of types of attachment to gendered objects gives way to exactly the typology not supposed to have solidified for several decades. That is, by moving to sequester all sexual ties in cross-gender relations (in amativeness), phrenological taxonomy accomplishes the assimilation of erotic difference to gender difference that yet defines our modern vocabulary of sexual definition (and which psychoanalysis would soon solidify). For by this calculus the only condition in which a properly sexual attachment can legitimately appear is that of a difference in gender between the two persons involved. Appearing here, well before the term "homosexual" was current in America, is a gender-based erotic economy of difference and sameness, hetero and homo.

Among the things even this loosely formed conceptual economy brings sharply into focus is the pertinence, the immense utility, of something like homophobia, even in 1860. We notice, that is, in the phrenological partitioning of human intimacy into mutually exclusive states of desire and not-desire, how remarkably vulnerable virtually everyone becomes (i.e., anyone who enjoys any attachments to persons of their own gender) to the charge of having stepped across the invisible, but now electric line that differentiates illicit bonds from licit ones—invisible because the very terms by which such a charge could proceed acquire meaning only in relation to a standard of sexual measure that is nowhere specified. Something qualitative must differentiate adhesive and amative attachments, but nothing in the phrenological account tells us what that something might be, only that gender difference is the proper condition of its emergence. What this constitutive uncertainty comes to mean, first, is that enormous reserves of coercive power will belong to anyone who can successfully wield such terms; and second, that such power will be manifested in an ability to "know" other people and their desires more intimately and authoritatively than they can hope to know themselves.[33]

By the light of such seizures as these, the dialectics of secrecy and disclosure in the "Calamus" poems, for all their playfulness, appear quite determined in the resistances they offer. For what the poet labors so painstakingly to neutralize in his readers—parading before us a world of attachments to which we are allowed, finally, no taxonomizing access—is exactly the interpretive security in which the invasive, regulatory powers of sexual knowledge are staked. His steadfast refusal to make the poems' same-sex attachments legible as simply or conclusively sexual, while it does not offer the solace of a valorized homosexual type, nevertheless assiduously frustrates the entire conceptual economy that would make homophobic proscription such an inordinately powerful coercive tool. Whitman deploys the lexicon of phrenology, then, but in a way that determinedly will not yield to the carefully partitioned sexual typology that the phrenological "sciences" intimate.

What's remarkable here as well is that the poet's impulse
against homophobia is, at the same time, an assertively nationalist impulse—is in fact very much a part of what Whitman himself
describes as the "political significance" of the "Calamus" poems.
That is, Whitman's sense of an impending foreclosure in the matter
of sexuality allows him, in turn, to begin to fashion sex as, precisely, a realm of as yet unforeclosed possibility; and these extrav-
agant possibilities for intimacy are, as we have seen, at the very
core of his nationalist aspirations. I've said that Whitman's calculated attenuations unsettle (even as they invite) attempts to
read his poems as an anatomy of a homosexual "type," and on this
point I differ most consequentially with Michael Lynch's powerful
account of "adhesiveness," and of the affordances it provides to
Whitman as he attempts to lay the groundwork for a "modern
homosexual" identity. Though Lynch's reading and mine concur
about the eagerness with which the poet makes himself and his
texts available to be recognized in the grain of their sexual specificity, I would nevertheless want to maintain that the concen-
tration of same-sex desires into a *type* is anathema to Whitman,
insofar as such typology depends quite entirely on a cleaving of
attachment into clearly defined, diametrically opposed states of
desire and not-desire. The homosexual "type," on this account,
would be one whose relations to some of the same sex are, definitively, desiring, but also one whose relations to the opposite sex
are, definitively, not-desiring. Or, to frame the matter differently,
the heterosexual type—the phrenologically "normal" type—would
not be one who desires every person of different gender, but who
desires no one of the same gender. What this partitioning threatens
to effect (along with a thorough enshrinement of heterosexuality
as the "proper" realm for sexual ties) is *a sweeping de-eroticization
of social attachments*, their demotion to the realm of the patently
not-sexual. That is, the phrenological model works to isolate the
sexual, to sequester its force and to identify it seamlessly with
male-female connubial attachment. Whitman, too, looks to figure
an urgent, physical, erotic need—he calls is "the need of comrades"—but his deliberate gestures of occlusion and concealment
have the effect of unmooring that passionate intimacy from the
constrictive teleologies of heterosexual reproduction that were
increasingly taken to define the sexual as such. What results from
these attenuations is, again, not a chastening but an extension
of the passionate, the physical, the erotic, across the whole range

of social ties. Refusing to draw a perimeter around "the sexual," Whitman instead releases erotic potentialities into every register of social life.[34]

There is thus a certain oddity about the claim that among Whitman's abiding ambitions was his desire to "make sex public."[35] It seems much more accurate to say that in Whitman sex is public by definition, since for him sociability—other-directedness—has as its foundation an erotic tie. Genital sexuality is simply at one end of a continuum that for Whitman is not divided according to the presence or absence of an erotic dimension, but scaled according to intensities. Sex, in other words, is the engine that drives the human capacity for relation to others, the *primum mobile* of human sociality—and so powerful is the force of this almost Deleuzian desire that it may bring persons into bond with each other almost at random.[36] This is what makes sexuality an ideal language to describe the nature and substance of American nationality. In poems like "Whoever You Are . . ." and "To A Stranger," Whitman underscores what Michael Warner calls the "mutual nonknowledge" of author and reader to argue that sexual desire allows even strangers to share an affective bond, to be intimate with one another.[37] The principal manifestation of such stranger-intimacy in the poems is of course *cruising*—the sexual solicitation of strangers seen most vividly in a poem like "Among the Multitude," where Whitman writes

> Lover and perfect equal!
> I meant that you should discover me so, by my faint indirections,
> And I, when I meet you, mean to discover you by the like in you.
> (*Leaves of Grass* 1860, 376)

By their mutual anonymity, these lovers exemplify not merely the enviably avaricious quality of American sexual appetites. Their cruising performs as well the utopian relation of citizen to citizen— the relations, that is, of nationality. In the world of "Calamus," one can enjoy a passionate bond with people one does not know (people, for instance, such as Walt Whitman). And this anonymous intimacy—extended across the great unpeopled spaces of the continent—is just what Whitman means to refer to when he broaches the word "America."

Epilogue
Nation Mourns

Mourning is immensely reassuring because it convinces us of something we might otherwise easily doubt: our attachment to others.

ADAM PHILLIPS, *TERRORS AND EXPERTS*

Whitman's America is and is not our own. In the nation's modern forms of coherence and vocabularies of belonging we find both unbridgeable dissensions from the past and points of startling continuity. Most obviously, race is not now what then it was, at least not in the prevailing epistemologies of national life. The matter is not simply that racial slavery no longer survives, but that race *means* in ways so fundamentally transformed that we cannot call on it to do the same work as we once expected it to do, even quite recently. No one makes this point more forcefully, or with a more bracing polemicism, than Paul Gilroy, who begins his *Against Race* with the assertion, "The modern times that W. E. B. DuBois once identified as the century of the color line have now passed."[1] Gilroy advocates something like the extirpation of "race-thinking"—or rather, he moves deliberately toward an imagining of modern political forms that would expand beyond the dichotomies of the color line. He does this for two basic reasons: first, because he believes that much of contemporary race-thinking is tainted by ineradicable, dangerously unethical presumptions about the nature of human diversity (it inhibits the "planetary humanism" he envisions); and second, because race itself, as he envisions it, has become inadequate to describe the complexity of relation, the intricate and hybrid forms of belonging, that now characterize both national and transnational contexts. Though race may continue to be a decisive element in the vocabularies that compose American nationality, it no longer *is* that vocabulary. Rogue states may be invoked, quasi-human "superpredators" may be imagined swarming the nation's urban horror-zones, but the diversifying imperatives of global consumer culture have seen to a pronounced diminishment in the currency of an American nation-language rooted in racial exclusivity and the tenuous mutuality it means to conjure. As Gilroy has it, "Blackness can now signify vital prestige rather than abjection in a global info-tainment telesector where the living residues of slave societies and the parochial traces of American racial conflict must yield to different imperatives deriving from the planetarization of profit and the cultivation of new markets far from the memory of bondage." For Gilroy, this is part of what makes for the "fading sign of 'race,'" as well as for his sense that, despite the continued utility of racial discrimination, "much of the contemporary discourse animating 'races' and producing racialized consciousness is an anachronistic, even a vestigial, phenomenon."[2] We might add to this that, as a racialized whiteness no longer provides for the anonymous mutuality of American nation-ness, its still considerable privileges appear once again to be best activated by laying claim not to whiteness itself but to the expansive putative racelessness to which it alone allows one unhindered access.

But if race and attachment no longer come jointly into meaning on the national stage with quite the same vividness and force, we ought not to imagine that intimacy and nationality have been in any way uncoupled in present-day America. On the contrary, the collusion of a notion of intimate attachment with a notion of nationality, which we have been observing in a variety of antebellum writings, has found for itself an impressive array of new terms and modalities. Lauren Berlant, for instance, argues powerfully that, in one major and still operative strain of American liberal democracy, subjects are bound to the nation "through a universalist rhetoric not of citizenship per se but of the capacity for suffering and trauma at the citizen's core." This version of what we might call traumatic nationality, Berlant suggests, "involves a fantasy scene of national feeling": "In this imaginary world," she writes, "the sentimental subject is connected to others *who share the same feeling*."[3] Such connectedness-to-others, I have argued thus far, is precisely the affect that race embodied so aptly and serviceably for antebellum nationalists, but that now, I want to suggest, travels under any number of different signs.

Not the least of these signs, it turns out, is "humanism" itself. In a remarkable turn, Gilroy himself opposes the "pseudo-solidarities" of race-thinking to what he sees as an altogether different mode of "identification and empathy," writing with a peculiar kind of sardonic optimism that "the recurrence of pain, disease, humiliation and loss of dignity, grief, and care for those one loves can all contribute to an abstract sense of human similarity powerful enough to make solidarities based on cultural particularity appear suddenly trivial."[4] Here, the solidarity of trauma replaces the pseudo-solidarities of race-thinking with a more expansive, seemingly less parochial vision of human kinship and mutuality, one rooted, for Gilroy, in the essential mortal vulnerability to wounding, suffering, loss, and extinction.

What's so startling about Gilroy's formulation is less its innovation than the strange way it seems to draw both from the most contemporaneous modes of postmillennial belonging and mutuality, and (if you are listening for them) from narratives of national cohesion several centuries old. If, for instance, we hear in Gilroy's "pragmatic, planetary," and, I would add, stridently affective humanism echoes of Richard Rorty and Jean-Luc Nancy, the resonances of Whitman's intimate nationality—a nationality made precisely of an "identification and empathy" turned passionate— are audible there as well.[5] But these are not the only points of reference. Indeed, if Berlant is correct, the story of an America given form by the affective bondedness of its mutually anonymous citizens was neither born nor died in the antebellum nation, though it did animate that era with a particular vibrancy. In fact, the antebellum dream of an intimate nationality accomplished a very great deal: above all else, it forever marked the social meaning of race in America, and it did so, as we have seen, by transforming race into a language of affiliation, aligning it thereby with a range of very basic human capacities (for self-relation, for attachment to others, intimacy, bereavement, etc.). But in the broader view of this tradition of nationalist imagining, the language of race— however consequential its encounter with the nation-languages of the antebellum era—appears to have been both predated and postdated by other, alternate visions of affective coherence. I want, then, to give a kind of frame to my readings of antebellum writing by looking at the story of an intimate, affectively rooted American nationality in several of its very earliest expressions, and tracking it up through some of its most contemporary forms. The moments I want to consider in collusion with one another—which range from 1630 to 1776 to 1852 to 2001—map out a terrain that, according to its authors, is made American by nothing so much as the qualities of loss, grief, shock, and mourning that traverse it. Together, that is, this colloquy of disparate voices sketches the contours of an *affect-nation*, older and more protean than the American state, and bearing toward it a relation that remains unsettled.

AGONIZING AFFECTIONS

Here is how John Winthrop imagined the American mission, before "America" itself was much more than a beachhead and an unforeclosed promise. Approaching the shores of Boston in 1630, on the deck of the Puritan flagship *Arabella*, Winthrop insisted to his congregation that their charge was not merely to be God's exemplars in the New World ("we shall be as a Citty vpon a Hill") but to do so by living their different lives with a profound sense of mutuality and compassionate connectedness. Of the "Covenant and sealed . . . Commission" given by the Lord to the Puritans, Winthrop writes

> wee must be knitt together in this worke as one man, wee must entertaine each other in brotherly Affeccion, wee must be willing to abridge our selues of our superfluities, for the suppply of others necessities, we must vphold a familiar Commerce together in all meeknes, gentlenes, patience and liberallity, wee must delight in eache other, make others Condicions our owne reioyce together, mourne together, labour, and suffer together, allwayes haueing before our eyes our Commission and Community in the worke, our Community as members of the same body, soe shall wee keepe the vnitie of the spirit in the bond of peace.[6]

In ringing biblical cadence, Winthrop insists that only the cultivated ties of "Affeccion"—which, he observes, will also include those of suffering and grief—can bind his followers into such cohesion that they might begin to acquit themselves of a task no less daunting, and no less supremely ambitious, than that of fulfilling God's promise in the fallen world. If this is the earliest expression of a particularly American exceptionalism—a glimpse of what one

critic calls "the infinite idealism of American democracy"[7]—it is
also a seminal description of a particular kind of American collectivity, one made whole and coherent by the specifically affective
ties that "knitt together" its citizens' disparities. It is these ties,
Winthrop suggests, whether affectionate or mournful, that will
allow us to "abridge our selues of our superfluities" and so forge
us into a sustaining mutuality.

It was not until nearly one hundred and fifty years later, though,
that the problem of American cohesion—of the nature of the American collectivity—was to be confronted as directly as it ever had
been, or would be again for some time. This happens most dramatically in Thomas Jefferson's initial draft of the Declaration of
Independence, a text that manages, by the meticulousness of even
its smallest movements, to tell a complicated story not only of the
delicacies of revolutionary rupture but of the urgency of the new
republic's need to imagine some viable mode of national belonging for a citizenry only very tenuously unified. And in a way that
echoes Winthrop intriguingly, Jefferson's version of the Declaration goes so far as to place affect at the very founding of America—
this despite the fact that the document's occasion would seem to
have warned against almost any invocation of the turbulent, dis-
ordering force of feeling.

Jefferson's premiere task in the Declaration of Independence
is, after all, a terrifically delicate one: he must endeavor to couch
a moment of revolutionary rupture in the terms not of violent
passion but rather of both moral and historical *necessity*, the better to remove from the revolutionary actors any of the stain of
reckless insurgency or self-interested usurpation. At the same time,
however, he must grapple with the equally daunting problem of
revolutionary authority: the problem, on which many critics have
commented, of how to declare independence on behalf of a nation,
when that nation does not properly exist, *as* a nation, prior to its
declared independence. His difficulty, in condensed form, is that
he cannot rightfully presume the unified peopleness of America
in the writing of the document—he cannot without trepidation
refer back to an already constituted "we"—since it is one of the
document's tasks to *create* Americans as a separate people.[8] Jefferson employs several rhetorical strategies in the document to
manage these twinned dilemmas, and they are worth considering
in some detail, particularly for their invocation of impassioned
feeling, not as an element threatening the very possibility of a

stable independent republic, but as that which might secure, definitively, its urgently desired cohesion.

With respect to the problem of revolutionary rupture, the passive voice, with its convenient dislocation of agency, serves Jefferson tremendously well. We see this in the very opening of the text: "When, in the course of human events, *it becomes necessary* for one people to dissolve the political bands which have connected them with another . . ."[9] We see here as well the beginnings of Jefferson's response to the problem of revolutionary rupture—of just who speaks this text, and on what authority. For here, Jefferson refers not to colonies, the state, or to America, but to an abstract, hypothetical "one people." Indeed, for most of the first two paragraphs, which Jefferson uses to lay out some general principles, his strategy is to refer again and again to this essentially hypothetical people, variously called "one people," "the people," "them," and "mankind." All the while, though, he allows the relation of that semi-imaginary "people" to an actual America to remain calculatedly unspecified, to exist in a state of unresolving indeterminacy. Consider the following sentences from the second paragraph:

> Prudence, indeed, will dictate that governments long established should not be changed for light and transient causes; and accordingly all experience hath shown that mankind are more disposed to suffer while evils are sufferable, than to right themselves by abolishing the forms to which they are accustomed. But when a long train of abuses and usurpations, begun at a distinguished period and pursuing invariably the same object, evinces a design to reduce them under absolute despotism, it is their right, it is their duty to throw off such government, and to provide such sufferance new guards for their future security. Such has been the patient sufferance of these colonies; and such now is the necessity which constrains them to expunge their former systems of government.

Here again, as in the opening, "these colonies" act not only under the strict constraint of necessity, but as a veritable extension of the principle guiding not any particular collectivity, but "mankind" itself. (As Jay Fliegelman has it, "The agent [of revolutionary rupture] is hidden and submerged in a sea of seemingly mechanical necessity.")[10] We note, too, an unsettled modulation between the circumstances of "mankind," a series of ambiguous references to "they," "them," and "their," and the specific case of "these colonies."

One effect of such modulations is to render uncertain the exact constituency of the "we" in the great loose-pentameter line, *We hold these truths to be self-evident.* It seems a *we* that might refer either to the invoked "mankind," or simply to the representatives of "these colonies," as they are named several sentences later, or to some unspecified correlation of the two. It is, at any rate, by these careful attenuations, this unresolved shuttling between the abstract and the particular, Jefferson manages to imply—without yet explicitly proposing—that America is indeed one people, though one whose principles and actions are neither idiosyncratic nor peculiar to it, but accord exactly with the laws of nature and history, God and man. In the same movement, that is, Jefferson both suggests the oneness of an American people and shields them from accusations of renegade violence or usurpation.

But it is in the final section of the Declaration (most of which was excised by Congress) that Jefferson makes his most strident effort to consolidate the wandering "we" to which he had earlier referred with such studied ambiguity. For it is here that he begins to describe exactly what form of cohesion has *already* forged the colonists into a like-minded collectivity capable of declaring itself. After spending several paragraphs laying bare the escalating offenses, moral and political, of the King of England, he makes an important turn:

> Nor have we been wanting in attentions to our British
> brethren. We have warned them from time to time of attempts by
> their legislature to extend a jurisdiction over these our states . . .
> we appealed to their native justice and magnanimity as well as to
> the ties of our common kindred to disavow these usurpations
> which were likely to interrupt our connection and correspondence.
> They too have been deaf to the voice of justice and of consanguinity,
> and when occasions have been given them, by the regular course
> of their laws, of removing from their councils the disturbers of our
> harmony, they have, by their free election, re-established them in
> power. At this very time too, they are permitting their chief mag-
> istrate to send over not only soldiers of our common blood, but
> Scotch and foreign mercenaries to invade and destroy us. These
> facts have given the last stab to agonizing affection, and manly
> spirit bids us to renounce forever these unfeeling brethren.

After so much perspicuous rationalism, this turn to the register of feeling, to sensibility and its violations, speaks with particular vehemence. Jefferson makes two important moves here. First, in his assault on the "brethren" in England, he accuses them in particular of violating the ties of consanguinity, of so betraying the specifically affective bonds that had naturally linked Americans to Britons that the former are compelled, Jefferson writes, "to renounce forever these *unfeeling brethren*." The suggestion here is that it is this betrayal more than any other, this failure of proper feeling, that marks the British, finally and conclusively, as unfit to rule or be ruled by. And this accords remarkably with the propositions about affective citizenship Winthrop had ventured so many years earlier, in his sermon on the deck of the *Arabella*.

But the passage does much more: it begins to explain precisely why a fledgling nation would want to imagine its own citizenry to possess a unique capacity for impassioned feeling, and for the intimacies it promises to provoke and sustain. For it is in exactly this register, the register of feeling and of affect, that Jefferson at last makes his move to give concrete form to the peopleness he had previously only implied. As the coldness and hard-heartedness shown to the colonists have given, in Jefferson's notably sentimental phrase, "the last stab to agonizing affection," he goes on to conclude that

> We must endeavor to forget our former love for them, and hold
> them as we hold the rest of mankind, enemies in war, in peace
> friends. We might have been a free and great people together; but
> a communication of grandeur and of freedom, it seems, is below
> their dignity. Be it so, since they will have it. The road to happiness
> and glory is open to us, too. We will tred apart from them, and
> acquiesce in the necessity which denounces our eternal separation.

The phrase is striking: *We must endeavor to forget our former love*. The dwelled-on regrets, very nearly the aggrieved "be it so" of a wounded lover, move the text similarly toward a pitch of high melancholic affect, one whose utility, for this document, only now comes into focus. Endeavoring to forget *together*, bound to one another by nothing so much as their shared grief, the agonized "endeavor" of their mourning, the varied and scattered colonial Americans find themselves, once and for all, consolidated—and consolidated as, precisely, a nation, a unified and mutually aware collectivity of fellow-grievers. As imagined here, in this climactic moment, Jefferson's is an American citizenry essentially traumatized into fellowship: wounded and bereaved by the severance of their dearest ties, and made one, in turn, by the bereavement they share. Nation-ness, on this account, is the precipitate of a mutuality of feeling, impelled in this case by the affective violence, the "agonizing affection," involved in the fraying of relations with the "unfeeling brethren" in England.

That it is *this* form of unity, this affective cohesion, that makes Jefferson's Americans "one people" is made clear by the dramatic change in rhetoric which follows hard upon his declaration of agonized affection. For now, after the moment of rupture and of unifying grief has been avowed, the obfuscations of agency (the passive-voice constructions, phrases like "we will . . . acquiesce in the necessity which denounces our eternal separation") all vanish, and are replaced by a voice much more decisive, and much more defiant.

> We therefore the representatives of the United States of America
> in General Congress assembled, do in the name, and by the
> authority of the good people of these states reject and renounce
> all allegiance and subjection to the kings of Great Britain and all
> others who may hereafter claim by, through or under them; we
> utterly dissolve all political connection which may heretofore
> have substituted between us and the people or parliament of
> Great Britain: and finally we do assert and declare these colonies
> to be free and independent states.

The rhetorical shift, from passivity to activity, from wariness to stridency, is unmistakable. If Jefferson resented the alterations to his document made by Congress (he later called them "mutilations") it might have been not simply because they saw fit to excise both his condemnation of the slave trade ("this execrable commerce," he called it) as well as his account of the sentimental agonies of separation. More distressingly Congress also unraveled his carefully plotted rhetorical movement, from obscure agency to dramatic decisiveness, and they did so by tempering each and every one of Jefferson's verbs in the concluding paragraphs. Where Jefferson's United States could *"reject and renounce," "utterly dissolve,"* and *"assert and declare,"* the rather more diffident Congress would only

> solemnly publish and declare, that these united colonies *are*, and
> of right *ought to be* free and independent states; that they *are*
> *absolved* from all allegiance to the British crown, and that all

political connection between them and the state of Great Britain
is, and *ought to be*, totally dissolved. (my emphasis)

The finalized draft, we might say, muddies Jefferson's well-
tempered construction; it loses the progressive steps of national
cohesion that lead Jefferson, move by move, to the consolidated
defiance of the final paragraphs. For in Jefferson's draft, America begins as an unclearly hypothetical "one people" and is then
founded in its nation-ness not by the declaration of the state but
affectively, in the grain of collective loss and rueful melancholy.
("We might have been a free and great people together . . .") Only
then, after that avowal of a specifically affective cohesion, can the
nation declare itself with all the directness and authority of a
grammatically secure "we." What's lost by Congress, in other words,
is Jefferson's meticulously fashioned narrative, his implicit chro-
nology: his sense that the nation is *first* a collectivity made of intimacies and affect, and *then* a state; or rather, his sense that the
nation-state invented in the Declaration merely ratifies a prior
affective collectivity, securing its future and deriving from it the
authority to declare itself in the first place.

What anchors the authority of Jefferson's imagined state, then,
is a specifically affective cohesion that, in this instance, depends
for its live existence on the capacity of a far-flung citizenry to feel
both an acute grief and, in the grain of that grief, an attachment,
an *intimacy* with unknown others. Jefferson's state is thus, in
a peculiar way, propped upon this prior affective cohesion, with
the result that the very labor and obligation of citizenship—the
"endeavor" of it, to use Jefferson's phrase—must be conceived in
terms of affect and intimacy, of feeling with the proper depth and
extension. A citizen's capacity for affect, here, is nothing less than
a capacity for national belonging. In this way, we could say that
the dream of an intimate nationality was already powerfully present to Jefferson—we hear it resoundingly in his conclusion to the
Declaration—just as it was, in more inchoate form, to Winthrop
before him. And, of course, it did not die with them.

We could, with little enough difficulty, trace a line from Jefferson's Declaration to the nationalisms of the following century,
many of which would flower in the high-canonical writings of the
American Renaissance we have been considering. Perhaps more
telling, though, is the continuity between Jefferson's text and the
vast and ongoing tradition of American sentimentality, which takes

its place on exactly the terrain Jefferson's document sketches, in the effort to imagine a national public unified affectively, joined by a mutual susceptibility to strong feeling. We need only think of Harriet Beecher Stowe, who brings *Uncle Tom's Cabin* to a close by reminding her readers that there is, in fact, "one thing that every individual can do,—they can see to it that *they feel right.*"[11] Stowe might be seen as retrieving a strand of nation-language from the seventeenth and eighteenth centuries, not only because of her affinity for the language of revivalism that marks both those centuries, but because, like Winthrop and Jefferson before her, her notion of an expansive but unified collectivity is centered around loss, suffering, trauma, and bereavement (for the dramatization of all of which, of course, slavery provides a spectacular vehicle). As Marianne Noble observes, "The sentimental project is one of unification": "sentimentalism," she writes, "describes a world in which pain is an avenue toward achieving that desired state." It is, finally, "a state of union . . . achieved through suffering."[12] For Stowe, the ideal of a nation made whole by the painful feelings bonding its citizens is particularly compelling inasmuch as it refuses the notion of a strictly *racial* coherence for America, a notion that had, in the decades previous, achieved such a remarkably swift ascendancy.[13] That the secret tissue of connectedness through which the dispersed citizens of the republic were bound to one another was nothing more than whiteness—this was not a nationalist vision to which Stowe was willing to subscribe. The unique strength of a model of nationality rooted in the human susceptibility to emotional wounding and loss thus lay, for Stowe and many other sentimental writers, precisely in the fact that anyone, white or black, could be grief stricken, and could therefore be included in the vast embrace of an affective nationality.[14]

I am trying to suggest, then, that what links this improbable collection of American authors, from Winthrop to Jefferson to Stowe, is above all the sense that loss, the affects of suffering and bereavement and the attachment to others they invoke, can be of central importance to the fellow-feeling of which American nationality is made. (And we might think here of Adam Phillips's canny remarks about mourning and the way its lacerations work steadily to remind us of "our attachment to others.")[15] Jefferson's sense of what, precisely, will bind into mutuality the distant and anonymous citizens of the republic—of what form of affect is best suited to such labor—is surely different from Winthrop's, and from

Stowe's, and for that matter from Whitman's. This is an important point to bear in mind. And while I want to be mindful of these contextual differences, which are real and telling, I would also emphasize that the story I am most interested to tell speaks *across* those differences, and as such is more a story of inheritances and astounding continuities than one of rupture or disjunction. Such a story is, in our own critical moment, not the easiest one to tell.

It is not unfair to say that the Americanist tendency of the last decade or so (borrowed in part from a New Historicist reading of Foucault) has been to emphasize rupture and discontinuity, in the hopes of better bringing into focus the peculiarities of a small, bounded, deeply particular moment of historical time. This move is of course prudent and, in a variety of ways, productive—not least, of a kind of scholarly rigor that is proof against untethered generalities about, say, "America." But there is a danger, too, in what Mark Seltzer has aptly called "overly-hasty historicizations," of too rigidly sequestering strains of the past, of estranging them from the languages they inherit, and which inherit them. This is especially true, I fear, of the history of affect and nation. For however distinct Jefferson's sense of grief might be from Stowe's or from our own, both the *invocation* of affective bondedness, and the harnessing of its energies for purposes explicitly nationalist, have persisted across the vast sweep of American self-narration with a consistency that is remarkable. From this perspective, there is perhaps less virtue than we tend to grant in a contextual particularism that would consign such telling continuities as these to only minor or negligible consequence. So while the readerly methods of the last three chapters have meant to argue against and around the potential short-sightedness of a historical practice that undervalues, or operates at too great a remove from, the shifty and multivalent relations of particular persons *to* the available terms of their moment, now I want to suggest that a too tightly contextualizing practice, while beneficial in many ways, may also foreclose some of the other kinds of stories we might wish to tell: stories, say, about the *persistence* of certain tropes and ideals; about the resistance, across gulfs of time, to certain kinds of transformation; and about the surprising, not always strictly linear patterns of inheritance—the kinds of "serial unpredictability," in Wai Chee Dimock's phrase—that are sketched across the centuries, even *within* the radically circumscribed arena of "nation-time."[16]

The consequences of these different kinds of stories can be, conceptually, quite substantial, if we are willing to hear them out. For instance: whatever the salient differences we might note between Winthrop, Jefferson, Stowe, and Whitman, this variability among the terms used to corroborate the dream of an intimate nationality does not, or does not necessarily, mean that these authors sustained mutually incompatible dreams of America. On the contrary, it may suggest that the notion of a nation given shape by the specifically affective ties binding its anonymous citizens has been less a historical peculiarity than an elemental *form* of American self-narration, a seemingly hard-wired grammar of mutual belonging adaptive to the pressures and affordances, however contradictory, of each new moment.[17] "Though wee were absent from eache other many miles," Winthrop writes, "and had our imploymentes as farre distant, yet wee ought to account our selves knitt together by this bond of love, and live in the exercise of it." To which challenge Walt Whitman responds, in 1860, by asking: "Do you know what it is, as you pass, to be loved by strangers?"[18]

AFFECT-NATION

This would begin to explain something of the eerie familiarity these dynamics have about them, the sense of their striking pertinacity. For ours, today, is quite plainly a moment that has neither seen through nor had done with the vexed promises of an intimate nationality. Such visions of belonging and mutuality have persisted, across a variety of media, though they tend now to travel under different names. Consider, to begin with, the tenor of so much of the "information" by which our age is said to be characterized. Consider the news, as it ranges from global and national organs like CNN and the networks down through local outlets, talk shows, and the tabloids. Mark Seltzer suggestively describes this contemporary American scene as a "wound culture." Thinking not only of the crush of suffering and death presented to us daily in the mass media, but also of the steady elevation of even inabstractably private catastrophe into public interest and national news (and we might think here of John F. Kennedy Jr. or, more routinely, of the affect-interviews of Oprah Winfrey or Barbara Walters), Seltzer writes: "The contemporary public sphere represents itself to itself, from the art and culture scenes to tabloid and talk TV, as a culture of suffering, states of injury, and wounded attachments." What results from this, Seltzer claims, is a peculiar "sociality of the wound," since here, in wound culture, "one discovers the sociality that gathers, and the public that meets, in the spectacle of the untoward accident and in an identification with the world in so far as it is a hostile place: the pathological public sphere."[19] It's worth returning again to Lauren Berlant's related contention about how subjects come to be bound to the nation "through a universalist rhetoric not of citizenship per se but of the capacity for suffering and trauma at the citizen's core." In the "fantasy scene of national feeling," she writes, "the sentimental subject is connected to others *who share the same feeling*."[20] All of this, we should remark, is argued in relation to America *before* September 11, 2001, before the rhetoric of a national citizenry made one by a mutual vulnerability to "terror" had become the sine qua non of American self-description. If these contentions were true then—and I believe they were—they are only more intensely so now.

So the mode of national citizenship these contemporary critics sketch is not new, but newly inflected: it is the citizenship of affective mutuality encouraged by Winthrop, implied by Jefferson, and presented as a moral demand by Stowe, the demand that we, each of us, *"feel right."* And this is, unmistakably, the grammar of contemporary national belonging, one proper to a public sphere so glutted with spectacles of horror, death, and suffering that the media critic Susan D. Moeller would feel compelled to invent a new term for the contemporary citizen's experience of it: not Benjaminian modernist trauma, but "compassion fatigue."[21] This, she argues, is one of the badges of our age, and it makes sense that it should be. For now, in the place of tarnished or discredited models of national belonging and mutuality, we have the bare inexhaustible fact of human loss, relentlessly abstracted into a kind of hypermediated publicness—Seltzer's "pathological public sphere." I would add to Seltzer's point only that this propagation of the image of grief and horror takes its place within the very long American tradition we have briefly sketched. That is, the often explicit aim of the productions of our current and expanding "wound culture" is to confirm in each of us a renewed sense of, precisely, national public belonging. This is so to the degree that grief and horror and bereavement, rather than a notion of race or of some more institutional allegiance, are now the principle adhesives with which our contemporary nationality is assembled. We are consolidated in our modern nation-ness, in other words, not by opinions or judgments, and even less by governments we profess not to trust and institutions we happily malign, but by affects, *feelings*: reactive responses (such as shock, horror, grief) which, as Berlant suggests, we are meant to understand ourselves as sharing in simultaneity with a multitude of anonymous others. The result is not only a peculiar form of nationality but of citizenship: it is not too much to suggest that today one participates in American nationality less by any mundane civic activities (such as, say, voting) than by grieving when anonymous others grieve, by weeping when they weep, by recoiling when they recoil. Similarly, we are encouraged to know ourselves as American, among Americans, because we grieve when others who are unknown to us personally grieve, weep when they weep, recoil when they recoil. This is the intimate connectedness of modern-day nationality, and the events of September 11, 2001, so wildly disorienting in so many ways, were not at all so in this one. The perennial headline, NATION MOURNS, is by now a redundancy.[22]

Such a modern-day utopia of affective cohesion is, of course, not without its complications. It's worth wondering, for instance, whether our affective nationality is capable of making the same sorts of demands—of *ethical* demands—that might be heard in Winthrop, or in Jefferson, or in Stowe. We might wonder, that is, how our own sense of grief and its extensions squares with those of our varied precursors. To be certain, we have democratized national belonging: the ideal, for instance, of a specifically racial American coherence—of a citizens made intimate with one another through nothing more than the whiteness they shared—no longer carries the civic weight it once did. The return to a mode of national belonging born of shared bereavement may seem to represent, for ourselves no less than Stowe, a way of imagining national affiliation which is attractive precisely for the way it sidesteps the brutal reductions and exclusions of race. Indeed, it is in exactly this spirit that Gilroy writes his tract on "the fading sign of 'race.'" Here again is his counterposing of the "pseudo-solidarities" of race to a more ample form of "identification and empathy": "The recurrence of pain, disease, humiliation and loss of dignity, grief, and care for those one loves can all contribute to an abstract sense of human similarity powerful enough to make solidarities based on cultural particularity appear suddenly trivial." Gilroy's notion essentially retrieves and updates Richard Rorty's utopian

172 EPILOGUE

rendering of "human solidarity," a "utopia" rooted in "the imaginative ability to see other people as fellow sufferers," and cultivated by "increasing our sensitivity to the particular details of the pain and humiliation of other, unfamiliar sorts of people." For Rorty, as for Gilroy, the possibility for a more progressive human solidarity lies in "the ability to see more and more traditional differences (of tribe, religion, race, customs, and the like) as unimportant when compared with similarities with respect to pain and humiliation." Hence, for him, "detailed descriptions of particular varieties of pain and humiliation (in, e.g., novels or ethnographies) . . . [are] the modern intellectual's principal contributions to moral progress."[23] In the place of hollow abstractions of human mutuality, then, what we have are *narratives*: stories of suffering and loss around which we might build more capacious, less narrow and exclusionary models of affiliation.

Such a notion is no doubt theoretically inviting—Gilroy, for one, does a great deal with it. But it is also tremendously vexed, and all the more pronouncedly so, it turns out, in the realm of the ethics of citizenship. For if, in the colloquy of American voices ranging from Winthrop and Jefferson to Stowe, Whitman, and up to today, there is an idealism to be heard, a dreaming toward a utopia of national harmoniousness and fulfillment, there is also the persistent specter of *betrayal*, in many modes and forms. As Greil Marcus has observed, the threat of collective failure, of betraying an expansive promise, was once a built-in element of American utopianism, a cautionary note meant to motivate and inspire. "'A city on a hill,'" Marcus writes, "was an image often invoked by Ronald Reagan during his presidency, as a sign of American triumphalism; it was found more than three hundred years before as a warning, as a prophecy of self-betrayal. The depth of the possible betrayal measures the breadth of the possible achievement."[24] For Winthrop, sustaining one another in the far-reaching mutuality of love was a task to be fulfilled, a *mission*; the labor of it comes not in the sense of mutual interconnectedness to be maintained but rather in the profound and potentially limitless *obligation* of citizen to citizen, an obligation that cannot be acquitted with "dissembling" or "dissimulation."

It is unclear, however, that our contemporary languages of national belonging—the affective languages of trauma—make any such demands, or sponsor any of the sorts of imaginative self-expansions Gilroy and Rorty theorize. For both of them, something like obligation is meant to follow, however indirectly or circuitously, from the experiences of "identification and empathy" produced in the encounter with another's suffering. In this, they are not at all unlike Stowe herself, whose program for national renovation begins with the basic imperative that all individuals "see to it that *they feel right.*" "An atmosphere of sympathetic influence," she writes, "encircles every human being; and the man or woman who *feels* strongly, healthily and justly, on the great interests of humanity, is a constant benefactor to the human race. See, then, to your sympathies in this matter!"[25] Stowe's prevailing sense here, problematic though it may have been, is that to feel is, of necessity, to be obliged—and in this both Gilroy and Rorty would, in their different manners, wish to bear her out. But if the contemporary spectacles of suffering and loss as documents of public concern have taught us anything, it is that feeling for the suffering of others is a much more knotty affair than any of these utopias can quite allow. The matter is not only that a multitude of forms of commodification have overtaken narratives of suffering, or that, consequentially, experiences of empathy and identification have become inevitably crossed with aspects of pity, condescension, self-aggrandizement, and no negligible degree of sadism.[26] More than this, affect is ever ready to stand *in the place of* obligation, feeling to become not the pathway to some greater sufficiency of other-attentiveness but the incontestable mark of it. Indeed, contrasted with the unending "endeavor" of citizenship as imagined by Winthrop or Jefferson, our contemporary languages of national belonging appear quite modest in what they demand: they solicit our immediate heartfelt response, and little beyond its parameters. Inasmuch as our citizenship is affective, it seems, the mere experiencing of our affects, and the recognition that we share them with unknown others, suffices *as* citizenship—and in this, we part company with the visions of Winthrop, or even of Stowe. An affective nationality rooted in wounding and bereavement promises to circumvent the unwanted discrimination and antidemocratic exclusivity of previous nation-languages, then, but it does so at a certain cost to citizenship itself. What results is a nation-language in which mutuality has grown increasingly separate from obligation, where national belonging no longer carries with it any but the thinnest of ethical demands.[27]

My intention here is not to rehearse an old story about the American state and the varied insidious ways it compels its citizens into conditions of acquiescence, submission, and more or less bovine complacency. I do not at all concur, for instance, with Russ Castronovo's claim that "the U.S. democratic state loves its citizens as passive subjects, unresponsive to political issues, unmoved by social stimuli, and unaroused by enduring injustices."[28] I am arguing that exactly the reverse is true: that the nation's current languages of mutuality and belonging prize and, indeed, revere citizens who are, precisely, responsive, moved, and aroused. The problem, rather, is that these solicited and much-desired affective responses function predominantly as the *ends* of national belonging, rather than the means to a civic practice productive of, for instance, less systemic inequity or suffering. To be aroused, in other words, is not necessarily to be thoughtful or ethical, which I take to be Berlant's point when she writes of the troubling contemporary situation in which we find "political ideas about the nation sacrificed to the development of feelings about it."[29] Ironically enough, one of the most vivid examples of the political "sacrifice" of affective citizenship appears in the current tendency to approach race itself as, in essence, a question of "feeling right." I am thinking of what Terence Whalen acutely describes as "the pervasive view of racism as a private sin or psychological malady rather than a long-standing, systemic condition perpetuated by powerful political and economic forces."[30] What Whalen calls "a private sin or psychological malady" we might also understand as a variety of *feeling*. Thus, in the context of a civic practice in which feeling adequates as ethical national citizenship, the whole panoramic matter of race in America—the "long-standing, systemic" political conditions, the lived intimacies and rivalries and attachments condensed in "race"—presents itself habitually in the guise of "racism," be it institutional or personal: a matter, that is, of failing to feel right, to which every citizen can address his or her feelings, and about the seeming intransigence of which every citizen may even feel a kind of anguish. Such painful feeling, as many writers of several centuries have suggested, may indeed bind us as a national citizenry into a sense of coherence and mutuality. But we do well to recall that this is currently a mutuality from which nothing—and certainly no utopia of dignity for all and unnecessary suffering for none—necessarily follows.

These are, at any rate, some of the perplexities of what has been, for more than 350 years, a dream of *fellowship*, of some manner of bond that would make kin of strangers, and in so doing distinguish the American collectivity—as well as the whole of the American project, with its proliferating utopias and endless betrayals—from anything else in the world. The authors of the antebellum nation are among the first to try to fashion an art, an expressive cosmology, from this unruly inheritance. What we will make of it here in America in the century before us—already the century of the global, the transnational, the techno-planetary, as well as the century of terror—will undoubtedly not avoid the entanglements and impasses they uncovered in their encounters with race and sex, attachment and loss, intimacy and nationality. We have before us, of course, the advantage of their example. With an eye to its troubles as well as its affordances, we might hope at least to be adequate, after our own fashion, to the breadth and complexity of their imagining.

Notes

INTRODUCTION

1. Walt Whitman, "The Eighteenth Presidency!," *Walt Whitman: Poetry and Prose*, ed. Justin Kaplan (New York: Library of America, 1996), 1333. Cited internally hereafter.

2. In the prefatory chapter of *The Scarlet Letter*, "The Custom-House," Hawthorne would, after much dealing with the state and its institutions, declare himself at last to be a citizen perhaps, but "*a citizen of somewhere else.*" The will to dissociate oneself and one's citizenship from the counterfeit languages of national belonging offered by the state flowered as well in Thoreau ("How does it become a man to behave toward this government to-day?" he asks in "Civil Disobedience." "I answer, that he cannot without disgrace be associated with it.") and even in Emerson, whose reserve with respect to overtly political matters was greater than most. See Emerson's essay of 1854, "The Fugitive Slave Law," in *Emerson: Essays and Poems*, ed. Joel Porte, Harold Bloom, and Paul Kane (New York: Library of America, 1996), 993–1008. Nathaniel Hawthorne, *The Scarlet Letter*, Centenary Edition of the Works of Nathaniel Hawthorne (Columbus: Ohio State University Press, 1962), 1: 55; Henry David Thoreau, *Walden and Civil Disobedience*, ed. Michael Meyer (New York: Penguin Books, 1986), 389. For an account of the varied political engagements, and more prominent disengagements, of canonical midcentury authors, see John Carlos Rowe, *At Emerson's Tomb: The Politics of Classic American Literature* (New York: Columbia University Press, 1997).

3. "Every nation that carries in its bosom great and unredressed injustice," Stowe writes at the conclusion of *Uncle Tom's Cabin*, "has in it the elements of [its] last convulsion." See Harriet Beecher Stowe, *Uncle Tom's Cabin, or, Life among the Lowly*, ed. Ann Douglas (New York: Penguin Books, 1981), 629.

4. On the antebellum disenchantment with political institutions, its causes and expressions, see Glenn C. Altschuler and Stuart Blumin, "'Where Is the Real America?': Politics and Popular Consciousness in the Antebellum Era," *American Quarterly* 49, no. 2 (June 1997): 225–67. On early articulations of American nationalism, see David Waldstreicher, *In the Midst of Perpetual Fetes: The Making of American Nationalism, 1776–1820* (Chapel Hill: University of North Carolina Press, 1997). On post-Jacksonian nationalism, and its anti-state inflections, see Edward L. Widmer, *Young America: The Flowering of Democracy in New York City* (New York: Oxford University Press, 1999). For a theoretical account of a nationlike structure of belonging that holds as its premise an antipathy toward the state and its institutions, see Michael Herzfeld, *Cultural Intimacy: Social Poetics in the Nation-State* (New York: Routledge, 1997).

5. Benedict Anderson, *Imagined Communities: Reflections on the Origin and Spread of Nationalism*, rev. ed. (New York: Verso, 1991), 36; Seymour Martin Lipset, *The First New Nation: The United States in Historical and Comparative Perspective* (1963; New York: Norton, 1979). Like Lipset, Anderson writes of America as a "creole state," whose national distinctiveness was always an open question, in part as a result of having been "formed and led by people who shared a common language and common descent with those against whom they fought" for independence (47).

6. Christopher Looby, *Voicing America: Language, Literary Form, and the Origins of the United States* (Chicago: University of Chicago Press, 1996), 14. "In America," Looby goes on, "racial and ethnic diversity, religious heterogeneity, population dispersal, geographical unboundedness, practical innovation, and exile from historical precedent all contributed to problematize (if not demolish) traditional notions of nationality."

7. Adam Phillips, *Terrors and Experts* (Cambridge, MA: Harvard University Press, 1995), 77–78.

8. On the elusiveness at the core of the concept of intimacy, see especially Lauren Berlant's introduction to *Intimacy*, ed. Lauren Berlant (Chicago: University of Chicago Press, 2000), 1–8. See also John D'Emilio and Estelle Freedman, *Intimate Matters: A History of Sexuality in America* (New York: Harper and Row, 1988); Anthony Giddens, *The Transformation of Intimacy: Sexuality, Love, and Eroticism in Modern Societies* (Stanford, CA: Stanford University Press, 1992); and Richard Wightman Fox's *The Trials of Intimacy: Love and Loss in the Beecher-Tilton Scandal* (Chicago: University of Chicago Press, 1999).

9. There is a vast body of critical literature attending to virtually every one of these terms. To name only a few: Glenn Hendler provides a splendid overview of sympathy and its cognates in *Public Sentiments: Structures of Feeling in Nineteenth-Century America* (Chapel Hill: University of North Carolina Press, 2001). In my definition of intimacy I borrow from his account of sympathy as, at its core, "a recursive emotional

exchange" (3). On "feeling," see especially Julia Stern, *The Plight of Feeling: Sympathy and Dissent in the Early American Novel* (Chicago: University of Chicago Press, 1997), as well as Elizabeth Barnes's *States of Sympathy: Seduction and Democracy in the American Novel* (New York: Columbia University Press, 1997). On "friendship" as a subcategory of sympathy, see especially Caleb Crain, *American Sympathy: Men, Friendship, and Literature in the New Nation* (New Haven, CT: Yale University Press, 2001). On the resonances of "allegiance" (particularly with respect to the "spontaneous allegiance" struck between white working-class men), see Theodore Allen, *The Invention of the White Race,* vol. 1, *Racial Oppression and Social Control* (London: Verso, 1994), 134. In a similar vein, see on "fraternity" Dana D. Nelson, *National Manhood: Capitalist Citizenship and the Imagined Fraternity of White Men* (Durham, NC: Duke University Press, 1998). On marriage, sex, and domesticity, see especially Barbara Welter, *Dimity Convictions: The American Woman in the Nineteenth Century* (Athens: Ohio University Press, 1976); Carroll Smith-Rosenberg, *Disorderly Conduct: Visions of Gender in Victorian America* (New York: Oxford University Press, 1985); Giddens, *The Transformation of Intimacy;* Fox, *The Trials of Intimacy;* and Leila J. Rupp, *A Desired Past: A Short History of Same-Sex Love in America* (Chicago: University of Chicago Press, 1999).

10. For a splendid account of "feeling" and the provision it makes for varied kinds of "affiliation," see Christopher Nealon, "Affect-Genealogy: Feeling and Affiliation in Willa Cather," *American Literature* 69, no. 1 (March 1997): 27–48.

11. Michel Foucault, *The History of Sexuality,* vol. 1, *An Introduction,* trans. Robert Hurley (New York: Vintage, 1978). For pertinent histories of intimacy, sexuality, and their transformation in nineteenth-century America, see especially Michael Warner, "Thoreau's Bottom," *Raritan* 11 (1992): 53–79. Thoreau, as Warner points out, is another author who, like Whitman, intuits exactly these coming shifts. See also Jonathan Ned Katz, *Love Stories: Sex between Men before Homosexuality* (Chicago: University of Chicago Press, 2001); as well as Rupp, *A Desired Past;* D'Emilio and Freedman, *Intimate Matters;* and Crain, *American Sympathy.*

12. Nelson, *White Manhood,* 6, 203, 11.

13. Ibid., 37.

14. Hendler, *Public Sentiments,* 213. See also Stern, *The Plight of Feeling,* and Burgett, *Sentimental Bodies: Sex, Gender, and Citizenship in the Early Republic* (Princeton, NJ: Princeton University Press, 1998).

15. Nelson, *National Manhood,* 3.

16. Christopher Nealon, *Foundlings: Lesbian and Gay Historical Emotion before Stonewall* (Durham, NC: Duke University Press, 2001), 45.

17. On race and the psychoanalytic conception of identification, see Diana Fuss, *Identification Papers* (New York: Routledge, 1995), particularly

her chapter "Frantz Fanon and the Politics of Identification." See also Glenn Hendler's suggestive remarks about American sentiment and the need for a "history of identification," *Public Sentiments*, 212–19.

18. Russ Castronovo, "Race and Other Clichés," *American Literary History* 14, no. 3 (Fall 2002): 551–65.

19. Adam Phillips, *On Flirtation* (Cambridge, MA: Harvard University Press, 1994), 79.

20. Eve Kosofsky Sedgwick, *Tendencies* (Durham, NC: Duke University Press, 1993), 74. Sedgwick uses the phrase while objecting to a critic whose methodology, she argues, "renders the formal and stylistic agency of James's texts invisible." I take Christopher Lane to be making a related point in his recent essay, "The Poverty of Context": "That literature troubles assumptions about historical causes," Lane writes, "calls for a subtler approach to imaginative writing and its aesthetic effects." Though I think Lane overstates the bellicosity of relations between historicism and its critics ("the more critics question the deterministic priority of context, the more they—and the works they study—are said to promote a form of retreat that tries to forget, suspend, or eviscerate the political realm"), his analysis of the leveling, ultimately reductive effects of a naïve reliance on "context" as an interpretive master-key is welcome and salutary. See Lane, "The Poverty of Context: Historicism and Nonmimetic Fiction," *PMLA* 118, no. 3 (May 2003): 452, 451.

21. See especially Clifford Geertz's account of "thick description"—a phrase he adapts from Gilbert Ryle—in his seminal essay, "Thick Description: Toward an Interpretive Theory of Culture," *The Interpretation of Cultures* (New York: Basic Books, 1973), 6–10, 3–30.

22. If we take "part of it" to underline, in its very vagueness, the indeterminacy of the relation, we may, in the abstract at least, grant Michaels's point about literature "as such" and culture "as such." But my point (and, as I take it, Geertz's initial point) is that it is surely incumbent on us as critics to find a more nuanced language with which to describe the nature of that "part-of-it" relation, or at the very least a language that exfoliates beyond the routinized dichotomies of resistant and acquiescent, subversive and hegemonic. As Hortense Spillers writes, in a brilliant and explicitly psychoanalytic critique of Fanon, the subject ensnared in colonial history nevertheless "executes an entire human being whose nuanced particularities escape calculation beforehand." It is to the nuanced particularities of these *texts*—to the particularity made evident in their signature movements of style—that I have most assiduously attended. See Walter Benn Michaels, *The Gold Standard and the Logic of Naturalism* (Berkeley: University of California Press, 1987), 27; on Michaels's historicism as "an unacceptable reduction," see James Chandler, *England in 1819: The Politics of Literary Culture and the Case of Romantic Historicism* (Chicago: University of Chicago Press, 1998), 144, 135–51. See also Hortense Spillers, "'All the Things You Could Be by Now, If Sigmund Freud's Wife Was Your

Mother': Psychoanalysis and Race," *boundary 2* 23 (Fall 1996): 96. For more on the stagnation of critical languages in the "kinda subservise, kinda hegemonic" dichotomy, see Eve Kosofsky Sedgwick, "Shame and Performativity: Henry James's New York Edition Prefaces," *Henry James's New York Edition: The Construction of Authorship*, ed. David McWhirter and John Carlos Rowe (Stanford, CA: Stanford University Press, 1995), 206–39. For the imperative, "Always historicize!," see Fredric Jameson, *The Political Unconscious: Narrative as a Socially Symbolic Act* (Ithaca, NY: Cornell University Press, 1981), 9. For the expression of these premises as explicitly textual concerns, see especially M. M. Bakhtin, "Discourse in the Novel," in *The Dialogic Imagination*, ed. Michael Holquist, trans. Caryl Emerson and Michael Holquist (Austin: University of Texas Press, 1981), 259–422.

23. On the dividends of looking to the "myriad small and local movements" of literary work, see Mary Kinzie, *The Cure of Poetry in an Age of Prose: Moral Essays on the Poet's Calling* (Chicago: University of Chicago Press, 1993), xii–xiii.

24. See Stokes, *The Color of Sex: Whiteness, Heterosexuality, and the Fictions of White Supremacy* (Durham, NC: Duke University Press, 2001), 13, 1–21.

25. Such a method has of course made immense affordances for incisive critical work and was itself initially motivated by precisely the need to open historicism out to new terms and modalities. But we have learned by now, I think, that as a way of imagining "history," it is a method not without significant remainders.

26. Nealon, *Foundlings*, 20.

27. Michel Foucault, *Discipline and Punish: The Birth of the Prison*, trans. Alan Sheridan (New York: Pantheon, 1977), 84.

28. See Peter Coviello, "Intimacy and Affliction: Du Bois, Race, and Psychoanalysis," *Modern Language Quarterly* 64, no. 1 (March 2003): 26. "The message of power," I write of Foucault's work and the misperceptions of it, "does not always or uninterruptedly reach its destination." What results from Foucault's understanding of power as an ideal form of operation, I argue, is a crucial kind of allowance with respect to the relational elements of even disciplinary forms of sociality. This tacit provision Foucault makes for the mobility of the relational is only one of the ways he is, in his work, perhaps more kin to Freud than his American followers have wished to grant. The methods I have pursued here—which attend to the mobility of identifications as made and sustained under the purview of disciplinary forms of authority—presume that something intellectually useful, as well as interesting, can be made of this underexplored kinship. See also Foucault's comments on "arts of existence" and "techniques of self" in *The Use of Pleasure*, vol. 2 of *The History of Sexuality*, trans. Robert Hurley (New York: Vintage, 1990), 8–13.

29. Claude Lévi-Strauss, *The Savage Mind* (Chicago: University of

Chicago Press, 1966), 259. I am indebted in my understanding of Lévi-Strauss, and throughout my discussion of the book's methodological aims, to James Chandler's magnificent and expansive meditation on the problematics of historicism, in *England in 1819* (see especially 51–93). On "history" as that which aggregates into discourse, see also Bryan D. Palmer, *Descent into Discourse: The Reification of Language and the Writing of Social History* (Philadelphia: Temple University Press, 1990).

30. Nealon, *Foundlings*, 14, 44, 22. I take Nealon's work to be exemplary in its desire to "extend our idea of 'the historical' to include the desire for its conditions" (13).

31. Toni Morrison, *Playing in the Dark: Whiteness and the Literary Imagination* (New York: Vintage, 1993). The authors cited as exemplary in white studies are taken up, and referenced fully, in chapter 1.

32. Julie Ellison, *Cato's Tears and the Making of Anglo-American Emotion* (Chicago: University of Chicago Press, 1999), 4; Ann Douglas, *The Feminization of American Culture* (New York: Knopf, 1977); Jane Tompkins, *Sensational Designs: The Cultural Work of American Fiction* (New York: Oxford University Press, 1985); Carroll Smith-Rosenberg, *Disorderly Conduct*; *The Culture of Sentiment: Race, Gender, and Sentimentality in Nineteenth-Century America*, ed. Shirley Samuels (New York: Oxford University Press, 1992); Claudia L. Johnson, *Equivocal Beings: Politics, Gender, and Sentimentality in the 1790s* (Chicago: University of Chicago Press, 1995); Julia Stern, *The Plight of Feeling*; Elizabeth Barnes, *States of Sympathy*; Lauren Berlant, *The Queen of America Goes to Washington City: Essays on Sex and Citizenship* (Durham, NC: Duke University Press, 1997); *Sentimental Men: Masculinity and the Politics of Affect in American Culture*, ed. Mary Chapman and Glenn Hendler (Berkeley: University of California Press, 1999).

33. F. O. Matthiessen, *The American Renaissance: Art and Expression in the Age of Emerson and Whitman* (New York: Oxford University Press, 1941).

34. W. E. B. Du Bois, *The Souls of Black Folk*, ed. Donald B. Gibson (1903; New York: Penguin Books, 1989), 86–87. The critic most attuned to this relational, protopsychoanalytic strand in Du Bois is Hortense Spillers, in two essays in particular: "Mama's Baby, Papa's Maybe: An American Grammar Book," *Diacritics* 17 (Summer 1987): 65–81; and "All the Things You Could Be by Now."

1. INTIMATE PROPERTY

1. Thomas Jefferson, *Notes on the State of Virginia*, ed. William Penden (Chapel Hill: University of North Carolina Press, 1982), 63–64. Cited hereafter as *Notes*.

2. George Combe, introduction, *Crania Americana*, by Samuel G. Morton (Philadelphia, 1839), 5.

3. Quoted in Reginald Horsman, *Race and Manifest Destiny: The Origins of Racial Anglo-Saxonism* (Cambridge, MA: Harvard University Press, 1981), 209.

4. Thomas Jefferson, *Writings*, ed. Merrill D. Peterson (New York: Library of America, 1984), 23. On mourning and early American national cohesion, see Julia Stern, *The Plight of Feeling: Sympathy and Dissent in the Early American Novel* (Chicago: University of Chicago Press, 1997).

5. Theodore Allen, *The Invention of the White Race: Volume 1: Racial Oppression and Social Control* (London: Verso, 1994), 134; Horsman, *Race and Manifest Destiny*, 251, 250–56 passim.

6. Du Bois's insight, in his 1935 *Black Reconstruction*, was that white workers in the antebellum nation clearly stood to benefit from an allegiance with similarly exploited black laborers. They chose instead to identify *against* African America, and to receive in compensation the "public and psychological wage" paid out by the privileges and permissions of their whiteness. See W. E. B. Du Bois, *Black Reconstruction in America: An Essay Toward a History of the Part Black Folk Played in the Attempt to Reconstruct Democracy in America, 1860–1880* (1935; New York: Atheneum, 1969). Du Bois's volume is especially important to David Roediger's *The Wages of Whiteness: Race and the Making of the American Working Class* (New York: Verso, 1991) and Theodore Allen's *The Invention of the White Race*.

Other seminal texts in the subgenre of white studies include Reginald Horsman's *Race and Manifest Destiny*, Alexander Saxton's *The Rise and Fall of the White Republic: Class Politics and Mass Culture in Nineteenth-Century America* (New York: Verso, 1990), Eric Lott's *Love and Theft: Blackface Minstrelsy and the American Working Class* (New York: Oxford University Press, 1995), Noel Ignatiev's *How the Irish Became White* (New York: Routledge, 1995), Michael Omi and Howard Winant's *Racial Formation in the United States: From the 1960s to the 1990s* (New York: Routledge, 1994), Ruth Frankenberg's *White Women, Race Matters* (Durham, NC: Duke University Press, 1996), Joseph Roach's *Cities of the Dead: Circum-Atlantic Performance* (New York: Columbia University Press, 1996), Matthew Frye Jacobson's *Whiteness of a Different Color: European Immigrants and the Alchemy of Race* (Cambridge, MA: Harvard University Press, 1998), and Dana Nelson's *National Manhood: Capitalist Citizenship and the Imagined Fraternity of White Men* (Durham, NC: Duke University Press, 1998).

7. The need for a critical discourse capable of describing the affective dimensions of race, perhaps from a specifically psychoanalytic vantage, has been suggested to me most powerfully by the work of Hortense Spillers, in particular her essay "'All the Things You Could Be by Now, If Sigmund Freud's Wife Was Your Mother': Psychoanalysis and Race," *Boundary 2* 23 (Fall 1996), and its predecessor "Mama's Baby, Papa's

Maybe: An American Grammar Book," *Diacritics* 17, no. 2 (Summer 1987). Similar necessities are suggested, if not wholly fleshed out, in a few of Kwame Anthony Appiah's remarks on the notion of "extrinsic racialism" in his *In My Father's House: Africa in the Philosophy of Culture* (New York: Oxford University Press, 1992).

8. A seminal description of whiteness as a kind of property in the self appears in Cheryl I. Harris's legal analysis, "Whiteness as Property," *Harvard Law Review* (June 1993): 1709–91. See also Nelson, *National Manhood*, 29–38. My account differs from these most prominently in its emphasis on the relational dimension of race-as-property—in its insistence that the forging of race as a kind of propertied self-relation prepares the ground for the emergence of race as a language of other-relation, of affiliation.

9. Spillers, "All the Things You Could Be by Now," 6.

10. Winthrop D. Jordan, *White over Black: American Attitudes toward the Negro, 1550–1812* (Chapel Hill: University of North Carolina Press, 1968), 579. For more on the projective fantasies of race in a nascent America, see Toni Morrison's *Playing in the Dark: Whiteness and the Literary Imagination* (New York: Vintage Books, 1992). On the racial inflections of an early American republican ideal of self-government that emphasizes the restraint the instinctive life and the triumph of rationalism, see Ron Takaki, *Iron Cages: Race and Culture in Nineteenth Century America* (Seattle: University of Washington Press, 1979), 5–15.

11. Jacobson, *Whiteness of a Different Color*, 25.

12. Jared Gardner has argued convincingly that the fractious politics of the postrevolutionary era in fact devolve on a discourse of proper whiteness, as it attends the idea of American national identity. On the one side, Gardner argues, republicans feared that the Federalists, by their ameliorating attitude toward Britain, would return America to a slavelike state of dependence, making American citizens nothing more than "white slaves." On the other side, Federalists feared that French-influenced radical republicanism, with its unsettling vision of "equality," would in effect return the American citizenry to a state of carnal savagery (which is precisely how the participants in Shays's Rebellion were imagined). Positioned uneasily between a servility that would make it black and a savagery that would make it red, the American national character, in Gardner's account, comes to be distinguished not least by its successfully embodied whiteness. See Jared Gardner, *Master Plots: Race and the Founding of an American Literature, 1787–1845* (Baltimore: Johns Hopkins University Press, 1998), 12–21.

For an excellent discussion of debates over slavery, factionalism, and the production of the Constitution, see Paul Finkelman, "Slavery and the Constitutional Convention: Making a Covenant with Death," *Beyond Confederation: Origins of the Constitution and American National Identity*, ed.

Richard Beeman, Stephen Botein, and Edward C. Carter II (Chapel Hill: University of North Carolina Press, 1987), 188–225.

13. Jacobson, *Whiteness of a Different Color*, 9.

14. After the Revolution, free black men voted in Maine, Massachusetts, New Hampshire, and Vermont. Free black men could also vote in New York if they met a special property requirement. But Eric Foner reminds us that "between 1800 and 1860, every free state except Maine that entered the Union, beginning with Ohio in 1803, restricted the suffrage to white males." See Eric Foner, "From Slavery to Citizenship: Blacks and the Right to Vote," *Voting and the Spirit of American Democracy: Essays on the History of Voting and Voting Rights in America* (Chicago: University of Illinois Press, 1992), 58. For more on the voting rights of free black men, see also Peter Kolchin, *American Slavery: 1619–1877* (New York: Hill and Wang, 1993), 82.

15. Daniel T. Rodgers, "Republicanism: The Career of a Concept," *Journal of American History* (June 1992): 11–38.

16. J. G. A. Pocock, "Authority and Property: The Question of Liberal Origins," *Virtue, Commerce, and History* (Cambridge, MA: Cambridge University Press, 1985), 70, 66. In his debate with C. B. Macpherson's notion of possessive individualism, Pocock provides what is probably the most subtle account of the eighteenth century as a period in which one saw less a melodramatic feud than an unending dialogue between polity and economy, between "political man" and "commercial man." If Pocock does rather unfairly ignore the manifestly political branch of Macpherson's theory of possessive individualism here (the better to show himself, and not Macpherson, the true dialectician), he nevertheless provides a pleasingly non-Manichean account of the *interconnectedness* of political and economic modes of social orchestration. Part of the emergent efficacy of race in the first third of the nineteenth century, we might say, comes with its capacity to act as a kind of conduit between political and economic spheres of obligation. See also C. B. Macpherson, *The Political Theory of Possessive Individualism: Hobbes to Locke* (Oxford: Oxford University Press, 1962).

17. Jacobson, *Whiteness of a Different Color*, 17.

18. Benjamin Franklin, *The Autobiography of Benjamin Franklin*, ed. Leonard W. Labaree, Ralph L. Ketcham, Helen C. Boatfield, and Helene H. Fineman (New Haven, CT: Yale University Press, 1964), 61–62.

19. Jay Fliegelman, *Declaring Independence: Jefferson, Natural Language, and the Culture of Performance* (Stanford, CA: Stanford University Press, 1993), 180.

20. Michael Warner, *The Letters of the Republic: Publication and the Public Sphere in Eighteenth-Century America* (Cambridge, MA: Harvard University Press, 1990), 42. This is why the franchise was extended after the war only to those citizens who proved their independence by the possession of property, understood in most cases to mean real estate: only

New Jersey, Georgia, and Pennsylvania had exemptions to the real estate requirement. Kirk Harold Porter, *A History of Suffrage in the United States* (Chicago: University of Chicago Press, 1918), 13.

21. Jacobson, *Whiteness of a Different Color*, 21, 20.

22. Women might generously be assumed to be equal citizens—women voted in New Jersey as late as 1807—though lurking behind such a proposition would generally be the rather less egalitarian assumption, located in the concept of "coverture," that women do always voluntarily transfer their political rights to the men to whom they attach themselves; unattached women therefore find themselves in possession of an "equality" incapable of being transferred, and so made active, without the mediation of a man. See Macpherson's account of the Leveller's position with respect to women's suffrage in "Note I," *The Political Theory of Possessive Individualism*, 296.

23. Hegel's famous analysis of master and slave succinctly unravels the supposition of full possession: he proposes, in *The Phenomenology of Mind*, that the master can know of his mastery only when it is opposed by the contrary will of the slave, which means that the master's mastery can only be substantiated in the one expression—the slave's will—which exposes the irremediable incompletion of his mastery. For a good account of Hegel's critique in the context of American slavery, see Eugene Genovese and Elizabeth Fox-Genovese, *Fruits of Merchant Capital* (New York: Oxford University Press, 1983), 352–55.

24. Jacobson, *Whiteness of a Different Color*, 28.

25. "If the Revolutionary era saw the first sustained attack on slavery in the South, that attack was met by the first sustained defense of it; what is more, whereas the attack was feeble and short-lived, the defense would prove remarkably hardy and persistent." Kolchin, *American Slavery*, 90.

26. Porter, *A History of Suffrage in the United States*, 40.

27. Jacobson, *Whiteness of a Different Color*, 26, 28.

28. Ibid., 41.

29. For more on the penchant of revolutionaries like Jefferson for Anglo-Saxon history, as opposed to a faith in the quality of Anglo-Saxon "blood," see Reginald Horsman, *Race and Manifest Destiny*, 9–42 passim.

30. Jay Fliegelman reproduces Jefferson's inscription in a surviving copy of the original, limited edition 1782 *Notes*, which reads: "Thomas Jefferson having had a few copies of these Notes printed to offer to some of his friends and to some other estimable characters beyond that line, begs the Abbé Morellet's acceptance of a copy. unwilling to expose them to the public eye he asks the favour of the Abeé Morellet to put them into the hands of no person on whose care and fidelity he cannot rely to guard them against publication." Jefferson's anxiousness about publication proved to be well-founded. See Fliegelman, *Declaring Independence*, 131.

31. Gardner, *Master Plots*, 18.

32. For more on this dynamic, as it occurs in early America, see Lora Romero, "Vanishing Americans: Gender, Empire, and New Historicism," in *The Culture of Sentiment: Race, Gender, and Sentimentality in Nineteenth-Century America*, ed. Shirley Samuels (New York: Oxford University Press, 1992), 115–27.

33. "Nothing Jefferson ever wrote has evoked more controversy than the passage and its revision on the murder of Logan's family," writes William Penden, editor of my edition of the *Notes*. For a detailed account of the minor scandal, see Jefferson's "Appendix No. 4: Relative to the Murder of Logan's Family," 226–58; and Penden's "Notes," 298–300. Jay Fliegelman has remarked as well, though in a different context, on "Jefferson's insistence on the interchangability of himself and Logan as 'Americans.'" See *Declaring Independence*, 97–98.

34. One of the things Jefferson begins to trace in outline here is the difference, in American usage, between *ethnicity* and *race*, a difference that has to do primarily with the perception of an ancestral nation-ness. By virtue of their nationlike social forms, Indians are invested in Jefferson's account with something like *ethnicity*—with differences that do not quite amount to something utterly alien or Other. African Americans, without any perceived ancestral nationality, read on the other hand as profoundly alien—what invests them are not the differences-within-similarity of ethnicity, but the uncanny similarities-within-Otherness of *race*. On the function of the racist epithet, Benedict Anderson writes: "It erases nation-ness by reducing the adversary to his biological physiognomy." That reduction, we might say, defines the very agency of "race" in Jefferson's account of blacks in America. See Anderson's *Imagined Communities: Reflections on the Origin and Spread of Nationalism* (New York: Verso, 1983), 135. See also Dana Nelson's account of race and nature in *Notes, National Manhood*, 53–57.

35. To the question, "Why not retain and incorporate the blacks into the state?," Jefferson responds: "Deep rooted prejudices entertained by the whites; ten thousand recollections, by the blacks, of the injuries they have sustained; new provocations; the real distinctions which nature has made; and many other circumstances will divide us into parties, and produce convulsions which will probably never end but in the extermination of the one of the other race.—To these objections, which are political, may be added others, which are physical and moral" (*Notes*, 138).

36. On Jefferson's faith in the political efficacy of silence, Christopher Looby notes: "Social and political differences, when they remained unspoken and unheard, would be as good as nonexistent." See Looby, *Voicing America: Language, Literary Form, and the Origins of the United States* (Chicago: University of Chicago Press, 1996), 87. Noel Ignatiev remarks in a similar vein on Jefferson's reiterated "opposition to placing

the slave question on the nation agenda." See his *How the Irish Became White*, 67.

37. For a different reading of the "Manufactures" chapter, appraising it as an instance of an "appealing, vivid . . . thorough statement of the case for the pastoral ideal," see Leo Marx, *The Machine in the Garden: Technology and the Pastoral Ideal in America* (New York: Oxford University Press, 1964), 118–44.

38. On this point, see especially Scott L. Malcomson's fine reading of Locke's tortured efforts to make sense of New World racial slavery in the terms of a political philosophy grounded in private property and individual self-possession, in *One Drop of Blood: The American Misadventure of Race* (New York: Farrar, Straus, and Giroux, 2000), 48–50.

39. Winthrop Jordan, *White over Black*, 429. For more on the influence of Jefferson's *Notes*, see Dana D. Nelson, *The Word in Black and White: Reading "Race" in American Literature, 1638–1867* (New York: Oxford University Press, 1992), 16–20.

40. As Jacobson writes, "Although merely implicit in much of the Revolutionary period, this critical link between race and republicanism would become increasingly explicit as the nineteenth century wore on, and especially as the slavery question gained prominence in public discussion." *Whiteness of a Different Color*, 30.

41. Karl Marx, "Critique of the Gotha System," *The Marx-Engels Reader*, ed. Robert C. Tucker (New York: Norton, 1978), 535.

42. Porter, *A History of Suffrage in the United States*, 93.

43. Ibid., 97.

44. Unlike property requirements, which ensured that those of a certain class could vote, residence requirements aimed generally at curtailing the ability of the many recent immigrants to contribute substantially to official public opinion. By the terms of the "Landholder's Constitution," white men who were native to America, and had lived in Rhode Island for more than one year, could vote without property restrictions. Immigrants were required to have resided in the state for at least three years after naturalization, and even then had to possess $134 worth of property.

45. Porter, *A History of Suffrage in the United States*, 99–100.

46. For a more detailed account of the Dorr War, which reads the events of 1842 in the context of the development of American constitutionalism, see George M. Dennison, *The Dorr War: Republicanism on Trial, 1831–1861* (Lexington: University Press of Kentucky, 1976).

47. See in particular Roediger's *The Wages of Whiteness*, especially chapters 3 and 4.

48. For more intricate assessments of the market revolution, its causes, its manifestations, and its effects, see Charles Sellers, *The Market Revolution: Jacksonian America, 1815–1846* (New York: Oxford University Press, 1991), and Paul E. Johnson, *A Shopkeeper's Millennium: Society*

and Revivals in Rochester, New York, 1815–1817 (New York: Hill and Wang, 1978).

49. Garrison wrote in an issue of the *Liberator* from August 1842: "It is not for me to espouse the cause of any politician, especially one like Thos. W. Dorr." Quoted in Noel Ignatiev's account of the Dorr Rebellion in *How the Irish Became White*, 82–84. For another detailed account of the Dorr War, and especially of the use made of Providence's black community by the opposing sides of the struggle, see Robert J. Cottrol, *The Afro-Yankees: Providence's Black Community in the Antebellum Era* (Westport, CT: Greenwood Press, 1982), 68–77.

50. Ignatiev, *How the Irish Became White*, 82.

51. Ibid., 76.

52. Thomas Jefferson, *The Portable Thomas Jefferson*, ed. Merrill D. Patterson (New York: Penguin Books, 1975), 432.

53. Daniel T. Rodgers, *The Work Ethic in Industrial America, 1850–1920* (Chicago: University of Chicago Press, 1979), 30–31.

54. See Roediger, "White Slaves, Wage Slaves, and Free White Labor," in *The Wages of Whiteness*, 65–92.

55. For more on the fiction of labor power and its exposition in Marx's "Critique of the Gotha System," see Carole Pateman, *The Sexual Contract* (Stanford, CA: Stanford University Press, 1988), 149–53. The notion of a labor power that is somehow separable from persons—the notion against which both Pateman and Marx direct their arguments—broaches a number of dilemmas. How, for instance, does one negotiate what seems to be a profound fissure opened up by market society between a person's energies and skills—a person's labor power—and the personhood of which he or she is not an integrated part? We might note here that the antebellum invention of domesticity as a sphere of life opposed and anterior to market relations is one way this self-bifurcation is managed in the period, and managed in such a way as to remove women still further from the realm of public affairs and public agency. See Gillian Brown, *Domestic Individualism: Imagining Self in Nineteenth-Century America* (Berkeley: University of California Press, 1990); Mary Ryan, *Women in Public: Between Banners and Ballots, 1825–1880* (Baltimore: Johns Hopkins University Press, 1990); and Christine Stansell, *City of Women: Sex and Class in New York, 1789–1860* (New York: Knopf, 1986).

56. On the "social death" imposed upon and lived by slaves, see Orlando Patterson, *Slavery and Social Death: A Comparative Study* (Cambridge, MA: Harvard University Press, 1982).

57. Macpherson, *The Political Theory of Possessive Individualism*, 48 (emphasis added).

58. See Harris, "Whiteness as Property," 1709–91. Walter Benn Michaels offers a related account of fantasies of inalienable property as they relate to Hawthorne, the romance, and the Free-Soil Movement, in "Romance

and Real Estate," in *The American Renaissance Reconsidered*, ed. Donald Pease and Walter Benn Michaels (Baltimore: Johns Hopkins University Press, 1985), 156–82; reprinted in Michaels's *The Gold Standard and the Logic of Naturalism: American Literature at the Turn of the Century* (Berkeley: University of California Press, 1987), 87–112.

59. Jacobson, *Whiteness of a Different Color*, 42, 42–43.

60. Roediger, *The Wages of Whiteness*, 57 (emphasis added). The sequestering of "dependence" among blacks seems to function in a way that recalls Foucault's account of the enclosure of illegalities, in the form of "delinquency," among France's lower classes. As it becomes an isolated or enclosed form of illegality, delinquency comes to function politically as a means for the upper classes to make use of the lower: the lower classes will be marked, because of the enclosure of delinquency within their milieu, with an innate criminality, whose potential to rise from dormancy to socially disruptive action must be supervised with such strictness as to allow "law" to gaze perhaps less steadfastly on the illegalities of a nondelinquent group. A notion of delinquency thus sponsors a differential distribution of illegalities. By redefining white masculinity as a quality of innate self-possession, labor republicanism also strictly isolates "dependence," and all of the corruption it carries, in non-white populations. The recurrence of race riots in this period is only one of the productions of this conceptual shift. See Michel Foucault, *Discipline and Punish: The Birth of the Prison*, trans. Alan Sheridan (New York: Vintage, 1977), 257–92.

61. "That Blacks were largely noncitizens will surprise few, but it is important to emphasize the extent to which they were seen as *anticitizens*. . . . The more powerless they became, the greater their supposed potential to be used by the rich to make freemen unfree." Roediger, *The Wages of Whiteness*, 57.

62. Alexis de Tocqueville, *Democracy in America,* vol. 1, ed. Phillips Bradley (New York: Vintage Books, 1945), 345.

63. Hortense Spillers remarks trenchantly about the *kinlessness* enforced by conditions of enslavement. In captivity, she writes, "'kinship' loses meaning, since it can be invaded at any given and arbitrary moment by the property relations." Hence, "we lose any hint or suggestion of a dimension of ethics, of relatedness between human personality and anatomical features, between one human personality and another, between human personality and cultural institutions." The extension of the anti-ethics of slavery to include all black persons is one of the major ideological thrusts of labor republicanism. See Spillers's "Mama's Baby, Papa's Maybe: An American Grammar Book," 74, 68.

64. George Fitzhugh, *Cannibals All! or, Slaves without Masters*, ed. C. Vann Woodward (Cambridge, MA: Belknap Press, 1960), 20. Cited internally hereafter.

65. Kolchin, *American Slavery*, 57. The most powerful contemporary counterexample to Fitzhugh's idyllic version of slavery is probably William Goodell's 1863 *The American Slave Code in Theory and Practice*, particularly chapter 17, "Facts Illustrating the Kind and Degree of Protection Extended to Slaves" (1863; New York: Johnson Reprint Corporation, 1968).

66. Horsman, *Race and Manifest Destiny*, 134.

67. James Kirke Paulding, *Slavery in the United States* (New York: Harper and Brothers, 1836), 42.

68. Spillers, "All the Things You Could Be by Now," 6.

69. Paulding, *Slavery in the United States*, 7, emphasis in the original.

70. James Kirke Paulding, *Letters from the South* (New York: Harper and Brothers, 1835), 1:34–35.

71. Eve Kosofsky Sedgwick, *Epistemology of the Closet* (Berkeley: University of California Press, 1990), 61.

72. For an especially fine account of the pain and ambivalence of antebellum African Americans' relation to the idea of America, see Eddie S. Glaude Jr., *Exodus: Religion, Race, and Nation in Early Nineteenth-Century Black America* (Chicago: University of Chicago Press, 2000), especially 160–67.

73. Of "white manhood" Dana Nelson writes that "it is a nearly impossible (however nationally / institutionally productive) subject position to achieve and to maintain." I think we can frame the matter more accurately, and a bit less melodramatically, by considering that in antebellum America race comes to prominence as much an *identification* as an identity—particularly as it is used to describe the forms of cohesion proper to nationality. As Freud theorizes it, in a text like *Group Psychology and the Analysis of the Ego*, the concept of identification manages to designate, in simultaneity, motions of seizure and of self-nomination, and as such it seems a notion particularly well-suited to redirect the by-now tired dialectic between constructivist and essentialist accounts of "where race comes from." Understanding race as an identification, we might lend to it a complex materiality that is reducible neither to "social fact" nor "social fantasy," though it is scored by both. See Nelson, *National Manhood*, 203; and Sigmund Freud, *Group Psychology and the Analysis of the Ego*, ed. and trans. James Strachey (New York: Norton, 1959).

2. THE MELANCHOLY OF LITTLE GIRLS

1. That so many should be exposed so early to Poe makes some sense of the enduring popularity of his macabre works among an audience that extends well beyond the walls of the academy. (Trade press editions of Poe's tales come in many varieties, and can today be found bending the shelves at virtually any commercial bookstore.) There is thus a certain

disingenuousness about accounts of Poe's unfair treatment in America, as when Shawn Rosenheim and Stephen Rachman write, "In Europe, in South and Latin America, and even in Japan, Poe has served as a crucial and much celebrated literary model for generations of writers and readers. In the country of his birth, however, Poe can hardly be said to be at home." The critical dismissal of Poe on trial here seems to me to have been perpetrated almost entirely by *academics*, who ought not to be confused with the generations of writers and readers, here in America, who have stood steadfastly by his tales and poems. See Fiedler, *Love and Death in the American Novel*, rev. ed. (New York: Stein and Day, 1966), 29; and *The American Face of Edgar Allan Poe*, ed. Shawn Rosenheim and Stephen Rachman (Baltimore: Johns Hopkins University Press, 1995), ix.

2. James's remarks are from a review of *Les Fleurs du Mal* first published in *The Nation*, April 27, 1876. Quoted in *The Recognition of Edgar Allan Poe: Selected Criticism since 1829*, ed. Eric Carlson (Ann Arbor: University of Michigan Press, 1966), 65. Eliot's remarks are from *Hudson Review*, Autumn 1949. Quoted in *The Recognition of Edgar Allan Poe*, 212.

3. See Vladimir Nabokov, *Lolita* (New York: Vintage Books, 1989), especially the remarks on "Monsieur Poe-Poe," 43.

4. Teresa Goddu, *Gothic America: Narrative, History, and Nation* (New York: Columbia University Press, 1997), 77–78.

5. F. O. Matthiessen, *American Renaissance: Art and Expression in the Age of Emerson and Whitman* (New York: Oxford University Press, 1941), xii.

6. See Meredith L. McGill, "Poe, Literary Nationalism, and Authorial Identity," in Rosenheim and Rachman, eds., *The American Face of Edgar Allan Poe*, 273.

7. On "psychobiography" and its textual blindnesses, see Jacques Derrida, "The Purveyor of Truth," trans. Alan Bass, in *The Purloined Poe: Lacan, Derrida, and Psychoanalytic Reading*, ed. John P. Muller and William J. Richardson (Baltimore: Johns Hopkins University Press, 1988), 176, 186–92. Rufus Griswald inaugurated the tradition of reading Poe's art as a function of his life and its pathologies on October 9, 1849, the day of Poe's funeral. In his slanderous and enduring biographical sketch (which came out in the New York *Daily Tribune*, and which Griswald signed "Ludwig"), he notes typically of "The Raven" that it "was probably much more nearly than has been supposed, even by those who were very intimate with him, a reflection and an echo of his own history." Quoted in Carlson, ed., *The Recognition of Edgar Allan Poe*, 33. Two of the more celebrated studies that followed Griswald's psychobiographical line were Joseph Wood Krutch's *Edgar Allan Poe: A Study in Genius* (New York: Knopf, 1926) and Marie Bonaparte's *The Life and Work of Edgar Allan Poe* (London: Imago, 1949), which first appeared in 1933 as *Edgar Poe: Etude psychanalytique*. Krutch's text is probably best summarized by

Edmund Wilson: "he believes that Poe was driven in the first instance into seeking a position of literary eminence by a desire to compensate himself for the loss of social position of which his foster-father had deprived him; that, in consequence, perhaps of a 'fixation' on his mother, he became sexually impotent and was forced, as a result of his inability to play a part in the normal world, to invent an abnormal world full of horror, repining, and doom" (from "Poe at Home and Abroad," quoted in *The Recognition of Edgar Allan Poe*, 143). Bonaparte's reading of Poe is less manifestly punitive, since the sexual pathologies of which Poe is the avatar are in her account less personal than universal (and this, she says, is why so many readers identify with and are attracted to the stories); but as Shoshana Felman observes, "she nonetheless, like Krutch, sets out primarily to diagnose that 'sickness' and trace the poetry to it." See Felman's "On Reading Poetry," *The Purloined Poe: Lacan, Derrida, and Psychoanalytic Reading*, 141.

8. See *The Purloined Poe*, and *Romancing the Shadow: Poe and Race*, ed. J. Gerald Kennedy and Liliane Weissberg (New York: Oxford University Press, 2001). Something of an exception to this appears in the work of Joan Dayan, particularly in "Amorous Bondage: Poe, Ladies, and Slaves," *American Literature* 66 (1994): 239–73, and "Romance and Race," in *The Columbia History of the American Novel*, ed. Emory Elliot (New York: Columbia University Press, 1991), 89–109. Dayan traces a link between the tropes of idealization, de-idealization, and servitude that populate Poe's romances, and their uncanny echo in his uneasy renderings of slaves and slavelike figures. Though interested, like Allan Tate before her, in Poe's treatment of white women, Dayan remains largely unconcerned with the question of sex—with what possibilities for sexual exchange, and what foreclosures, follow from Poe's imaginings of gender.

9. Perhaps the most concisely skeptical of Poe's modern-day critics is Harold Bloom, who, as he wonders over the ineffable quality that allows a story like "William Wilson" to "survive its bad writing," concludes: "The tale is somehow stronger than the telling, *which is to say that Poe's actual text does not matter.* What survives, despite Poe's writing, are the psychological dynamics and mythical reverberations of stories about William Wilson and Roderick Usher." Psychology, in Bloom's account, travels at one remove from a textuality with which we need only dismissively concern ourselves. I will be arguing the reverse: that it is in the very rhetorical textures of Poe's writing that any investigation of his significances (psychological or otherwise) must begin. See Harold Bloom, "Introduction," *Edgar Allan Poe*, ed. Harold Bloom (New York: Chelsea House, 1985), 3–4; my emphasis.

10. Edgar Allan Poe, *Poetry, Tales, and Selected Essays*, ed. Patrick F. Quinn and G. R. Thompson (New York: Library of America, 1996), 317–18. Cited internally hereafter.

11. A deafness to the comic tonalities even of Poe's "serious" pieces seems particularly prevalent in the more adversarial accounts of his work. For a vivid example, see Yvor Winters's altogether angry dismissal of Poe as an "explicit obscurantist" in "Edgar Allan Poe: A Crisis in the History of American Obscurantism," from *American Literature*, January 1937 (reprinted in Carlson, ed., *The Recognition of Edgar Allan Poe*, 176–202).

12. "Induction, and a microscopic power of analysis, seem to be the pervading characteristics of the mind of Edgar Poe." From the London *Literary Gazette*, January 31, 1846. Quoted in Carlson, ed., *The Recognition of Edgar Allan Poe*, 19.

13. These sentences are taken from "The Premature Burial," "The Pit and the Pendulum," and "The Facts in the Case of M. Valdemar," respectively.

14. Joan Dayan writes that in Poe's macabre tales "one thing remains certain: the dead do not die. They will not stay buried. In Poe's tales these awfully corporeal ghosts are always woman." This latter sentence, I am going to argue, is accurate though not exactly *right*, since the consciousness that one is, oneself, almost-already-dead—that one is, in effect, an awfully corporeal ghost—seems to describe perfectly the condition of *morbidity* that afflicts a great number of Poe's hyperacute male narrators. See Dayan's "Amorous Bondage," 244. For further accounts of Poe, death, and its relation to the living, see Daniel Hoffman, *Poe Poe Poe Poe Poe Poe Poe* (New York: Doubleday, 1972), 220–22; and J. Gerald Kennedy, *Poe, Death, and the Life of Writing* (New Haven, CT: Yale University Press, 1987), particularly chapter 2. A useful account of death as it functions in Poe's verse appears in Debra Fried's "Repetition, Refrain, and Epitaph," *ELH* 53 (Fall 1986): 615–32.

15. Many of the terms I've used to describe morbidity in Poe are taken from Foucault's account of "morbid anatomy" in *The Birth of the Clinic*. At the turn of the nineteenth century, Foucault argues, the dissectionist "revitalized the concept of death: he volatized it, distributed it throughout life in the form of separate, partial, progressive deaths, deaths that are so slow in occurring that they extend even beyond death itself." Those odd "cataleptic disorders" and temporary cessations of vitality that so plague Poe's narrators thus realize, with uncanny exactness, the "phenomena of partial or progressive death" that morbid anatomy discovers at the turn of the nineteenth century. The point here isn't to show that Poe's writing is somehow abstractly "influenced" by the accounts of morbid anatomy to which he no doubt had access; rather, I would suggest that Poe's distinctive narrative *style* offers us what may be the purest literary embodiment or codification of what Foucault calls the "anatomo-clinical gaze," with which morbid anatomists were suddenly able to see death in all its organic and embodied mobility. Like Foucault's revolutionary clinicians, then, Poe is enabled by the idiosyncrasies of his microplotted, radically

temporalizing style to speak compellingly "of the permeability of life by death." See Michel Foucault, *The Birth of the Clinic: An Archaeology of Medical Perception*, trans. A. M. Sheridan Smith (New York: Vintage, 1973), 144, 171.

We might note as well that Poe's interest in the deathliness of life has made him a particularly serviceable example within an entire tradition of metaphysical thought. Foucault argues, for instance, that the signal importance of morbid anatomy lies in its sweeping ratification of the very idea of individuality. After Bichat, he writes, death is suddenly "constitutive of singularity . . . in the slow, half-subterranean, but already visible approach of death, the dull, common life becomes an individuality at last; a black border isolates it, and gives it the style of its own truth" (171). Addressed at least implicitly to the current in twentieth-century philosophy that takes death as the Archimedean point from which reflections on the subject and its conceptual fragility must proceed—a current which, derived from Heidegger, continues through Sartre, Blanchot, and especially Lacan—Foucault's remarks suggest how Poe's fixation with the death one carries, living, within oneself might render him particularly attractive to theorists of subjectivity such as Alexandre Kojeve, Lacan's teacher, who argues in a vein Poe would surely appreciate that "*human Being* . . . is the death which lives a *human* life." For Lacan on death, see *The Seminar of Jacques Lacan: Book II*, trans. Sylvana Tomaselli (New York: Norton, 1988), especially chapter 18, "Desire, Life and Death." For Lacan's relation to a philosophical tradition whose terminus is Heidegger, see Mikkel Borch-Jacobsen, "In Place of an Introduction," *Lacan: The Absolute Master*, trans. Douglass Brick (Stanford, CA: Stanford University Press, 1991). Kojeve quoted in *The Absolute Master*, 15.

16. Henry David Thoreau, "Slavery in Massachusetts," *Reform Papers*, ed. Wendell Glick (Princeton, NJ: Princeton University Press, 1973), 109.

17. For more on the already-deadness attributed to non-white persons in the wake of American slavery, see Orlando Patterson's magesterial *Slavery and Social Death: A Comparative Study* (Cambridge, MA: Harvard University Press, 1982). Of the "social death" inflicted upon slaves, Patterson writes: "The master's authority was derived from his control over symbolic instruments, which effectively persuaded both slave and others that the master was the only mediator between the living community to which he belonged and *the living death that his slave experienced*" (8, my emphasis).

18. The becoming-equivalent of white hero and black servant is thus emphatically *not* a moment of racial radicalism or critique in Poe—is not an "exposure" of the underlying dependence of white power on black servitude, as Joan Dayan contends—since it is precisely in that equivalence that the General is, by the story's logic, *demeaned*, made a suitable object for ridicule and satire. He is ridiculed, that is, not for being dependent on

Pompey, but for being so unsettlingly *like* him; the sentiment of the story, on this reading, is far less racially uplifting. See Dayan's "Amorous Bondage," especially 257.

19. On the fears of white antebellum laborers and artisans that "they were becoming 'blacker' with every increment of industrial advance," see Eric Lott, *Love and Theft: Blackface Minstrelsy and the American Working Class* (New York: Oxford University Press, 1995), 71.

20. For an excellent account of Poe's generic hybridity, and of the appeals of melodrama to a Southern intellectual confronted with, but unable to speak forthrightly about, slavery, see Julia Stern, "Double Talk: The Rhetoric of the Whisper in Poe's 'William Wilson,'" *ESQ* 40 (1994): 185–218. See also Jonathan Elmer's "Terminate or Liquidate?: Poe, Sensationalism, and the Sentimental Tradition," in Rosenheim and Rachman, eds., *The American Face of Edgar Allan Poe*, 91–120.

21. A fine, detailed account of this aspect of the gothic appears in Eve Kosofsky Sedgwick's *The Coherence of Gothic Conventions* (New York: Arno Press, 1980), as well as her *Between Men: English Literature and Male Homosocial Desire* (New York: Columbia University Press, 1985), especially chapter 5.

22. Elisabeth Bronfen, *Over Her Dead Body: Death, Femininity, and the Aesthetic* (New York: Routledge, 1992), 69. Bronfen's is a more oedipally centered account than mine—and one that has nothing to say about race—though we come to related conclusions about the utility of gender in Poe's death-ridden world.

23. We see the rigidity of sexual difference perhaps most vividly in the very fact that had appeared to erode it: Roderick and Madeline are twins and, beyond that, share in a certain cadaverous embodiment; but so entirely different are the deaths by which they are defined—Roderick's seemingly incidental next to the supreme grotesqueness of Madeline's—that the decisive gendering of Madeline's death effectively discloses an elemental distinction between them, a *gender* distinction, where none had seemed to exist.

24. The entendres that almost laughably populate the narrator's descriptions of his daughter draw their force from the coincidence of these two registers of horror.

25. Joseph Wood Krutch, *Edgar Allan Poe*, 27.

26. Edmund Wilson, "Poe at Home and Abroad," from *New Republic*, December 8, 1926 (quoted in Carlson, ed., *The Recognition of Edgar Allan Poe*, 147).

27. Elisbeth Bronfen, *Over Her Dead Body*, 366.

28. For more on Poe, pedophilia, and Nabokov, see Elizabeth Freeman, "Honeymoon with a Stranger: Pedophiliac Picaresques from Poe to Nabokov," *American Literature* 70 (December 1998): 863–97.

29. It bears mentioning that the grossly reductive (if not, on occasion,

unappealingly lurid) psychoanalytic readings of Poe offered by Krutch and Bonaparte have certainly been bettered in that most famous recent volume of Poe criticism, *The Purloined Poe: Lacan, Derrida, and Psychoanalytic Reading,* edited by Muller and Richardson. But certain defining tendencies remain, foremost among them: first, a thoroughgoing abstraction of the stylistic particularity of Poe's prose or poetry; and second, an unwillingness to read Poe's figures in relation to any historically contingent node of meaning, such as race. For instance, the earlier critics' tendency to leave behind the peculiarities of the written text in favor of what Derrida sneeringly calls "psychobiographism" finds its analogue in the Lacanian/Derridean tendency to reduce all the discursive textures of Poe's obviously intricate works to a mere handful of, by now, quite familiar dramas, chief of which involves the default of signification and the concomitant revelation of "the limit of language," the eruption of the Real, and so forth. This is of course to generalize a bit too flippantly (and of all the essay contributors, Lacan is by far the *most* attentive to the contours of Poe's text), but the point remains that in their hurry to read Poe's recursiveness and his insistent paradoxicality as commentaries on the nature of "language" writ large, and on certain aporias of psychic economy generally, the critics gathered in *The Purloined Poe* seem unperturbed by the specific varieties of language Poe sets into motion in his tales, or by their social embeddedness, and least of all by his management in the poems of mundane concerns like measure and rhyme. (The latter oversight is particularly dispiriting in Felman's piece, "On Reading Poems," which conceives of "a direct reading of a poetic text by Poe" to be an effort "to locate in the poem itself a signifier of poeticity and to analyze its functioning and its effects; to analyze—in other words—how poetry as such works through signifiers" [153]. The investigation of "poetry as such," in other words, has curiously little to do with the particular formal means of its assembly.) This is not to say that there is little of value in a book that has so effectively taught us actually to *see* the recursiveness of many of Poe's narrative strategies as textual problems in and of themselves; it is, however, to note that even at its most inventive and dazzling, the critical work in *The Purloined Poe* serves fundamentally to extend and complicate, rather than redirect, the thrust of an age-old psychoanalytic interpretation of Poe, which has tended toward silence about the problems of textual particularity and historically inflected meaning this chapter has tried to address. I have for this reason persisted in steering away from, say, an exactingly Oedipal interpretation of Poe's figures, even (especially) when those figures promise to yield themselves with exemplary thoroughness to such a reading.

30. The historian of the Jacksonian era Harry L. Watson writes of these dynamics, "Enfranchised citizens defined who they *were* by emphasizing who they were *not*." The call for full white manhood suffrage in this

way produced a more vehement emphasis on the civic incapacities not only of free blacks but of women, who were in most instances already disenfranchised. See Watson, *Liberty and Power: The Politics of Jacksonian America* (New York: Hill and Wang, 1990), 52. For more on women and civic enfranchisement in the antebellum era, see Mary P. Ryan, *Women in Public: Between Banners and Ballots, 1825–1880* (Baltimore: Johns Hopkins University Press, 1990).

31. The forms of this outsiderness have included, most prominently: his psychological ill-health; his Southernness amid a coterie of New Englanders; as well as his (partially self-fashioned) persona as "a subject who stands outside history," politics, nations, etc. (McGill, "Poe, Literary Nationalism, and Authorial Identity," 272). We notice, though, that these explanations, however various in content, all tend to presume for Poe an "outsider-ness" that resides almost entirely exterior to his writing and *its* peculiarities—as though it were really to some disagreeable aspect of Poe's personality that Matthiessen meant to refer. For more on these matters, see McGill; Perry Miller, *The Raven and the Whale: Poe, Melville, and the New York Literary Scene* (1956; Baltimore: Johns Hopkins University Press, 1997); and, on Poe's Southernness, Allen Tate, "Our Cousin, Mr. Poe," in *Poe, A Collection of Critical Essays*, ed. Robert Regan (Englewood Cliffs, NJ: Prentice Hall, 1967).

32. J. Gerald Kennedy and Liliane Weissberg, "Introduction: Poe, Race, and Contemporary Criticism," *Romancing the Shadow*, xiii.

33. *Edgar Allan Poe: Essays and Reviews*, ed. G. R. Thompson (New York: Library of America, 1984), 1027–28. Cited internally hereafter as *Essays and Reviews*.

34. On the dialectic in American poetry between Germanic and Latinate inheritances, see Robert Pinsky, "American Poetry and American Life," *Poetry and the World* (New York: Ecco Press, 1988), 122–39.

35. Miller's is a particularly meticulous and detailed account of the allegiances and rivalries surrounding Poe in the antebellum literary world. See Miller, *The Raven and the Whale*, especially 121–52.

36. McGill, "Poe, Literary Nationalism, and Authorial Identity," 273.

37. Describing Poe's hesitancy to take up with any stridency divisive matters like race and slavery as part of a strategy of "literary nationalism," Whalen mistakes the wish for a nonfactional mass audience—a national readership—with the very different desire to forge a set of expressive forms adequate to the distinctiveness of American life and American cohesion. "Literary nationalism," in the antebellum era, referred more directly to the latter set of impulses, and it is toward these impulses, and not the desire for a wide readership, that we find Poe ranging between ambivalence and hostility. See especially Whalen's remarks on "The Wages of Nationalism," in his "Average Racism: Poe, Slavery, and the Wages of Literary Nationalism," in Kennedy and Weissberg, eds.,

Romancing the Shadow, 28–35. On Poe's relation to mass culture more generally, see Whalen's *Edgar Allan Poe and the Masses: The Political Economy of Literature in Antebellum America* (Princeton, NJ: Princeton University Press, 1999).

38. Reginald Horsman, *Race and Manifest Destiny: The Origins of American Racial Angle-Saxonism* (Cambridge, MA: Harvard University Press, 1981), 159, 158–86 passim.

39. Horsman, *Race and Manifest Destiny*, 166. For a detailed account of Poe's involvement in a flap among Northern writers concerning the *Southern Literary Messenger*, his advocacy of it, and its perceived pro-slavery sentiments, see *The Poe Log: A Documentary Life of Edgar Allan Poe, 1809–1849*, ed. Dwight Thomas and David K. Jackson (Boston: G. K. Hall, 1987), 520–25. In 1846, some four years after his anti-nationalist piece in *Graham's*, Poe would write for the *Messenger* a notably unkind review of his one-time advocate, James Russell Lowell, noting of the review in a letter, "Lowell is a ranting abolitionist and *deserves* a good using up" (792). Such opinions, as well as his own occasionally erratic behavior in public, were enough to make uneasy Poe's relations, even among would-be supporters, in the New York literary scene. Whalen's "Average Racism" is an especially fine reading of the local politics of race in the antebellum literary marketplace (*Romancing the Shadow*, 3–40).

40. W. G. S. [William Gilmore Simms], "Progress in America; or, a Speech in Sonnets, on the Relations between Great Britain and the United States, Not Delivered either in Parliament or Congress," *Democratic Review* 19 (January 1846): 91–94, 92–93. For more on Simms and his relation to Poe, as well as to Young America, see Miller, *The Raven and the Whale*, 104–9, 130–47; and Edward L. Widmer, *Young America: The Flowering of Democracy in New York City* (New York: Oxford University Press, 1999), 93–124.

41. On Poe's vexed relation to whiteness, particularly as it is expressed in *The Narrative of Arthur Gordon Pym*, see Toni Morrison, *Playing in the Dark: Whiteness and the Literary Imagination* (New York: Vintage, 1993), 31–54.

3. BOWELS AND FEAR

1. Quoted in Perry Miller, *The Raven and the Whale: Poe, Melville, and the New York Literary Scene* (1956; Baltimore: Johns Hopkins University Press, 1997), 89. This volume reprints Miller's 1956 edition, which was titled *The Raven and the Whale: The War of Words and Wits in the Era of Poe and Melville*.

2. On originality in Melville, and its relation to orphanhood, inheritance, and genealogy more generally, see Leo Bersani, "Incomparable America," *The Culture of Redemption* (Cambridge, MA: Harvard University

Press, 1990), 136–54; Wai Chee Dimock, *Empire for Liberty: Melville and the Poetics of Individualism* (Princeton, NJ: Princeton University Press, 1989); and Michael Paul Rogin, *Subversive Genealogy: The Politics and Art of Herman Melville* (New York: Knopf, 1983).

3. Herman Melville, "Hawthorne and His Mosses," *Moby-Dick: An Authoritative Text, Reviews and Letters by Melville, Analogues and Sources, Criticism*, ed. Harrison Hayford and Hershel Parker (New York: Norton, 1967), 546. Melville's letters and criticism will be quoted from this edition, and cited internally; citations from *Moby-Dick* itself will come from the 1988 Northwestern-Newberry edition.

4. The novel's vastly absorptive quality has itself sponsored, perhaps unsurprisingly, a kind of referential, bibliophilic, and downright Nabokovian mania among its critics. In one of the historical notes to the Northwestern-Newberry edition of *Moby-Dick*, the editors supply the following recipe for the novel's concoction, which might well have appeared somewhere in *Pale Fire*: "By the count of Mary K. Bercaw in *Melville's Sources*, critics . . . have named more than a hundred and sixty works as Melville's sources for *Moby-Dick*, more than a source for every chapter, if that had been the way Melville worked." What follows is a several-pages-long detailed list, whose component parts are matched, point by point, to the effects they generate in the novel. See "Historical Note, IV," in *Moby-Dick, or the Whale*, ed. Harrison Hayford, Hershel Parker, and G. Thomas Tanselle (Chicago: Northwestern University Press and the Newberry Library, 1988), 646–47. All quotations from the novel are drawn from this edition and will be cited internally.

5. Ann Douglas, *The Feminization of American Culture* (New York: Knopf, 1977), 304.

6. Bersani writes: "Cetological erudition in *Moby-Dick* is only the first step in an enterprise of cannibalistic encyclopedism. Like its monster-hero, Melville's novel opens its jaws to devour all other representations from Lear's Fool to Vishnoo the Hindu god" ("Incomparable America," 139). My reading of the novel's ironic appropriations, and of their relation to the project of American nationalism and American originality, follows from many of Bersani's insights about Melville's effort to so glut the book with sources and precedents as to render it, and the nation it invokes, incomparable. Where I part from Bersani's reading most consequentially is in its account of the motive forces behind the novel's cannibalistic, encyclopedic nationalism. For Bersani, it is the paradox within the idea of a democratic nationalism—of the survival of an idea of *supremacy* within a democracy, which, for Bersani, is the form meant to banish hierarchy—that impels the novel's comprehensive negations. But this presumes that for Melville "democracy" means something like "the absence of all hierarchy," when in fact for him, as for even the most radical Democrats of his day, democracy was meant to guarantee an equality before the

law and before the nation, which did not itself preclude hierarchy in any way. Bersani's reading thus makes a leveling and, for 1850, anachronistic idea of "equality" the tenor of Melville's democracy, the better to show nationalism's paradoxes. I argue that Melville's complicated enthusiasm for, and simultaneous wariness of, any but the most voided American nationalisms was a response to much more immediate dilemmas, not the least of which was the rise, in the ranks of Young America, of a particularly virulent strain of racial nationalism. In one sense, the novel's negations aim to preserve and protect nationalism, as a premise, from the racialism that had more and more come to define it.

7. There is, of course, a great deal more one could say about Melville's distinctive prose, and about the relations it establishes with various forms of literary authority. His neologisms, for instance, provide an interesting vantage on the disparate rhetorical goals the novel seems to have set for itself. These nonce words come in essentially two varieties: first, the nouns turned into adjectives (as in "Leviathanic" or "atheistical"), in which we hear the note of farce, of giddy absurdism, toward which the prose more than occasionally tends; otherwise, we find adjectives turned into polysyllabic nouns ("unfulfilments," "immensities") that seem to capture the novel's Shakespearean reach toward a grandeur that outpaces conventional language. And we might show as well how Melville's is a writing that, though it flirts with pentameter and is often taken over by it, is yet happy to let the iambic impulse emerge *against* the insisted-on rhythms of the demotic, the spoken. A seminal account of the exigencies of Melville's style, and its varied inheritances, appears in F. O. Matthiessen, *American Renaissance: Art and Expression in the Age of Emerson and Whitman* (New York: Oxford University Press, 1941), 421–31.

8. Walt Whitman, *Leaves of Grass*, ed. Malcolm Cowley (New York: Penguin, 1959), 5. Cowley's text reprints the first 1855 edition of *Leaves of Grass*.

9. A polemical reading of Ishmael as a "disoriented intellectual," driven to despair and passivity by his "doubt and fear and guilt and isolation from people," appears in C. L. R. James's impassioned *Mariners, Renegades, and Castaways: The Story of Herman Melville and the World We Live In* (New York: C. L. R. James, 1953), 46, 47.

10. Samuel Otter, *Melville's Anatomies* (Berkeley: University of California Press, 1999), 160.

11. Bersani, "Incomparable America," 152. The phrase of Crane's comes from his 1926 poem "At Melville's Tomb":

And wrecks passed without sound of bells,
The calyx of death's bounty giving back
A scattered chapter, livid hieroglyph,
The portent wound in corridors of shells.
(*The Poems of Hart Crane*, ed. Marc Simon [New York: Liveright, 1986], 33)

12. Douglas, *The Feminization of American Culture,* 307. For an exceptionally strong account of the volatile reader-relations of dependency and anxiety in Melville, see Eve Kosofsky Sedgwick, "Some Binarisms (I): *Billy Budd*: After the Homosexual," *Epistemology of the Closet* (Berkeley: University of California Press, 1990), 97–104.

13. "The extraordinary originality of Melville's work is that it somehow subsists—materially—as a book orphaned by its content." Bersani, "Incomparable America," 153.

14. C. L. R. James, for one, writes very powerfully of *Moby-Dick* as a novel that is heroically *anti*-nationalist. In the dedication that prefaces *Mariners, Renegades, and Castaways,* he bequeaths all the insight and revelation of Melville's novel to his son, Nob, "who will be 21 years old in 1970, by which time I hope he and his generation will have left behind them forever all the problems of nationality."

15. On inexpressibility in Melville, see also Richard H. Brodhead, *Hawthorne, Melville, and the Novel* (Chicago: University of Chicago Press, 1973); and John T. Irwin, *American Hieroglyphs: The Symbol of the Egyptian Hieroglyph in the American Renaissance* (New Haven, CT: Yale University Press, 1980), 285–349.

16. Duyckinck called the book "an intellectual chowder of romance, philosophy, natural history, fine writing, good feeling, bad sayings." Parker suggests that the review finds Duyckinck "straining to be fair" throughout. Quoted in *Moby-Dick,* ed. Harrison Hayford, Hershel Parker, G. Thomas Tanselle, 720, 721. For an exhaustive account of the immediate critical reception of *Moby-Dick,* see in this volume Parker, "Historical Note, VII," 689–732; see also Hugh H. Hetherington, "Early Reviews of *Moby-Dick,*" in *Moby-Dick: Centennial Essays,* ed. Tyrus Hillway and Luther S. Mansfield (Dallas: Southern Methodist University Press, 1953), 89–122.

17. [George Sanders], review of *Moby-Dick, Democratic Review* 30 (January 1852): 93. On Sanders's relation to literary nationalism and Manifest Destiny, see Rogin, *Subversive Genealogy,* 148–51. On Melville's own relation to the political crises of the midcentury, see also Alan Heimert, "*Moby-Dick* and American Political Symbolism," *American Quarterly* 15 (1963): 498–534; and James Duban, *Melville's Major Fiction: Politics, Theology, and Imagination* (DeKalb: Northern Illinois University Press, 1983), 82–148.

18. Herman Melville, *Pierre; or, The Ambiguities,* ed. Harrison Hayford, Hershel Parker, and G. Thomas Tanselle (Evanston: Northwestern University Press, 1995), 244–56.

19. The tradition of accounting for the racial salience of whiteness in *Moby-Dick* has its most prominent origin in D. H. Lawrence's *Studies in Classic American Literature* (New York: Thomas Selzer, 1923), where he reads the novel as a proclamation of the "doom of our white day." Toni

Morrison refines and revises Lawrence's reading in "Unspeakable Things Unspoken: The Afro-American Presence in American Literature," *Michigan Quarterly Review* 28 (Winter 1989): 1–18, as well as in her *Playing in the Dark: Whiteness and the Literary Imagination* (New York: Vintage Books, 1993). Strong accounts appear as well in Rogin's *Subversive Genealogy*, 102–51; Dimock's *Empire for Liberty*, 3–41, 109–31; and throughout Carolyn L. Karcher's *Shadow over the Promised Land: Slavery, Race, and Violence in Melville's America* (Baton Rouge: Louisiana State University Press, 1980). For summary accounts of the treatment of race in Melville scholarship, see Arnold Rampersad, "Melville and Race," in *Herman Melville: A Collection of Critical Essays*, ed. Myra Jehlen (Englewood Cliffs, NJ: Prentice-Hall, 1994), 160–73; and David Bradley, "Our Crowd, Their Crowd: Race, Reader, and *Moby-Dick*," in *Melville's Evermoving Dawn: Centennial Essays*, ed. John Bryant and Robert Milder (Kent, OH: Kent State University Press, 1997), 119–46. A useful survey of more than a century's worth of interpretations of whiteness in the novel, mainly along lines other than racial, appears in Khali Husni, "The Whiteness of the Whale: A Survey of Interpretations, 1851–1970," *College Language Association Journal* 20 (1976): 210–21.

20. See in particular Reginald Horsman's *Race and Manifest Destiny: The Origins of American Racial Anglo-Saxonism* (Cambridge, MA: Harvard University Press, 1981), 240–52, 284–86. Eric Lott provides another useful account of anti-slavery racism among Democrats in his *Love and Theft: Blackface Minstrelsy and the American Working Class* (New York: Oxford University Press, 1995), 208–10.

21. For more on this double movement, see David Roediger's *The Wages of Whiteness: Race and the Making of the American Working Class* (New York: Verso, 1991), 43–92; and Noel Ignatiev's *How the Irish Became White* (New York: Routledge, 1995), 62–89.

22. Walt Whitman, "The Eighteenth Presidency!," *Walt Whitman: Poetry and Prose*, ed. Justin Kaplan (New York: Library of America, 1996), 1345, 1335, 1338.

23. Horsman, *Race and Manifest Destiny*, 252.

24. See Dimock, *Empire for Liberty*, especially 3–41.

25. [John D. O'Sullivan], "Annexation," *Democratic Review* 17 (July–August 1845): 5–10, 5, 8. See also Horsman, *Race and Manifest Destiny*, 219–24.

26. Quoted in Miller, *The Raven and the Whale*, 110.

27. On the escalation of the racialist, imperialist dimensions of Young America's nationalism, particularly as it is expressed in the career of O'Sullivan himself, see Edward L. Widmer, *Young America: The Flowering of Democracy in New York City* (New York: Oxford University Press, 1999), 185–209. Widmer underplays the degree to which the Young America coterie was, from the first, inflected by racialist nation-languages, the

better to prove a decisive split between what he views as two distinct stages of the Young America movement (he calls these Young America [I] and Young America [II]). Citing O'Sullivan's "pet interest in pacifism," he leans toward a kind of apologism when he writes that, for O'Sullivan, "it was democracy, not Anglo-Saxonism, that he wished to spread across the continent and around the world" (51). But as the quote from as far back as 1845, in "Annexation," clearly indicates, democracy and Anglo-Saxonism were not so easily separable for O'Sullivan, and in his rhetoric were in fact mutually dependent.

28. Morrison, "Unspeakable Things Unspoken," 18. Arnold Rampersad summarizes Morrison's point nicely: "For daring to put these ideas in fiction," he writes, "Melville was punished with neglect, silence, and then misappropriation and misinterpretation." Rampersad, "Shadow and Veil: Melville and Modern Black Consciousness," in *Melville's Evermoving Dawn*, 177.

29. Ahasuerus was the Old Testament king who, according to the first chapter of the Book of Esther, "reigned from India even unto Ethiopia, over an hundred and seven and twenty provinces."

30. As discussed in chapter 1, a vivid example of the logic of white racelessness appears in Thomas Jefferson's *Notes on the State of Virginia*. Pondering the "difference . . . fixed in nature" between the races, Jefferson addresses himself not to any difference between black and white natures but to the difference broached, in his oddly tautological phrase, by "the black of the negro." The crucial difference, then, is between a people with, and one without, race. *Notes on the State of Virginia*, ed. William Peden (Chapel Hill: University of North Carolina Press, 1982), 138. For more on race as it intersects with questions of embodiment and citizenship, see Lauren Berlant, "National Brands / National Body: *Imitation of Life*," *Comparative American Identities: Race, Sex, and Nationality in the Modern Text*, ed. Hortense J. Spillers (New York: Routledge, 1991), 110–40; in the context of American republicanism, see Michael Warner, *The Letters of the Republic: Publication and the Public Sphere in Eighteenth-Century America* (Cambridge, MA: Harvard University Press, 1990), 48–49.

31. Morrison, "Unspeakable Things Unspoken," 15. Or, as Samuel Otter has it, Melville endeavors in "The Whiteness of the Whale" to "think about what it would mean to think about what white 'means'" (*Melville's Anatomies*, 138).

32. Nathaniel Vinton, "Civic Misreadership: Deformity, Isolation, and Prophecy in Melville's *Moby-Dick*," unpublished manuscript, 25.

33. Otter, *Melville's Anatomies*, 161. Otter writes of the same dilemma, in a slightly different critical key: "If fiction is intimately concerned with conveying character, with offering the reader the possibility of standing in the skin and getting inside the heads of others, then in the nineteenth

century, when the racial lines were vividly drawn and announced to be indelible, 'race' was the test case for the reach of fictional endeavor" (163).

34. The phrase *terra incognita* comes from Stephen E. Ambrose's description of the early American wilderness. See Ambrose, *Undaunted Courage: Merriweather Lewis, Thomas Jefferson, and the Opening of the American West* (New York: Simon and Schuster, 1996), 55. I am grateful to Nathaniel Vinton for the reference and the term, and for conversations about its resonances in *Moby-Dick*.

35. Andrew Delbanco, "Introduction," *Moby-Dick, or The Whale* (New York: Penguin Classics, 1992), xix.

36. The remark on the novel's innocent homoeroticism comes from Leslie Fiedler's *Love and Death in the American Novel* (New York: Stein and Day, 1966), 370. For less purgative accounts of desire between men in Melville, see Robert K. Martin, *Hero, Captain, and Stranger: Male Friendship, Social Critique, and Literary Form in the Sea Novels of Herman Melville* (Chapel Hill: University of North Carolina Press, 1986), as well as Martin's more recent "Melville and Sexuality," in *The Cambridge Companion to Herman Melville*, ed. Robert S. Levine (New York: Cambridge University Press, 1998), 186–201; Eve Kosofsky Sedgwick, "*Billy Budd*: After the Homosexual," 91–130; James Creech, *Closet Writing / Gay Reading* (Chicago: University of Chicago Press, 1993), 93–179; and Caleb Crain, "Lovers of Human Flesh: Homosexuality and Cannibalism in Melville's Novels," *American Literature* 66 (March 1994): 25–53.

37. For two splendid accounts of the ways tactical deployments of ignorance can structure essentially homophobic responses to sexual suggestions, see Eve Kosofsky Sedgwick's "The Privilege of Unknowing," *Tendencies* (Durham, NC: Duke University Press, 1993), 23–51; and the opening strains of D. A. Miller's *Bringing Out Roland Barthes* (Berkeley: University of California Press, 1992).

38. B. R. Burg, *Sodomy and the Pirate Tradition: English Sea Rovers in the Seventeenth-Century Caribbean* (New York: New York University Press, 1983), xii; Michel Foucault, *The History of Sexuality*, vol. 1, *An Introduction*, trans. Robert Hurley (New York: Vintage, 1990), 101.

39. On sex and the new forms of medical discourse, see especially Stephen Nissenbaum, *Sex, Diet, and Debility in Jacksonian America: Sylvester Graham and Health Reform* (Westport, CT: Greenwood, 1980). On the shifting sexual ideologies of nineteenth-century America, see also Carroll Smith-Rosenberg, *Disorderly Conduct: Visions of Gender in Victorian America* (New York: Oxford University Press, 1985); John D'Emilio and Estelle B. Freedman, *Intimate Matters: A History of Sexuality in America* (New York: Harper and Row, 1988); and Lelia J. Rupp, *A Desired Past: A Short History of Same-Sex Love in America* (Chicago: University of Chicago Press, 1999). For a reading that places the shift into a rigid system of sexual taxonomy rather too decisively in the very late nineteenth

century, and so ignores the evidence of an *encroaching* regime of sexual specification that its own fantastically rich archival work provides, see Jonathan Ned Katz, *Love Stories: Sex between Men before Homosexuality* (Chicago: University of Chicago Press, 2001). These transformations in antebellum sexual meaning are taken up again, in detail, in chapter 4.

40. Bersani, "Incomparable America," 147.

41. For a related account of the interdependencies of Ishmael and Ahab, and of their mutual projects, see Donald Pease, "*Moby-Dick* and the Cold War," in *The American Renaissance Reconsidered*, ed. Walter Benn Michaels and Donald Pease (Baltimore: Johns Hopkins University Press, 1985), 144–51.

4. Loving Strangers

1. Walt Whitman, *Poetry and Prose*, ed. Justin Kaplan (New York: Library of America, 1996), 1034. The Library of America edition reprints the 1892 *Complete Prose Works*, in which the famous 1876 preface is included. Cited internally hereafter.

2. Whitman's long-held dream of becoming a touring orator has been amply documented, as has his career as a printer and journalist. See especially C. Carroll Hollis, *Language and Style in "Leaves of Grass"* (Baton Rouge: Louisiana State University Press, 1983), as well as the "Oratory" section from *Walt Whitman: Notebooks and Unpublished Prose Manuscripts*, vol. 6, *Notes and Index*, ed. Edward F. Grier (New York: New York University Press, 1984).

3. Walt Whitman, *Leaves of Grass*, ed. Malcolm Cowley (1855; reprint, New York: Penguin Books, 1959), 43. Cowley's version reproduces the initial 1855 edition of *Leaves of Grass*; quotations from "Song of Myself" come from Cowley's text and are cited internally by page number (*not* by section number).

4. The contraction of address in "Song of Myself" moves typically from a national public that might include "you" to a much more special "you" with whom the narrator promises to exchange secrets. What often gets described as Whitman's capacity to "enfold" his readers is largely an effect of these sudden reductions and expansions of discursive scope. Michael Warner addresses just this drama when he writes of the intimacy-effects of Whitman's second-person address, arguing that "'you' is, after all, not you but a pronominal shifter, addressing the in principle anonymous and indefinite audience of the print public sphere." He goes on to suggest that Whitman's anonymous "you" is also not "complacently generic": "while we remain on notice about our place in nonintimate public discourse, we are nevertheless solicited into an intimate recognition exchange." See Warner, "Whitman Drunk," in *Breaking Bounds: Whitman and American Cultural Studies*, ed. Betsy Erkkila and Jay Grossman (New

York: Oxford University Press, 1996), 41. See also Tenny Nathanson's excellent description of Whitman's "presence" and its capacity to "compound the physical and the vaporous," in *Whitman's Presence: Body, Voice, and Writing in "Leaves of Grass"* (New York: New York University Press, 1992), 3.

For a fine elaboration of the key idea that "Whitman wishes to disseminate affectionate physical presence from [author] to the [audience], fervently and directly," see Michael Moon's *Disseminating Whitman: Revision and Corporeality in "Leaves of Grass"* (Cambridge, MA: Harvard University Press, 1991), 3.

5. For more on the antebellum disenchantment with political institutions, and on Whitman's own brand of anti-state nationalism, see Glenn C. Altschuler and Stuart Blumin, "'Where Is the Real America?': Politics and Popular Consciousness in the Antebellum Era," *American Quarterly* 49 (June 1997): 225–67.

6. Benedict Anderson has written eloquently about "that remarkable confidence of community in anonymity which is the hallmark of modern nations." Whitman, I would suggest, tends to conceive such "confidence in community" in markedly physical, passionate terms: for him, nationality can exist only as a quality of intimacy between persons who, though members of the same nation, *are likely unknown to each other*. The singular depth and forcefulness of that unlikely bond, as it occurs in the United States, seems finally to account for Whitman's fervent belief in the exemplarity, the superiority of American nationality. See Benedict Anderson, *Imagined Communities: Reflections on the Origin and Spread of Nationalism,* rev. ed. (New York: Verso, 1991), 36.

7. For an account of Whitman's catalogs and their "agglomerative syntax," see Nathanson, *Whitman's Presence*, chapter 2. See also Quentin Anderson's *The Imperial Self: An Essay in American Literary and Cultural History* (New York: Knopf, 1971), chapters 3 and 4.

8. For more on the particularity of Whitman's style, see C. Carroll Hollis, *Language and Style in "Leaves of Grass,"* and Mark Bauerlein's *Whitman and the American Idiom* (Baton Rouge: Louisiana State University Press, 1991); Matthiessen's account of the poet's language, I would say, remains a touchstone here as well. See F. O. Matthiessen, *The American Renaissance: Art and Expression in the Age of Emerson and Whitman* (New York: Oxford University Press, 1941). Another truly fine account of the force of Whitman's verbal idiosyncrasy appears in Randall Jarrell's "Walt Whitman: He Had His Nerve," in *Critical Essays on Walt Whitman*, ed. James Woodress (Boston: G. K. Hall, 1983), 231–43.

9. For more on the dialectic in Whitman's poetry between embodied particularity and general availability, read in the context of "the opposition between particular and special interest and general representativeness that was the premiere concern of American politics in Whitman's

time," see Mitchell Breitwieser, "Who Speaks in Whitman's Poems?" in *The American Renaissance: New Dimensions*, ed. Harry R. Gavin and Peter C. Carafiol (Lewisburg, PA: Bucknell University Press, 1983), 121–34. See also Wai Chee Dimock's excellent account of the conflict in Whitman "between the opposing claims of universality and particularity in the definition of personhood" in *Residues of Justice: Literature, Law, Philosophy* (Berkeley: University of California Press, 1996), 113–20. Useful here as well is Robert Pinsky's acute description of Whitman's rhythm of whispered description and shouted list in his *Poetry and the World* (New York: Ecco Press, 1988), 41–44.

10. *The Complete Poems of D. H. Lawrence,* ed. Vivian de So la Pinto and Warren Roberts (London: William Heinemann, 1964), 2: 653. The line Lawrence is satirizing comes from section 48 of "Song of Myself," where Whitman writes, "And whoever walks a furlong without sympathy walks to his own funeral, dressed in his shroud" (82).

11. In *Studies in Classic American Literature*, Lawrence chastises Whitman for having mistaken tired old Christian charity for the vastly more noble virtue of sympathy. Doing so, Lawrence suggests, Whitman forces the soul into improbable attachments and thereby falsifies its instinctual inclinations. And what are those inclinations? Lawrence ventriloquizes the soul thus: "'Look at that prostitute! Her nature has turned evil under her mental lust for prostitution . . . She likes to make men lose their souls. If she tried to make me lose my soul, I would kill her. I wish she may die.'" Whitman's sympathy, by this account, falsifies the elemental misogyny of the soul, whose phallic defensiveness Lawrence fairly shudders to see compromised. See his *Studies in Classic American Literature* (New York: Penguin Books, 1964), 184. An excellent reading of Lawrence's response to Whitman appears in Eve Kosofsky Sedgwick's *Between Men: English Literature and Male Homosocial Desire* (New York: Columbia University Press, 1985), 201–15. For a fuller account of Whitman and the relation of his work to women, see Sherry Ceniza, *Walt Whitman and Nineteenth-Century Women Reformers* (Tuscaloosa: University of Alabama Press, 1998), and Vivian R. Pollak, *The Erotic Whitman* (Berkeley: University of California Press, 2000), 172–93.

12. On the appropriativeness of Whitman's sympathetic stances, in the context of antebellum expansionism, see David Simpson, "Destiny Made Manifest: The Styles of Whitman's Poetry," in *Nation and Narration*, ed. Homi K. Bhabha (New York: Routledge, 1990), 177–96. For a recent account of Whitman's nationalism that counters Simpson's, see Charles Altieri, "Spectacular Antispectacle: Ecstasy and Nationality in Whitman and His Heirs," *American Literary History* 11 (Spring 1999): 34–62.

13. Such Manichaean pairings are not difficult to find in historicist criticism of Whitman. It seems by now something of a rule that the poet will be considered either a genius made distressingly human by his

supremacist advocacy of "the racialist theory," as in Alan Trachtenberg's account, or (more commonly) a democratic prophet and revolutionary who boldly "celebrated the liberation of male and female, sex and the body, workers and poor persons, immigrants and slaves," as Betsy Erkkila contends. Accounts that take the poet's "stances" and "gestures" thus in hand, though illuminating in many important ways, also seem to me worryingly lacking in the ability to describe the differences between one achieved "gesture" and any other. Thus, for Martin Klammer, the passage from "Song of Myself" in which Whitman claims "I am the hounded slave"—a passage whose striking rhetorical laxity we are about to discuss—reads as an unbroken extension of the (I believe) much more poised, and very differently calibrated, passage concerning the runaway slave. In the face of criticism of Whitman's gesture of sympathy (Lawrence's, in fact), Klammer turns not to nuances of the verse itself but to "recent scholarship on slave narratives" which, in his estimation, shows clearly that "Whitman's imaginative entry into the runaway slave's life may well be the most compassionate response possible." Nothing of the unevenness in Whitman's execution of such gestures is allowed to come into meaning. See Trachtenberg, "The Politics of Labor and the Poet's Work: A Reading of 'A Song for Occupations,'" in *Walt Whitman: The Centennial Essays*, 131, 120–32; Erkkila, *Whitman the Political Poet* (New York: Oxford University Press, 1989), 7; and Martin Klammer, *Whitman, Slavery, and the Emergence of "Leaves of Grass"* (University Park: Pennsylvania State University Press, 1995), 134. For a scrupulous account of the reverent valorization of Whitman in recent scholarship, see William Vance, "What They're Saying about Whitman," *Raritan* 16 (1997): 127–49.

14. Vivian R. Pollak's description of Whitman's "Ethiopia Saluting the Colors" is exemplary in this respect: "In naturalizing an African-born, female figure's sexual and racial subservience, Whitman reverts, appropriately enough, to the traditional, full end-rhyme closure, internal rhyme, and stanzaic regularity of his pre-*Leaves* verse. The poem stands out formally and representationally as a retreat from a more egalitarian social vision." The assumption that forms themselves—*not* rhetorical maneuvers within them—communicate transparent ideological positions, which are more or less egalitarian in nature, seems to me to simplify the often rather knotty relations between form, rhetoric, and political disposition. See Vivian R. Pollak, "'In Loftiest Spheres': Whitman's Visionary Feminism," in Erkkila and Grossman, eds., *Breaking Bounds*, 96 (reprinted and expanded in Pollak, *The Erotic Whitman*, 172–93).

15. See Warner, "Whitman Drunk," 39. Bersani is describing Joyce, whose powers of realist character evocation are often slighted or ignored in the rush to anatomize his "fancy narrative techniques." Bersani, *The Culture of Redemption* (Cambridge, MA: Harvard University Press, 1990), 157.

16. Wai Chee Dimock, who reads this passage similarly as "one of the most compelling moments of democratic affections in 'Song of Myself,'" offers an especially fine account of Whitman's manipulation of temporality—in particular, of memory—in the stanza. See Dimock, *Residues of Justice*, 117–19.

17. "The Slave in the Dismal Swamp" comes from Longfellow's 1842 volume *Poems on Slavery*. See *The Poetical Works of Henry Wadsworth Longfellow* (Boston: Houghton Mifflin, 1880), 1: 174.

18. The only moment where the enunciating voice adopts some of Whitman's particularity—in the phrase "my gore dribs thinned with the ooze of my skin"—is chastened by virtue of being bookended by two of the most confected lines in the stanza: "I clutch the rails of the fence" and "I fall on the weeds and stones."

19. The *Brooklyn Daily Times*, May 6, 1858. Quoted in *I Sit and Look Out: Editorials from the Brooklyn Daily Times*, ed. Emory Holloway and Vernolian Schwarz (New York: Columbia University Press, 1932), 90.

20. For more on racial nationalism and the various meanings of whiteness within it, see Reginald Horsman, *Race and Manifest Destiny: The Origins of White Anglo-Saxonism* (Cambridge, MA: Harvard University Press, 1981), 158–86; on antebellum racial politics and Whitman's Free-Soil partisanship, see Eric Lott, *Love and Theft: Blackface Minstrelsy and the American Working Class* (New York: Oxford University Press, 1993), 78–79, 208–10, and Alexander Saxton, *The Rise and Fall of the White Republic: Class Politics and Mass Culture in Nineteenth-Century America* (New York: Verso, 1990), 152–54; on Whitman and the project of "ethnology," see Dana Phillips, "Nineteenth-Century Racial Thought and Whitman's 'Democratic Ethnology of the Future,'" *Nineteenth-Century Literature* 49 (December 1994): 289–320.

21. "As stunning as Whitman's representations of African Americans may be in *Leaves of Grass*, no less remarkable is his almost immediate retreat from these new and radical claims in the years following." Klammer, *Whitman, Slavery, and the Emergence of "Leaves of Grass,"* 159.

22. Walt Whitman, *Leaves of Grass: Facsimile Edition of the 1860 Text*, ed. Roy Harvey Pearce (Ithaca, NY: Cornell University Press, 1961), 342. Cited hereafter internally as *Leaves of Grass* 1860. For the sake of clarity, I will be referring to many of these poems not by number—as they are given in the 1860 text—but by the titles later attached to them.

23. A most vivid example is Malcolm Cowley's account of the poet in an article called, aptly enough, "Walt Whitman: The Secret." Having discovered (mostly from journals) Whitman's desire for other men, Cowley confesses that he finds it impossible not to feel toward the poet "almost as Proust's narrator felt toward the Baron de Charlus, when he saw him crossing a courtyard where the Baron thought he was unobserved. 'I could not help thinking how angry M. de Charlus would have been,' the

narrator said, 'could he have known that he was being watched.'" Cowley here imagines himself to have acquired a knowledge the poet could never have intended for him to have; his embarrassment before the anger he might instill in the poet is second only to his (and to Proust's) self-congratulation for having been so penetrating. See "Walt Whitman: The Secret," *New Republic*, April 8, 1946, 482.

24. Genealogies of this tradition appear in Betsy Erkkila's "Whitman and the Homosexual Republic," in *Walt Whitman: The Centennial Essays*, ed. Ed Folsom (Iowa City: University of Iowa Press, 1994), 153–71; in Robert K. Martin's introduction to *The Continuing Presence of Walt Whitman: The Life after the Life*, ed. Robert K. Martin (Iowa City: University of Iowa Press, 1992), xi–xxiii; in Erkkila and Jay Grossman's introductory and concluding essays in *Breaking Bounds*, 3–20, 251–64; and in Jay Grossman's "The Canon in the Closet: Matthiessen's Whitman, Whitman's Matthiessen," *American Literature* 70 (December 1998): 799–832. The most prominent, most recent example of urbane reading can be found in David Reynolds's award-winning *Walt Whitman: A Cultural Biography* (New York: Knopf, 1995), in which he offers the strikingly noncommittal claim (to which we will have occasion to return) that "in the free, easy social atmosphere of pre–Civil War America, overt displays of affection between people of the same sex were common. Women hugged, kissed, slept with, and proclaimed love for other women. Men did the same with other men" (198). The unspecified contrast to today leaves us to wonder exactly what this "commonness" means to attest to: that such attachments were differently meaningful than they are today, or simply less so? If different, how? Reynolds allows that a different kind of significance might invest these "common" activities, but by his desexing, domesticating gestures he seems pointedly to insist that we not imagine those significances to be in any way continuous with what we would now call homosexuality. For a vehement dissent from Reynolds's account, see Gary Schmidgall, *Walt Whitman: A Gay Life* (New York: Dutton, 1997), 89–92.

25. *Between Men*, 202.

26. The exercises I have in mind here are those in which we discover that Whitman's great secret is, after all, his desire for men; that Whitman's homoerotic attachments need to be rescued from the guardians of the canon who want only to expurgate them; that by his secret codes (which *we* have cracked) the poet means to outfox and finally redeem a repressive nation. Each of these readings, though surely at one time or another invaluable, seems to me by now to have been fairly exhausted, and to offer little new insight into the complexity of Whitman's corpus. If the concern is that Whitman's desires will be denied or belittled by the still quite healthy ranks of dismissive biographers and critics, then we would probably do well to describe those desires not at their most formulaic (roughly: homosexuality equals liberation equals American utopia)

but as they operate less neatly, less transparently, in resistance to such pat equivalences.

27. This is an especially prominent element in, for instance, David Kuebrich's account of "Calamus," in his *Minor Prophecy: Walt Whitman's New American Religion* (Bloomington: Indiana University Press, 1989).

28. See, inevitably, Michel Foucault, *The History of Sexuality*, vol. 1, *An Introduction*, trans. Robert Hurley (New York: Vintage, 1978).

29. Reynolds, *Walt Whitman*, 199.

30. Michael Warner, "Thoreau's Bottom," *Raritan* 11 (1992): 54. Two useful, more recent accounts appear in Caleb Crain's *American Sympathy: Men, Friendship, and Literature in the New Nation* (New Haven, CT: Yale University Press, 2001), and David Deitcher's amazing collection of photographs, *Dear Friends: American Photographs of Men Together, 1840–1918* (New York: Harry N. Abrams, 2001). For these authors, the kinds of unresolving ambiguity we have observed in Whitman reflect more generally the *nature* of antebellum sexuality: of our distance from it (a distance impossible not to fill with desire, envy, and anxiety), and its own not-yet-hardened codes and prohibitions. As Crain elegantly frames the matter: "They dwelt in possibilities we cannot help but reduce to prose. Whether or not a couple had sex is a natural question to ask, but the answer will not allow us into the private meaning of their bond" (33). This is a useful point, a kind of attentive agnosticism that means, in a decidedly nonphobic way, to guard against unscholarly anachronism in sexual attribution. At the same time, though, I fear that such studious hesitancy threatens to miss the degree to which ambiguity, extended nondisclosure, and cultivated inspecificity might be *deployed* by particular authors, for particular purposes—and so perhaps ought not to be taken solely as a priori facts of antebellum sexuality. Whitman's sexual persona is indeed elusive and irreducible—but it is also a persona he fashioned, with evident care and calculation. This elemental ambiguity, in other words, might have been part of what made sex such an apt expressive vehicle for many. It would for these reasons be a mistake to underemphasize the deliberateness of such insistences on possibility unforeclosed, especially since they often operated, as Warner suggests, in response and in resistance to an already encroaching system of codification.

31. By far the most nuanced and informative account of Whitman, phrenology, and its relation to sexuality is Michael Lynch's "'Here Is Adhesiveness': From Friendship to Homosexuality," *Victorian Studies* 29 (1985): 67–96. Other sources that discuss the poet's relation to phrenology are: Edward Hungerford, "Walt Whitman and His Chart of Bumps," *American Literature* 2 (1931): 366–81; Madeline B. Stern, *Heads and Headlines: The Phrenological Fowlers* (Norman: University of Oklahoma Press, 1971); Betsy Erkkila, "Whitman and the Homosexual Republic," 153–71; and David Reynolds, *Walt Whitman*, 395–98.

32. Lorenzo Fowler, *Marriage: Its History and Ceremonies; with a Phrenological and Physiological Exposition of the Functions and Qualifications for Happy Marriages* (New York: Fowler and Wells, 1847), 76, 98. The range of phrenological tracts that produce exactly these lists of faculties and attributes is unmanageably vast. A few of the titles most relevant to Whitman would include: Orson S. Fowler, *Fowler's Practical Phrenology* (New York: Fowler and Wells, 1856); Fowler derived much of his text from George Combe's *A System of Phrenology* (New York: William H. Coyler, 1846), which itself synthesized J. G. Spurzheim's *Phrenology, or the Doctrine of Mental Phenomena* (Boston: Marsh, Capen, and Lyon, 1833). For a detailed account of the developmental history of phrenology, see Lynch, "'Here Is Adhesiveness.'" It is of course worth recalling that Whitman had his head "read" by Lorenzo Fowler in 1849, and that Lorenzo and Orson Fowler, along with Samuel Wells, distributed the first edition of *Leaves of Grass*, and published the second.

33. I have borrowed a great many of my terms here from Eve Kosofsky Sedgwick's seminal description of homophobia as "a mechanism for regulating the behavior of the many by the specific oppression of a few." Explaining the interpretive slippage that gives to homophobic accusation and attack its broadly regulatory power, Sedgwick writes of a patriarchal dispensation in which intense bonds between men are simultaneously mandatory *and* reprobated. What results from this, she argues, is an endemic, and tremendously manipulable, state of uncertain or inadequate self-perception; in short, of panic: "Not only must homosexual men be unable to ascertain whether they are to be the objects of 'random' homophobic violence, but no man must be able to ascertain that he is not (that his bonds are not) homosexual. In this way, a relatively small exertion of physical or legal compulsion potentially rules great reaches of behavior and filiation." Sedgwick, *Between Men*, 88, 88–89; see as well her *Epistemology of the Closet* (Berkeley: University of California Press, 1990).

34. See Lynch, "Here Is Adhesiveness." For more on Whitman and the fashioning of a homosexual identity or "type," see Robert K. Martin's pioneering *The Homosexual Tradition in American Poetry* (Austin: University of Texas Press, 1979). For a critical response to Lynch, which disagrees with him to somewhat different purposes than my own, see Betsy Erkkila's "Whitman and the Homosexual Republic."

35. The phrase "Whitman wants to make sex public" comes from Michael Warner's "Whitman Drunk," 40.

36. The profound power Whitman attributes to sexuality goes a long way to explain his attraction to sexual sciences—such as those found in the male-purity movement—whose aims seem so sharply contrary to his own. Anti-onanist writers such as Sylvester Graham, though they demonize it tirelessly, nevertheless present sexuality as a potentially world-altering force, powerful enough to bring civilization itself to its knees. The

attractiveness of these authors to Whitman thus seems to lie not in their proscriptions but in their presumption—which Whitman is keen to elaborate on as well—that sex is a power that makes and unmakes worlds. See Sylvester Graham, *A Lecture to Young Men* (Providence, RI: Weeden and Cory, 1834), and Stephen Nissenbaum, *Sex, Diet, and Debility in Jacksonian America: Sylvester Graham and Health Reform* (Westport, CT: Greenwood Press, 1980). On the uses of a variety of medical paradigms and discourses later in Whitman's career (following the Civil War), see Robert Leigh Davis, *Whitman and the Romance of Medicine* (Berkeley: University of California Press, 1997).

37. Warner, "Whitman Drunk," 39.

EPILOGUE

1. Paul Gilroy, *Against Race: Imagining Political Culture beyond the Color Line* (Cambridge, MA: Harvard University Press, 2000), 1.

2. Gilroy, *Against Race*, 36, 47, 37.

3. Lauren Berlant, "Poor Eliza," *American Literature* 70 (September 1998): 636, 646, my emphasis.

4. Gilroy, *Against Race*, 6, 17.

5. See Richard Rorty, *Contingency, Irony, and Solidarity* (Cambridge, MA: Cambridge University Press, 1989), and Jean-Luc Nancy, *The Inoperative Community* (Minneapolis: University of Minnesota Press, 1991).

6. John Winthrop, "A Modell of Christian Charity," in *The Puritans*, ed. Perry Miller and Thomas H. Johnson (New York: American Book Company, 1938), 198.

7. Greil Marcus, *Invisible Republic: Bob Dylan's Basement Tapes* (New York: Henry Holt, 1997), 89.

8. See Jacques Derrida, "Declarations of Independence," *New Political Science* 15 (1986): 7–17. See also Jay Fliegelman's splendid account of the "necessitarian context" of the Declaration in his *Declaring Independence: Jefferson, Natural Language, and the Culture of Performance* (Stanford, CA: Stanford University Press, 1993), 140–47. For a different account of Jefferson's text, as a document concerned with problems other than those of national unity, see Garry Wills, *Inventing America: Jefferson's Declaration of Independence* (New York: Doubleday, 1978). Wills's interesting claim, with which I differ here, is that our vision of Jefferson as the great unifier of the unruly colonies is essentially an inheritance from Lincoln and his eloquent, idealized view of the Declaration.

9. Thomas Jefferson, *Writings*, ed. Merrill D. Peterson (New York: Library of America, 1984), 19. All quotes from Jefferson's draft of the Declaration of Independence will be taken from his account of it in his *Autobiography*, as produced in this edition, 19–24.

10. Jay Fliegelman, *Declaring Independence*, 144.

11. Harriet Beecher Stowe, *Uncle Tom's Cabin; or, Life Among the Lowly*, ed. Ann Douglas (New York: Penguin, 1981), 624.

12. Marianne Noble, *The Masochistic Pleasures of Sentimental Literature* (Princeton, NJ: Princeton University Press, 2000), 64, 62, 65.

13. Martha C. Nussbaum usefully defines "compassion"—which, not least through the ethical inflection she wishes to give it, resembles very closely Stowe's ideal of "sympathy"—as a specifically *"painful* emotion occasioned by the awareness of another person's undeserved misfortune" (my emphasis). See Nussbaum, *Upheavals of Thought: The Intelligence of Emotions* (Cambridge, MA: Cambridge University Press, 2001), 301.

14. One of the projects of sentimentality, as Philip Fisher notes, was to "experiment with the extension of full and complete humanity to classes of figures from whom it has been socially withheld." Fisher, *Hard Facts: Setting and Form in the American Novel* (New York: Oxford University Press, 1985), 99. For a fine overview of the paradoxes of a humanity that must be "extended"—of the twinned elements of "reciprocality and coercion" within sentimentality—see Glenn Hendler, *Public Sentiments: Structures of Feeling in Nineteenth-Century American Literature* (Chapel Hill: University of North Carolina Press, 2001), 218, 212–19, 3–11.

15. Adam Phillips, *Terrors and Experts* (Cambridge, MA: Harvard University Press, 1995), 78.

16. Wai Chee Dimock, "Non-Newtonian Time: Robert Lowell, Roman History, Vietnam War," *American Literature* 74 (December 2002): 921. For similarly against-the-grain models of rendering historical time, see also Dimock's "Deep Time: American Literature and World History," *American Literary History* (December 2001): 755–5. On "overly-hasty historicizations," see Mark Seltzer, "Serial Killers (I)," *differences* 5, no. 1 (1993): 120. For an exceptionally subtle account of what we might call the persistence of "history" across the epochs into which we retrospectively divide it, see again Chris Nealon's introduction to *Foundlings: Lesbian and Gay Historical Emotion before Stonewall* (Durham, NC: Duke University Press, 2001), 1–23.

17. There are at least two factors that have made, and continue to make, America susceptible to such utopian imaginings of intimate national belonging. There is, first, the provenance of the nation in a turn *against* ancestry and inherited structures of order and mutuality; and second, a historically pervasive distrust of government and governmental institutions and, along with them, of state-bound models of nationality. As live elements of American national life, these tendencies have shown an impressive persistence. Hence, so too have visions of an affectively constituted, eternally present-tense national coherence been remarkably pertinacious. See Benedict Anderson, *Imagined Communities: Reflections on the Origin and Spread of Nationalism,* rev. ed. (New York: Verso, 1991), 36. On the first factor, see Seymour Martin Lipset, *The First New Nation:*

The United States in Historical and Comparative Perspective (1963; New York: Norton, 1979); and Anderson, *Imagined Communities,* particularly his chapter "Creole Pioneers," 47–65. On the latter, see Garry Wills, *A Necessary Evil: A History of American Distrust of Government* (New York: Simon and Schuster, 1999).

18. Walt Whitman, "Song of the Open Road," *Poetry and Prose,* ed. Justin Kaplan (New York: Library of America, 1996), 301.

19. Mark Seltzer, *Serial Killers: Life and Death in America's Wound Culture* (New York: Routledge, 1998), 254, 278. Marianne Noble argues along similar lines that in masochistic discourses, violence and wounding can function as "a metonymn for intimacy." The "physical exposure" of pain, she writes, works as "a prelude to a sensation of rhapsodic union." Noble, *The Masochistic Pleasures of Sentimental Literature,* 56, 58. See also Wendy Brown's *States of Injury: Power and Freedom in Late Modernity* (Princeton, NJ: Princeton University Press, 1995). On mass suffering and death as reported in the major media, see Susan D. Moeller, *Compassion Fatigue: How the Media Sell Disease, Famine, War, and Death* (New York: Routledge, 1999). On aspects of the gothic, and of gothic sadomasochism, in contemporary culture, with particular attentiveness to the talk show, see Mark Edmundson, *Nightmare on Main Street: Angels, Sadomasochism, and the Culture of the Gothic* (Cambridge, MA: Harvard University Press, 1997).

20. Lauren Berlant, "Poor Eliza," 636, 646, my emphasis. See also the first two chapters of Berlant's *The Queen of America Goes to Washington City: Essays on Sex and Citizenship* (Durham, NC: Duke University Press, 1997).

21. Moeller, *Compassion Fatigue.* See especially 7–53.

22. Reporting on the one-year anniversary of September 11, the *New York Times* offered this perfectly apt headline: "A Single Grief Knits Together a Vast Country." See Dean E. Murphy, "A Single Grief Knits Together a Vast Country," *New York Times,* September 12, 2002, 1.

23. Rorty, *Contingency, Irony, and Solidarity,* xvi, 192.

24. Marcus, *Invisible Republic,* 209.

25. Harriet Beecher Stowe, *Uncle Tom's Cabin,* 624.

26. Berlant is very strong on these points. "In a sense," she writes, "the sentimental bargain has constantly involved substituting for representations of pain and violence representations of its sublime self-overcoming that end up, often perversely, producing pleasure both as a distraction from suffering and also as a figure for the better life that sufferers under the regime of nation, patriarchy, capital, and racism ought to be able to imagine themselves having . . . This ravenous yearning for social change, this hunger for the end of pain, has installed the pleasures of entertainment, of the star system, of the love of children, and of heterosexual romance where a political language about suffering might have

been considered appropriate." And it has installed as well, I would add, a linked desire for exactly those "detailed descriptions of . . . pain and humiliation" in which Rorty places such political and ethical hope. See Berlant, "Poor Eliza," 664.

27. Martha C. Nussbaum, like Rorty and Gilroy and Stowe, sees something ethically promising in what she calls "compassion." "Compassion is frequently linked to beneficent action," she writes. "If one believes that the misforturnes of others are serious, that they have not brought misfortune upon themselves, and, in addition, that they are themselves important parts of one's own scheme of ends and goals, then the conjunction of these beliefs is very likely to lead to action addressing the suffering. It may not do so, if there is no available course of action that suggests itself. But if there is, it will be difficult to believe that the compassionate person really does have all three judgments, if she does not do something to address the victims' vulnerability" (*Upheavals of Thought*, 335). Here again is the premise that an individual should be obliged—"is very likely" to act—as a result of the feeling of compassion (or, begging the question, that if the individual is not obliged it is not real compassion). The preponderance of evidence from contemporary American life seems to me to suggest that the chief occasions for public acts of compassion, in part because they are inevitably staged through the organs of national culture and mass media, are almost a priori ones in which no immediate course of ameliorative action suggests itself to the individual subject of mass culture, with the result that feeling *more*, feeling *again*, or feeling shocked at any perceived lack of feeling anywhere else comes eventually to stand for the subject as, precisely, the best available course of "action." This is part of the recursivity of sympathy, particularly as mediated by mass culture, that leads me to feel less optimistic about its public and ethical extensions than these other theorists.

28. See Russ Castronovo, *Necro-Citizenship: Death, Eroticism, and the Public Sphere in the Nineteenth-Century United States* (Durham, NC: Duke University Press, 2001), 4.

29. Berlant, *The Queen of America Goes to Washington City*, 7–8.

30. Terence Whalen, "Average Racism: Poe, Slavery, and the Wages of Literary Nationalism," *Romancing the Shadow: Poe and Race*, ed. J. Gerald Kennedy and Liliane Weissberg (New York: Oxford University Press, 2001), 11.

Index

Peter Coviello is associate professor of English at Bowdoin College. He is the editor of Walt Whitman's *Memoranda during the War*.